COPENHAGEN
– PEOPLE AND PLACES

PERNILLE STENSGAARD
PHOTO **ANNE PRYTZ SCHALDEMOSE**
TRANSLATED BY **W. GLYN JONES**

COPENHAGEN
– PEOPLE AND PLACES

GYLDENDAL

Gyldendal Publishers

Klareboderne 3, DK-1001 Copenhagen K, Denmark

www.gyldendal.dk

© 2002 Pernille Stensgaard, Anne Prytz Schaldemose and Gyldendal A/S, Copenhagen

2. udgave, 1. oplag

Printed in Bosnia and Herzegovina 2015

Cover: Steen Frimodt and Anne Prytz Schaldemose

Editors: Lisbeth Frimodt and Dorte Einarsson

Translator: W. Glyn Jones

Reader: Anne Marie Køllgaard

ISBN 978-87-02-17818-0

Typeset in Swift Metro by Steen Frimodt and Anne Prytz Schaldemose

Content

Foreword

This book is the result of a series of field studies. In town, this has meant going out in the streets, up into apartments, around the parks, down into the courtyards. I am grateful to many of the people I have turned to. They have given me a good reception when, with or without an appointment, I have forced myself on them to ask how far back they can remember. Most of them have also willingly tried to answer question such as: "How do people tend to dress round here" or "Do people round here tend to have big dogs or small ones?"

Without the locals, it could never have been done, for I personally have managed only to live in Colbjørnsensgade, Vesterbrogade and Toldbodgade as a child, and as an adult in Christianshavn and Nørre Farimagsgade, from which I can't ever envisage moving. I don't know the other places in that way. Others have had to tell me what the essence of their districts really is. The thesis of the book is that such a thing exists: People move to where they have roots or where they think they will find others like themselves. In this way a special, self-reinforcing conception of the place arises. Someone who moves to Nørrebro doesn't expect the same as some-one moving to Frederiksberg even though the two districts are cheek by jowl with each other. The various parts of Copenhagen are essentially different from each other, and their residents have fixed ideas as to "how we do things here". It is often not like that in reality, but that makes it only more interesting. The idea of the place lives on, and that is what I am trying to describe.

I am also grateful to all the researchers and writers on whose excellent work I have drawn. Vast numbers of books have been written about the history of Copenhagen, its culture, its architecture, its ways and byways, pubs and brothels, parks, harbour etc. Mine differs from them in starting out from the present – and then here and there looking back over the centuries. Who were the different districts originally built for, and who lives there now? Why do houses, parks and building complexes look as they do? The book is not exhaustive, and many will discover that their house, street or near neighbourhood is not included. My justification is the lack of space.

The focus is on Copenhagen's attractions and charms. They represent the essential Copenhagen.

Pernille Stensgaard

A view of the city

Copenhagen is the local America. At times it's a dreadful place and at others a land of possibilities. In novel after novel, the capital of Denmark plays the role of a dangerous place, a place you go to in order to disappear into anonymity and become a prey to temptation.

"But this is Hell!" mutters the itinerant Jutlandic clergyman in Henrik Pontoppidan's *The Realm of the Dead* (1916). He has arrived in the Central Station and is now standing looking at an enormous flashing neon advertisement high up above the roofs proclaiming that "Søholm's Coffee is the best". The first person he meets is a pimp. Copenhagen is like America, Hell, damnation. The bigger Copenhagen becomes in the 19th and 20th centuries, the brighter and more beautiful is life in the country described. The leading authors are antagonistic to the city and defend their beloved rural society as it loses significance and industry expands. The little Danish smallholder with his white-headed cow and four hens is the happiest person in the world. Copenhagen is a modern den of vice, run by rapacious capitalists. And Vesterbro is the worst.

"Vesterbro Passage is devoid of innocence, but if one's nerves have a little understanding of the bitter-sweet poison of our particular century, this is still the place to be," wrote Jacob Paludan in 1940. The broad street is lit up and sleepless until over midnight. The glare from its lights can be seen far out into the country. "And if you made your way out into the side streets, you thrilled to the authentic mood of city gloom and mental gloom; you could glimpse the street names that were linked in your memory to unsolved murders. The green lights of the police station kept watch over their unpleasant back streets ... And the stooping figure you met was perhaps a Raskolnikov trying to vanish into thin air when a policeman allowed his eyes, laden with memorised descriptions, slowly to look over him."

A hundred years ago the new districts arising around the old bridges leading into Copenhagen and collectively known as the bridge districts, where the equally new proletariat was forced to live in overcrowded conditions, could scarcely be said to be attractive. The Home Mission evangelical movement considered Copenhagen to be in the power of sin, a training ground for all popular vices. Clergymen and missionaries arranged meetings in church premises on the theme of "Work for the Unbelieving Copenhagen Masses". There were factories and workshops just around the corner or down in the courtyard, and black smoke rose from chimneys everywhere. The city was destined to play a fateful role in the lives of many people. There was a great deal of misery in the country districts, too, but it was better hidden.

In literature and in reality, the city is the destination to which people migrated from the provinces. It's the place where you start afresh and create a new life. Out in the country people's future lay in such a predictable and desolate framework that they got away from it. Life in the city offered boundless opportunities. Desperadoes from Jutland and peasants from Funen came in their hundreds, lost their innocence to the calculating Copenhagen girls of the novels, went to the dogs or rose to the top. Anything could happen in this fantasy about freedom. Johannes Jørgensen wrote five novels in the 1880s and 1890s, all of which tell the same story: A young man from the provinces comes to Copenhagen to study – and goes to the dogs. Sex plays an important part when the city is to be portrayed as dangerous: desire becomes acute amid strangers in the street, while at home in the provinces people were content to court their childhood sweethearts.

"It was a Saturday evening, when all men have money and all the girls are out. It was one of those evenings when the Prince of Darkness walks invisible through the streets with their electric lighting sowing the seeds whose fruit is sin," writes Jørgensen in *The Tree of Life*. And many other authors freaked out in the same way. One provincial student after the other was devoured by the city whose dreadful reputation remained with it far, far up into the 20th century. In 1886, Copenhagen imported bad nerves from America, "for our capital has just now achieved the status of a major city where a complicated and intensified life is the expression of an over-excited nervous system," wrote the psychiatrist Knud Pontoppidan, suggesting that people should learn to shake off the impressions and show a certain reserve in relation to the crowd that was forcing itself on them. Merely to cross the street could set "a whole lot of nerves" off. Pontoppidan became a consultant in the Municipal Hospital.

On the other hand, Copenhagen also saved many, many people from a spiritual death in the provinces. "There's room for village idiots in here. I think it's an advantage that people don't care about each other, and that you're left in peace. In the country people talk about each other so much," says the author and film director Christian Braad Thomsen, who grew up in a village consisting of five houses and three large farms. "I felt very isolated, but that was also because I knew I didn't want to be a farmer. My great dream was to come to town. There's no doubt that I would have become a village idiot if I'd stayed there."

The author Søren Ulrik Thomsen was also saved: "My greatest nightmare is to have to settle in the provinces. I never spend the night there, either. I'm always reminded of how people behave in those places. I really hate the Danish provinces. I *hate* them."

But why?

"They are evil. Everything's simply banal. They can't tolerate anyone who is not exactly the same as they are. So either that's what you become, or you leave. Or you go to the dogs if you haven't the energy to get away. I clearly remember these outsiders who lived in their own way and were always called "Daft" as their first name: Daft Agnes, Daft Birthe and so on... Of course, people in the towns have exactly the same tendencies, but the city makes it possible for those affected to disappear round the next corner," he says to Peter Øvig Knudsen in the book *Børn skal ikke lege under fuldmånen (Children should not Play under the Full Moon)* from 1996.

A 19-year-old girl from Southern Jutland, Marit Jessen, spent the summer of 2001 at home in Højer studying the Kraks Map of Copenhagen. She had been there once before but now she was going there to study. The city's famous and infamous anonymity frightened her: "We're all close to each other in Højer. That's probably what I'm most afraid of. That people just don't care and don't bother with you. When I walk down the street in Højer I always meet some old lady who asks how I'm getting on. I don't think that sort of thing exists in Copenhagen," she said to a newspaper before leaving. "Some young people deliberately go away because they want to start somewhere new, where no one knows them. Conversely, there is something in the idea that some

Arriving at a new life in Copenhagen, the only large city in Denmark. Advantages: Here you can at once be yourself and meet lots of different people. The city is big enough to make a dominant common mentality impossible.

people only go to Copenhagen because they want to show off and are a bit stuck up. So it's extra pressure on them if they fail an exam and the others start talking about them at home."

The 21-year-old Stine Larsen was also preparing the leave Jutland. She'd been in Copenhagen twice before: "I simply can't think I'm going to Copenhagen. I've got to have all my things with me, and I know that I'll not be coming back for the time being. But that's exactly what hasn't dawned on me yet. That I'm

going to be away for such a long time. My relatives keep saying, 'You'll probably not be coming back from Copenhagen.' 'Oh, no. I'll probably stay over there,' I say. It's a bit crazy."

Modern, progressive thinking in the 1930s said: "Light! Air! Residential areas here, institutions there. That ideology was fine for the suburbs, but it was a death knell for the city. The only real solution was to get away as soon as you could afford to, in practi-

Students kissing on Kongens Nytorv. A frightening number of novels describe the ruin of students from the provinces in a city that is big, ugly and far too modern. This demonisation persists – both in literature and in the provinces.

cal terms to move to a small house with a garden. The concept of a "city break" would have been met with derision. The front cover of the book *Kvinde, kend din krop (Woman, Know Your Body) from* 1976 still shows it as sheer misery. The city is drawn on to the woman's body in the form of smoking factory chimneys, tranquillisers and an aggressive boss. A dirty, capitalist hell as low as you can get. Her children and an undulating landscape are the only positive values. Even hippies moved out into the country, and the academics went into small houses built close together in the suburbs. Losers and fanatics stayed behind in the shop-less city in the 1970s.

In the 1980s, Copenhagen's artistic circles suffered from

paranoia and dressed in black, while its (few) wealthy individuals danced at Anabel's in rehabilitated suits. Crisis-ridden Copenhagen was worn down and poor and had to take out loans in order to be able to honour people's social security payments. Authors continued to demonise the city and destroy young men in their books, while the police confronted the inhabitants on the question of how the Nørrebro district is to look. The Mayor won the battle and built monotonous low structures in the heart of the old district with its traditional tall buildings.

Quite slowly, there came a new interest in the city – the real, dense city with tenements, streets and squares. The ideal changed so that anonymity, the cafés and city life were suddenly no longer wretched. At the end of the 80s, students in the schools of architecture stopped designing run-of-the-mill idylls and turned their attention to boulevards, squares and parks. The old-fashioned street with rows of houses on either side reappeared in planning instead of free-standing blocks surrounded by greenery. All this greenery, which almost did for the city. This change really made it self felt at the beginning of the 90s, irrespective of artists' and writers' pessimism. People had money, and industry was completely gone. Copenhagen had become multi-ethnic with 76,000 citizens from non-Western countries as opposed to 18,000 in 1980. The small proletarian flats were combined and modernised to the tune of a million kroner apiece. But the police didn't fight with the citizens about how Vesterbro was to look – and Vesterbro was saved in its entirety – though at considerable cost.

Despite Jutlandic warnings to the contrary, the city was becoming thoroughly nice and peaceful. The few buildings in the city that had not been subject to the great renovation stood out like eyesores. There was scaffolding everywhere. Squares and markets were being emptied of cars and discreetly renovated. Copenhagen was becoming more and more beautiful all the time and had been subjected to urban regeneration. That was suddenly an expression regularly heard. The unthinkable had happened: Even knowledgeable foreigners were looking at Copenhagen. *Lonely Planet* finally gave Copenhagen something of a mark of distinction. So did another international city guide, *Time Out*.

"It's a bit like when we were included in the CNN weather forecast," says a happy head of PR of Wonderful Copenhagen. And the extremely hip international lifestyle magazine, *Wallpaper*, appoints Antwerp, Barcelona and Copenhagen as the three best cities in the world to live in: Copenhagen is "a bit Scando, a bit Euro". The airport is one of the best in the world, the Metro is here and there is a sufficient network of cycle paths. The once rough districts are exciting, the prices of houses surprisingly low compared with London and New York, and nowhere else can you by such wonderful Scandinavian furniture classics as in Copen-

hagen. Downsides: the restaurants close too early, the weather is dubious and the taxes too high.

The international firm of consultants, William M. Mercer, ranks the city as number five for quality of life among the major cities of the world. Top of the list are Zurich, Geneva, Vancouver and Vienna. Copenhagen wins on traffic conditions and public transport and loses on entertainment and leisure. The list is used by multinational companies when they are working out local

During the second half of the 1990s, Copenhagen came into money and abandoned its image as long-haired, poor and left-wing.

allowances for their foreign postings. Baghdad is the worst and so attracts the highest allowance.

Copenhagen has been partly retrieved from the car, which had freedom to go as it pleased for more than half a century. "The first motorcar seen in Strøget", wrote a newspaper at Easter 1900. "Yesterday an elegant little motorcar chugged up through Vimmelskaftet to Højbro, where it deftly turned down Købmagergade. It is the first time this modern means of transport has been seen in Strøget; the hissing and chuff-chuffing disturbed the peace of the Sabbath."

Until 1962, when Strøget became the mother of all pedestrian precincts, cars drove and stopped everywhere in streets and squares while people squeezed past on narrow pavements. That was what things ought to be like: "We're Danes, not Italians", and "The use of public space conflicts with the Nordic mentality", argued the opponents of pedestrian precincts. They were mistaken: Strøget (1962), Fiolstræde (1968), Købmagergade (1973) and Strædet (1992) are all successful pedestrian precincts. 18 squares and streets, where cars once parked in serried ranks, were emptied and made beautiful in a long, difficult process. Others in the series included Gammeltorv and Amagertorv in 1962, Gråbrødretorv in 1968, Kultorvet and Nytorv in 1973, Nyhavn in 1980, Højbro Plads in 1986, Gammel Strand and Axeltorv in 1991 and Ved Stranden in 1995. Since 1962, car-free areas in the city have expanded six-fold, and such Italian phenomena as outdoor serving have turned up everywhere. That we *are* Italians is demonstrated by figures from the Royal Danish Academy of Fine Arts School of Architecture, which regularly surveys city parameters. The city has as many as 126 pavement cafés and 5,000 seats. In 1986 there were 3,000. People used to go to town to walk around and look at the shops and then go home again. Now they have far more things to do. Something is happening. Copenhagen has become more welcoming to people and is less at the beck and call of the car, and that has not kept people out, quite the opposite.

During the same period bicycle traffic has risen by 65 per cent, and we boast of that as part of the spirit of the city. There are other attitudes. When the American author Douglas Coupland caught sight of all the Copenhageners cycling around the lakes, he rolled down his widow and shouted: "Buy a car, losers!"

The big city is a draw now, even though it is dangerous to your health: People drink, smoke and weigh more than people in the country. The life span of a Copenhagener is noticeably shorter than that of other Danes, and Copenhageners are forced to choose between a constant selection of vices, sins and forms of entertainment: "An ever-renewed palette of possibilities for satisfying or at any rate moderating your curiosity, your appetite, your lechery, your longing for adventure, your restlessness, your thirst or your ambitions," is a list rattled off by the journalist Henrik List in Berlingske Tidende. Common sense, thrift and moderation – life with belt and braces, bicycle helmets and padded sleeves for protection – belong in the provinces.

"A special feature in city life has always been intensity, speed, complexity and modernity. People of all kinds can meet here. Here we learn to mix distantly but courteously with people with other opinions and values than our own – we learn to be "urbane" and "civilised" as it is called," says the writer Frederik Stjernfelt. "But a centuries-old tradition has always hated the city. It is seen as rootless, cosmopolitan, far too modern, the centre for the erosion of natural, established experiences."

Copenhagen is a city of single people. More than half the apartments in the city are only lived in by a single person, who wants to go out and meet another. The price of town houses, owner-occupied flats and detached houses rose markedly in the 1990s because Copenhagen has become modern and people in general have plenty of money. A new feature is that some families with children want to live there. Copenhagen politicians flock around them, at least in thought, because they have a stabilising effect on the place. When such families disappeared in the 1960s

"Café" – perhaps the word that best describes the new, hip city life. The first, Café Sommersko, only dates from 1976. On the other hand, taverns and pubs are dying out.

and 1970s, Copenhagen went into steep decline, so now it's a question of holding on to them. They work, pay their taxes, go shopping, go to the cinema and are interested in the city. The places where they live must be pleasing to look at and offer security. These people seem to be *normal* after decades as marginalised city dwellers, but most of them move out again the moment the blue line shows itself in the pregnancy test. Copenhagen's old reputation clings to it: the dangerous, stressed city in which the worn-out single mother comes along on her bicycle with the baby in tow and where child molesters are standing waiting in the entrances. No one thinks of the sense of community that arises in stairways leading up to apartments and in the courtyards. Green courtyards.

The vanished children are the biggest mystery in town for all older Copenhageners. They are amazed and talk of how the streets were *milling* with children in their childhood. In the back yards, where there are now tall trees and organic herb gardens, they used to jump around on the dustbins. As late as the 1960s there were enough boys living in Esplanaden to form a full football team, and the schools were full to bursting. Even the romanticisation of the city that took place in the 1990s has difficulty competing with "green fields" as the only suitable place for children. A city without children is strange and incongruous, but there are signs of change. André Maltesen from Vesterbro is 33 years old. He was the last child born on those particular flats in Sønder Boulevard, and it was 30 years before the next one. But now, after the urban revival, the flats are coping with a veritable baby boom of four children. And there are many places like it in the city. The ultimate test of the new Copenhagen is whether parents will let their children live in it.

There have only been cars in Copenhagen for 100 years.

Children bathing in a courtyard in Nørrebro. The term backyard can hardly be used any longer with its negative associations. The numbers of Copenhageners have dropped by 300,000 since the 1950s, partly because the tightly packed back yards have been cleared of back buildings and partly because small flats have been combined. But also because the little detached house in the suburbs has been an attraction.

The locals

The locals are overwhelmed in Copenhagen every day by hundreds of thousands of people coming in from outside. No other Danes share their patch with so many others. People live in the heart of Copenhagen, but it is simply not theirs alone. It is the country's political, administrative and cultural centre, and the few local residents only play a subsidiary role even though they make an effort to show that they do in fact live there.

Copenhagen brings in strangers from the suburbs, provinces and the whole world. They pour out of Nørreport Station and spread all over the workplaces in the City. If you ask people in Strøget where they come from only seven out of hundred will say that they live in the City.

"We live in a place that is really hired out in bits to the rest of the Danish population," says a woman from Ny Vestergade. "So it's important to us to show the others that we actually live here. We're busy inventing all kinds of special Copenhagen features to distinguish us from the others. That must be because we're proud to live here."

One way of showing tourists who is in charge in the City is to stand with someone inside the Illum department store and say very loudly, "I don't think I can manage that bloody thing on my bike." Or demonstratively to manoeuvre your Christmas tree out of the window during the rush hour. You water your potted plants so that the water runs down the outside wall a little. You cycle around with a small carton of milk in your cycle basket, or you go down the street with a look that clearly demonstrates that you've seen all this before. This is just everyday.

At Whitsun you get away from the carnival, while the main flow is in the opposite direction – towards the city. And in many circles it is also in vogue loudly to dissociate yourself from the Jazz Festival. Nor are the locals likely to stand and discuss global environmental politics with the insistent grass roots people on Kultorvet. That sort of thing is for the *others*. Only when you have visitors from outside or are looking after the grandchildren do you go up the Round Tower or visit Thorvaldsens Museum. During the summer, the town is populated by tourists and people from the provinces, and *they* take a boat trip round the harbour. In general, locals don't use the city like others do – they are just there. "The others have too much time, and that is why they can walk that slowly. They walk in no specific direction," says a woman from Badstuestræde, who thinks people should get out of the way when she comes along with her bicycle and shopping bag, for that's where she lives. "During the evening, I might well think of cycling in Fiolstræde, and that's my privilege, for this is my town and I'm on my way home. Others are not allowed."

And it is "the others", too, who come in by train at weekends and throw pizza boxes and cigarette ends on the street and piss in the doorways. What these others like and come a long way to enjoy – for instance a walk along Strøget on a Saturday – is something most locals are not interested in. They draw lots to decide who has to run the gauntlet on a Saturday down to Magasin or Illum to buy food and stand in a queue behind 20 Swedes who don't know what currency to pay in. The locals know all the rat runs so as to avoid Strøget. During the summer they go in constant danger of being run down by Italian tourists, who are notoriously bad at cycling.

The paradox is that people move in to the centre of the capital in order to enjoy anonymity, and that at the same time they insist on living in a local community. "It's wearing to be among so many people and to feel a stranger among them. You look for someone you know: There's a caretaker I know. And there's a kiosk where they know me. You look for enclaves," says a woman pointing to a wine dealer down on the corner. That's a hive of information for the few people who live in Frederiksholms Kanal. Several men are sitting in the shop, rocking their feet while listening to jazz. You can be elective in your haunts. Christian Braad Thomsen, of Lavendelstræde, says that he lives an isolated life and only goes to four places in town: Irma, the Grand Theatre, Cinema, Filmhuset and Jazzhouse.

"We have to keep together here in the village," is a phrase typically heard in the special Copenhagen circles where you buy your fish from the last fishwife on Gammel Strand. There are of course similar groups at Frederiksberg and Østerbro, where people love their district in a special cultural and local-historical sense. High-

ly educated complainers who can take over if something goes wrong or regeneration threatens. The residents are surrounded by spectacular events. Great, important happenings in the country's history pass immediately in front of the door. You notice it when kings and statesmen visit Denmark. The American president makes a speech on Nytorv, the Royal Guard march past every other moment, and when there is a New Year levee at Christiansborg, every parking space along the canal is occupied by nervous folk in clothing that is far too fine for them. Expensive fireworks are for ever going off all around, the Town Hall bells boom out, and the Queen's horses are trained every day in the city streets.

The old town is the place for Copenhagen's most affluent citizens. They are predominantly middle-aged and predominantly Danes. They earn an average of 226,000 kroner a year, whereas the poorest – living in Kongens Enghave – earn 135,000 kroner. Staff don't have very much to do in the mandatory but minute Social Security Office, for the residents don't have any problems: they have work, are highly educated and have plenty of money. They are not on drugs, and their children are not forcibly removed. There are only three elementary schools now to serve what once, not all that long ago, simply *was* Copenhagen.

Until the ramparts were demolished in the 1850s, the old town constituted the whole of Copenhagen. Everyone huddled together there. Now hardly anyone lives in the actual old town, where everything started. It's unusual to live there. One doesn't know many who do. They live in the exception, in the tourists' wonderful, wonderful Copenhagen – a cross between an animated historical museum and a shopping centre. Two large groups in the medieval town are the affluent middle-aged and the affluent singles between 26 and 40 years of age. Students can hardly keep up with that class, for the city is constantly being done up

In town, you have to behave in an urbane manner (from urbs, meaning town), i.e. in a cultured, well-bred and polite way. There is no space for anything else.

Playing pétanque in Sankt Annæ Plads. Copenhagen in summer is entirely different from Copenhagen in winter. As soon as the opportunity presents itself, people pour into the streets. The citizens of Copenhagen have the reputation of being the Italians of the North.

Girls with strawberries, beer and laced shoes on Kastellet ramparts on the evening before what was once a day of prayer, "Store Bededag". Walking on the ramparts on that evening is an old Copenhagen tradition.

and made to look good. New to the city are the 50- and 60-year-olds who are fed up with their detached houses with gardens and are moving in from the dormitory towns longing for noise and culture. They want to be able to walk to the Royal Theatre, to university extension courses and Statens Museum for Kunst, the Danish national gallery. Now they can take it easy in the shade in Kongens Have sitting in their own deckchairs and enjoy an old age steeped in culture. They have done their duty out in the green areas. For the sake of their children.

Grandparents are moving in, and the grandchildren are moving out. The young parents just manage to give birth before getting out. Half of all children have left the old town before reaching the age of six. As things stand now, researchers see no possibility of repopulating the old town with families with children. The competition from local authorities offering facilities for families and green surroundings is too intense. And perhaps parents simply refuse. They have had fun in town and perhaps will do so again, but not with children. The number of people aged between 50 and 59, however, is growing all the time, for there is everything they need. Everything suggests that the trend will continue. "The middle-aged want their second youth. They sell their house up in the north and move into town, which is finally becoming a European capital city. It would have been unthinkable five or ten years ago," says one estate agent.

This is the Copenhagen that people write and sing about – and sell. They live in historical and charming – and often listed – buildings. Three out of four dwellings are more than a hundred years old, and the floors often slope so much that you can't sleep with your head in just any direction, while occupational therapists are worried about locals who day in and day out use their whole bodies to resist sliding down to the bottom of the study on the desk chair. Only you don't end in an apartment in the medieval town just by chance, but because you *want* to live there and you make a great effort to have your will. You choose aesthetically, not practically.

The dwellings in the old town are special. As time has passed, some famous Dane has lived in almost every one of them – or at least in the flat above or the one next door – and the people living there know that. You can read about your district in Holberg, Kierkegaard, Hans Christian Andersen, Herman Bang and all the others, only a minority of whom have had no link with the square kilometre that constitutes the medieval town. There, you live surrounded by good taste and roof terraces that are as good as the most beautiful in Rome. You have winding staircases and collar beams, original dados and a view across the roofs and towers in the city, "quietly situated in the old Latin quarter" or "with Gråbrødretorv as your back garden". Estate agents sell history, charm, patina and *soul*. You don't live like the rest, thank God, and every day you walk about in the footsteps of history. A woman says that it is exciting to live in "the literary Løvstræde", where a whole lot of booksellers used to have their shops. Another says that Mikkel Thøgersen wandered around in her street looking into the gardens in Johannes V. Jensen's novel *The Fall of the King*. A third refers to Holberg's chestnut tree in Fiolstræde, where she lives. A fourth says that in her Badstuetræde lay one of the city's bath-houses, and the hairdresser maintains that her shop is above nothing less than the king's sauna. The sauna was closed in 1509, so there is nothing short-term about such a place, and you can trace your street back through an extraordinary number of generations. The "bridge" districts have no chance in that competition. They are not even 150 years old yet.

Some people live above an old Franciscan monastery, others above the local pond or the town privies and others again on the bones of medieval Copenhageners. And they all tell you about it, for it is a great thing to live in town: You are not alone, others have been there before you.

Right up to the time when the ramparts were removed in the middle of the 19th century, the number of Copenhageners was rising to quite intolerable levels. People were layered in cellars and lofts, in hovels in backyards, buildings tacked on the to the sides of tenements and in new upper storeys that were added, while the military kept the city gates closed for the sake of security in this city-fortress. The city was primarily the home of the royal family, the government and the fleet, and most Copenhageners plied some skilled trade. But things changed about 1840. Industrialism and its smoking chimneys could no longer be overlooked. Limited companies were formed, the Industrial Society was founded, and enterprising men had one crazy idea after the other. Only then did the population begin to grow in earnest.

Scarcely were the city gates and ramparts gone and the "bridge districts" made available for building before the medieval town lay almost deserted. People moved out to the suburbs Vesterbro (Westbridge), Nørrebro (Northbridge) and Østerbro (Eastbridge), "so the old town more and more came to consist of business districts with shops, offices and warehouses", notes the Salmonsen Encyclopaedia, describing this strange phenomenon as a "flight from the centre". Copenhagen was in the process of transforming itself into a city. The word "city" appears for the first time in Danish in 1885. It was known from London City, where the population had disappeared and dwellings had been transformed into business premises. The Copenhagen Krak guide talks of "the tendency there obviously is to change the inner part of Copenhagen into a City". Copenhageners moved first from the main business streets – Amagertorv, Strøget, Købmagergade, Pilestræde – and then also from the smaller streets, something Krak explains by saying that the apartments in the small streets now became stores and workshops, "whereby the poverty-stricken population was partly driven out".

The City was established between 1895 and 1911, when depopulation was at its height. After this, it was gently and progressively expanded. "City" means that ordinary, local life was no longer to be found as before, and that offices, shops, organisations, institutions and culture account for most of the space. The Copenhagen speculators were filled with "City" fever. They wanted to tear down all the old rubbish and build City streets with City premises according to City plans – and they also went far along this road. Emma Gad complained: "City! A name that is so alien at the heart of our Danish town."

The population reduced at an alarming rate, for instance in the politically left-wing district of Trinitatis, which was the home of 5,000 people in 1880 and only 535 in 1950. Now there are fewer than ten. The City now consists of the central medieval town and is about one kilometre square. 6,800 people live there, most of them in the Latin Quarter around the Cathedral and in Pisserenden. The smallest number – under 500 – live in the financial district behind Kongens Nytorv and Holmens Kanal.

Typically, people live on the top floors in each individual building, while businesses and offices occupy the ground floor and the first and second floors. At about 10 o'clock on an ordinary winter's evening, students of architecture counted lights in the windows of 6,300 dwellings, strictly speaking one per inhabitant, so there is life. It is much worse in Stockholm. The centre of the Swedish capital is completely deserted, and the 900 inhabitants make a desperate attempt to fill it out a little. The similar number is doing its best in Oslo. 2,700 shudder a little in Hamburg.

Copenhagen is well off in comparison with such empty cities, but cities like Amsterdam and Vienna have managed to keep their populations. Twice as many people live in the central part of Amsterdam as in Copenhagen, and in Vienna three times as many.

The houses

One Tuesday evening in October 1728, some children were playing with fire in a house near Vesterport and set this crowded district of half-timbered houses and narrow streets alight. Unfortunately, a strong wind was blowing, and unfortunately some of the town's water conduits were under repair and therefore empty, and unfortunately the city fire brigade were all blind drunk. There was a desperate need for water from the moat, but the city commander-in-chief daren't open the city gate without asking the king's permission. And the king had already gone to bed. Everything went wrong. Hour by hour the streets burnt down. The wind was blowing, so fire rained down over the city, on yards containing large stores of wood, in across St. Peter's (Petri) Church, the Town Hall on Gammeltorv, the Bishop's

Gabled houses in Gråbrødretorv, a tiny relic of the old, colourful Copenhagen. These so-called "fire houses" were built after the 1728 fire, but most of them burned down again in the second great fire of Copenhagen in 1795.

Palace, the University, the Cathedral and on to Købmagergade and Trinitatis, where the University Library was housed in the loft. That, too, succumbed to the flames. The fire burnt throughout Wednesday, Thursday and Friday. Not until the night between Friday and Saturday, when the wind had dropped, was it possible to put out the flames. By then 69 streets, most of Copenhagen, lay in ashes. Of the three fateful fires, this was only the first. Each time, Copenhagen changed its appearance, and more and more of the colourful medieval town disappeared. That is why, in view of Copenhagen's age, the centre is so shockingly young to look at. Roughly speaking, it is possible to count on one hand what is left from the Middle Ages. And on two or three what is left from the Renaissance. Although Copenhagen is almost a thousand years old, its main nucleus of housing is from the 18th and 19th centuries.

After the first great fire, the authorities tried to persuade people to erect brick-built houses instead of the half-timbered structures that were much more likely to go up in flames. They were successful in certain areas. The city arose again, higher, more modern and less likely to burn down. The national director of buildings, Johan Cornelius Krieger, launched a standard house that people could copy if they wished. This so-called "fire house" was a narrow building of two or three storeys with a broad gable, typically with three windows and a small oval window at the top. The designs (with an estimated price) inspired builders throughout the city, and some of their charming houses still stand, for instance on the southern side of Gråbrødretorv.

What was spared in the first great fire was destroyed in the second. One afternoon in June 1795, fire broke out in a store of timber, boards and coal in Gammelholm, which at that time was an enclosed area under the control of the navy. It is now the district behind the Royal Theatre. Unfortunately, a gale blew the fire in across the city, where it was confronted with the same lack of talent as before. Unfortunately, everything was dry tinder after a lengthy drought; unfortunately the fire crews had gone home; and unfortunately the chief fire officer had to be brought in from far-away Frederiksberg. Nor did it do any good when he came. Everyone was confused and incompetent. Most of the city's fire pumps were not used, and the flames had it almost all their own way for three days. This time, 53 streets were destroyed and almost 6,000 people left homeless.

However, the building of a new Copenhagen was a success, an artistic achievement. To begin with, people had money because trade was prospering. Secondly, an elegant new architectural style – neo-classicism – was ready for use. Architects, builders and apprentices had it off pat. The apprentices had gone to evening classes in classical ornaments in the Royal Danish Academy of Fine Arts and over the following years they built one of the most attractive sights in Copenhagen: the ordinary burgher's house. This *is* the special ambience that is Copenhagen. Over half the listed buildings in Copenhagen are from the neo-classical epoch. It coincides with the period of artistic and intellectual achievement known as the Golden Age. "To wander through the streets of Copenhagen is to experience one of the greatest joys in Europe: the revelation of endless panoramas in an unspoilt city from the beginning of the 19th century," wrote the British art historian Giles Worsley in *Klassicisme i København* (1998). "Here we have the quiet street scene that was captured so beautifully and fittingly in the gentle works of the Golden Age. There is no sign of the self-satisfied boasting that is characteristic of the London or Paris of the time."

The long rows of simple, bright houses in the inner city area were constructed after the fire in 1795 and all were built after the same model: ancient Rome and Greece. Architects spent years studying in those countries and scrutinised the old buildings in detail. They admired the columns, ornaments and triangular gable ends, the symmetry, the peace and quiet. Then they imported the style to Denmark or looked it up in the textbooks that were available on the European market.

As time went by, the city's stucco workers produced finished friezes with Greek key patterns to be installed between the first and second floors, often the only decoration on the building at all. Everything else was removed, even the old-fashioned gables from the fire houses. People were suddenly tired of baroque and rococo, which they found decadent, exuberant and overdone. The new style was stringent. Not only Denmark, but all Europe sketched and tried to imitate the ideals of beauty from Classical Antiquity. In Denmark, the style acquired not only a Danish, but a special Copenhagen form: after the fire, the authorities ordained that all new rows of houses must have obliquely cut corners so that fire engines could more easily get through if things went wrong again. In this way, tiny octagonal plazas were formed all over the city where two streets intersect. Such oblique corners are not often found in other cities.

The author R. Broby-Johansen is alone in making another suggestion: "These oblique corners were ordained by law in 1795. The explanation is naturally that the military should be able to shoot round corners if the population rebelled. We are in the decade of

the great French Revolution," he wrote in his art guide to Copenhagen, *København inden for voldene* (1986).

Other capitals such as Paris and London were able to build long, new streets consisting entirely of the same neo-classical houses. This was not possible in Copenhagen, where each individual house made a thing out of being slightly different from the neighbours. The houses are not all of exactly the same height, and neither are they of the same colour. The windows and cornices are not in line, and nor are there always the same number of storeys. When Frederik VI donated a strip of land in Kongens Have to Copenhagen after the fire, this provided the opportunity to build an elegant long street of identical buildings along the park, but Kronprinsessegade was to be just as individualistic as the others: perfect, beautiful and harmonious, but not uniform. A typical Copenhagen feature is the twisting medieval streets which, irrespective of how many times the houses burnt down, always arose with the same twisting characteristics. The owners of the sites would not surrender a single square metre, not even if they were paid. This painful lesson resulted in some streets nevertheless being widened, and new squares were established as fire breaks. Højbro Plads arose in this way.

Some neo-classical key words are clarity, moderation, symmetry and propriety. When the style had gone out of fashion, it was criticised as limiting and suppressing on account of certain rules that must be observed, for instance the five orders of columns. You had to know those in order to use the right columns in the right places. You went in for Greek or Roman and eagerly discussed the choice between the two. You don't chop and change in neo-classicism; there is something stern and academically correct

Højbro Plads was established in the City as a firebreak intended to prevent flames from spreading. Before the 1795 fire, there were houses and narrow streets here.

A row of houses in Kronprinsessegade. The neo-classical houses were built after the second great fire in 1795 on a broad strip of land that Crown Prince Frederik (VI) donated to the city. In England or France a row of identical houses would have been built now the chance had presented itself.

about it. A neo-classical burgher's house has neither columns nor triangular gable ends nor ornaments like the expensive and monumental houses of the time. Fundamentally, it has nothing, and that is why it is so beautiful. It is covered with smooth plaster in pale colours, especially grey or white. The windows are made to stand out and are not framed by anything. The only decoration is the shelf above the entrance to the basement and a narrow cornice or frieze. The building is smooth and bare, no balconies, no bays.

The first neo-classicist in Denmark was the French architect N.H. Jardin, who was summoned to Denmark to finish Frederikskirken (better known now as the Marble Church). He never completed the task, for the money ran out, and he was sent home in 1771. But his pupils had been inspired. Jardin's pupil, the professor of architecture Caspar Frederik Harsdorff (1735-99), persuaded to king to give him a site on Kongens Nytorv, for he was eager to build a full-size model of a neo-classical house. This was just so that his students could have something good to copy (and he himself could have something to live in). The king agreed, and in 1779 Harsdorff built a unique white house with a temple motif between Charlottenborg and the Royal Theatre. It demonstrates three different façades in one and the same house. Ready to use.

A few years later, the fire did its damage, and the model was used more than Harsdorff had ever imagined. He had taught the artisans in the Academy, and now they were to build several hundred houses. It couldn't be better. The city had only just managed to catch its breath after the great fire when the British surrounded it in 1807 and demanded the surrender of the fleet. They launched a devastating bombardment of the city lasting three nights in order to achieve their objective. The Cathedral was struck and burned down along with the University and the Latin Quarter with its professorial houses and halls of residence.

This time, Christian Frederik Hansen (1756-1845) stood ready with all the simple neo-classical apparatus. He loathed decorations for example in the form of bay windows and proposed a tax

Slutterigade behind the Law Courts in Nytorv. Built at the time when a prison had to scare the life out of people with its brutality and enclosed appearance. Designed by C.F. Hansen and built 1813-16.

Magstræde is one of the oldest streets in Copenhagen. The name is known from 1563 and refers to a "mag", a privy situated at the edge of the water. As in the rest of the old part of Copenhagen, the houses were mostly built after the second great fire of 1795.

of six *rigsdaler* per bay and ten for the particularly ugly ones. The money was to go to an institution for orphan children. His style was even simpler than that of his teacher, Harsdorff, undoubtedly because this time there were no longer people with money. He made a virtue of necessity and was himself forced to re-use and build further on ruins when he was faced with his greatest tasks – a new Christiansborg Palace (once more burnt down), a new town hall and a new cathedral. An architect could not aspire to more than this.

Specialists today call him a world-class genius. It is thanks to him that Copenhagen is reckoned among the major neo-classical cities. He placed his huge, fantastic landmarks among the quiet burghers' houses: the Town Hall and Law Courts on Nytorv with the colossal ionic columns and behind them the tall steps leading up to the three entrance portals. Then came the hugely frightening and brutal prison with small windows in the enclosed Slutterigade, finished by an arch at either end. Christiansborg Palace Chapel was a Roman temple, the Cathedral Church of Our Lady, Vor Frue Kirke, with the compact tower and no spire a mixture of a Roman basilica and a Greek temple. The Metropolitan School on Frue Plads is also by Hansen.

C.F. Hansen was the arbiter of taste for almost 50 years. Younger architects saw him as a dictator and were relieved when the old man died at a ripe old age in 1845. He had lived to become out-dated and unpopular. People found his buildings too heavy and stringent, their walls too enormous. They longed for colour and Romanticism.

When the old sculptor Bertel Thorvaldsen stood delightedly looking at his exuberant ochre, blue and white museum on Slotsholmen, he is said to have exclaimed: "See, the museum is smiling like a flower". It was cheek by jowl with C.F. Hansen's deadly serious Christiansborg Palace, which later burnt down. Thorvaldsens Museum, opened in 1848, betokened a breach with what its architect, Gottlieb Bindesbøll, called Copenhagen's "embarrassing grey architecture". That was now a thing of the past.

At more or less the same time came the Constitution, a period of growth, industry and cholera. And the ramparts were levelled. Copenhagen was no longer a fortress city, unhealthily hidden behind high green ramparts and damp moats. Nor was it any longer closed down for the night, and the keys were no longer taken to the king. Nowadays, the ramparts have been replaced by entry phones and locks that buzz when you can open them.

Hardly had C.F. Hansen been laid in his grave before the reaction against him came with full force. People were thirsting for colour, decoration, bays and a feeling of charm. Hansen just managed to see Thorvaldsen's polychrome museum and the new university in Frue Plads, where Gothic pointed arches suddenly sneaked in. They were certainly not classical. Copenhageners started painting their houses in other colours than grey and white. Italy and ochre came into fashion, the bright blues, reds and greens of Pompeii. From the 1850s it was the rule that there no longer were any rules. People stole ideas from all historical periods in all countries. The style is known as historicism. Architects built taller and taller buildings in the Gothic style, Romanesque style, Italian, Dutch and French Renaissance, the Viking style and whatever – European or Nordic. Characteristic towers of zinc or copper made their appearance everywhere on the tops of buildings. They are from the period about 1900, built by the self-confident middle classes. In the main streets the richly decorated façades were intended to tempt tenants to rent the large, expensive apartments. Nørre Farimagsgade is from the 1870s and is pretentious and decorated from end to end. On the other hand, the side streets to it and Nansensgade behind it are not. The poor nevertheless rented apartments there.

A new district arose behind the Royal Theatre in the 1860s when the navy left its old enclave of Gammelholm. The model was the stuccoed area of Berlin, and it showed itself in all its splendour in the broad streets, where prefabricated mermaids, garlands of flowers and cherubs adorn the façades. According to a well-established Copenhagen custom, the further you moved into

Copenhagen is considered one of the leading
classicist cities. The style is quite simple,
without ornament.

A view through the colossal Greek Doric columns at the entrance to Copenhagen Cathedral, designed by the great name of Danish and international neo-classicism, C.F. Hansen.

the back yards of the tenements, the darker, more crowded and impoverished things became. With the exception of the Frederiksstad district around Amalienborg, where no poor people lived, rich and poor lived in close proximity to each other in a clear hierarchy, where the front of the building was the best and the first floor the best of all.

Out in the suburbs of Vesterbro and Nørrebro, historicism flourished in a more modest manner, and here people moving in from the country districts also began to congregate in extensive working-class and poor districts. Cement replaced sandstone everywhere. Historicism continued until the First World War, after which the urge for decoration died down and has not since returned to Copenhagen.

The list of losses of wonderful old streets with Renaissance houses, merchants' houses, gabled houses, mansions, inner courtyards with beautifully carved external galleries and wooden staircases, all demolished by a modern age, is poignant and long. Entire districts in the central area were demolished in the 20th century and replaced with dreary blocks of apartments or rows of offices and broad, wind-swept streets – Copenhagen's fourth great catastrophe after the fires in 1728, 1795 and 1807.

When beautiful houses are worn out, they must either be renovated or pulled down. In the 19th century, they were always pulled down, especially around the turn of the century, when the city was affected by growing pains and an urge to become a City, and old things were insignificant and embarrassing. "Clear out and pull down! The rotting old shacks in the unhealthy districts in the city are an eyesore to Copenhagen," wrote one newspaper in 1890. "When we move into the New Year and look forward to all those splendid things that are to decorate the city's façade, asphalt and electric light, we must not forget that immediately behind this beautiful façade there is the reverse side of the coin: old alleyways that are a disgrace to our city. Where are those resolute men who will make an effort to remove these miserable shacks? Where are those dynamic forces that can overturn these marks of shame? Where are the powerful lungs that can blow away all the filth from our city?"

Things proceeded at a great pace right up to the 1970s, when opposition at last made itself felt with debates in the newspapers and a torchlight procession when the publishing house, Gutenberghus, sought to swallow up the last remaining part of Landemærket. Another turning point was the furrier Birger Christensen's purchase of houses and courtyards around his shop in Østergade, whereby he single-handedly saved and revivified Pistolstræde in 1971 and showed speculators that you could also make money in *that* way.

Nevertheless, the city is well preserved. Other cities, for instance Stockholm, managed to achieve more damage in this senseless period. They were more thorough and moved faster. Copenhagen also got through the first and second world wars without destruction, and pressure on the old part of the city had been relieved when the centre was moved to the new Rådhusplads in 1905. There was room there for all those modern things that needed space: the rational, American-inspired office buildings around the Freedom Column and Vesterport Station.

Despite the long list of losses, Copenhagen displays its restrained neo-classicism in street after street. We quite happily call the oldest part of the city the medieval city out of reverence for its old, winding network of streets which were made to fit the contour lines or to go at right angles to them. The market squares also lie where they lay in the Middle Ages. But in reality, it is the neo-classical city we walk around in.

The painter Paul Gauguin lived there for six months or so in 1885: "I hate Denmark, profoundly and passionately. Its climate, its residents ... I am sorry, I forgot to mention the admirable houses that are built to be warm in the winter and cool in the summer, and that the city is beautiful."

The Port of Copenhagen when the ferry Sjælland was still there and the Royal Library, the Black Diamond, further away on the left. On the right, Christianshavn. The water is clean enough to bathe in.

The Latin Quarter

Out on the Amager tundra the humanists weep over the Latin Quarter, which they were foolish enough to leave in the 1970s and move to the "Copenhagen University Temporary Extension on Amager" as it was originally called.

Meanwhile, law students stay behind to crow in the main building on Frue Plads, only disturbed by the Cathedral bells and the nearby cafés. They can stand chatting outdoors on the monumental square, while the outstanding figures of science and the Church keep watch over them from their pedestals fronting the University. The real bishop lives beside them in his bishop's palace, Bispegården. The new academic power brokers, united in the Association of Danish Lawyers and Economists, have taken the place over. This is *too much* for the arts people, who think it is they who have the right to their historical place in the old city. They are also far better at being bohemians. There is a powerful, romantic idea in the Latin Quarter of how to study in the right way: It must be done here in the heart of the city in dignified old buildings, and it must be redolent of spirit and tradition. You ought to live in the old hall of residence, Regensen, stroll to lectures, bury yourself in boxes of books and tiptoe to your permanent seat in the cathedral-like building of the University Library overlooking Fiolstræde. The place still lives on that idea, and everyone seems agreed to keep the dream alive, even the estate agents who, with something approaching aesthetic linguistic invention, sell "love in the attic", "the student's dream lodgings" and "your nest in the Latin Quarter". Francophile Copenhageners go in for the *Quartier latin* and the *Dôme*.

The Latin Quarter is the Cathedral and the University and the books. "Here, in silence, learning speaks out. Here stands the stern, grey Metropolitan School; here budding grandees have fought with their problems and worn their sleeves shiny by carrying books; here they have later strolled to the waiting lecture hall with thoughts concentrated on the day's lecture. And a few of them now stand on Frue Plads in bronze, in the shadow of the Cathedral, serene and hard of hearing, with a slumbering, full-of-days smile, while a new generation mills about beneath them like a school of dancing," wrote Jacob Paludan in 1940.

There was a special aura to students. Right until the 1920s and 1930s it was common for the better-off Copenhagen families to have a student living in their homes as a kind of charitable gesture, or else they might have a student who came and had dinner once a week.

The Tower of Copenhagen Cathedral. The architect C.F. Hansen was not keen on towers and certainly did not like spires.

Copenhagen University in Frue Plads at the heart of the Latin Quarter. A square does not simply emerge of its own accord: from the Middle Ages and until the British bombardment in 1807, the cemetery was situated here.

The Latin Quarter is mainly the area between Nørregade and Købmagergade, but there are no precise boundaries. At the very least it encompasses the square round the cathedral, Fiolstræde, Store Kannikestræde, Krystalgade and Studiestræde. A broader definition brings in Gråbrødretorv, Skindergade and Sankt Peders Stræde as well.

In other old European cities the area around the university is also known as the Latin Quarter. This is where they once spoke Latin. The snooty students disputed in Latin in the streets to practise and to show that they were something special. Latin was also the only real language in which to address God if you were a Catholic, but even after the Reformation, Latin was still *the* language. The literature and culture of Antiquity were viewed as the basis of an elite education.

This part of the city went up in flames in 1807 when the British used the tall steeple of the Cathedral as a target and brought it down in flames, setting yet other buildings alight. So the Latin Quarter is generally under 200 years old, although it is felt to be the very old part of the city.

The significance of this district is learning and faith.

From the moment the first university in The Kingdom Denmark/Norway/Sweden was established with the Pope's blessing in this part of the city in 1479, Church and University were closely related. The whole aim of the University was to train Catholic priests. Students could also read a little law and medicine, but there was no possibility of graduating in anything but theology. The Cathedral Church of Our Lady is the old Catholic St Mary's Church, which was prey to the iconoclasts during the Reformation. In those days it was full of relics – a piece of the Cross in a glass case that was often kissed, a finger of Abbot Vilhelm, a piece of a sacred tunic and the banner an angel presented to Saint Olaf.

Pictures of saints, sepulchral monuments, forty altars and wax images were massed in what is now a stern, bare Protestant church. It has stood on the same spot since the 12th century, but has been rebuilt, burned down and bombarded. It has changed its style four times since Absalon started on it: In the Middle Ages it was first Norman and then Gothic. Later it was turned into a baroque church – destroyed by the British – and now it stands there as a mighty neo-classical church with the façade of a temple and dates only from 1829. And inside stands the most copied figure of Christ in the world with his arms outstretched. Thorvaldsen's Jesus is a man as big as a rocket on a launching pad. A small-scale version stands on coffee tables the world over.

The Cathedral is slowly moving back towards semi-Catholic conditions: After five years of vain discussions with the previous bishop, it was given permission under his successor in 1993 to erect a globe for candles, where people can light a

On the initiative of the founder of Copenhagen, Bishop Absalon, Frue Kirke – the church of Our Lady – was built on the highest point of the village. It is the city's oldest still-existing church, but in a quite different shape than in the Middle Ages. Consecrated to the Virgin Mary when we were Catholics.

candle and in this way say a wordless prayer. The earlier bishop thought this was a lot of Catholic rubbish completely out of place in the Lutheran tradition. On Friday and Sunday evenings, Copenhageners gather for Midnight Mass under the barrel vaulting, while their hand-written prayers are read out. Feeling and spirituality are on their way back into the Church of the Word. And when the Cathedral dares to do this, others will follow.

The handsome low-built Metropolitan School on the one short side of the square, Fiolstræde, is the oldest school in Copenhagen, possibly as old as the church and is mentioned for the first time in 1246 as Vor Frue Latinskole – Our Lady's Grammar School. It was strict to the very end. Here.

The Metropolitan School has moved out to Nørrebro; the University has taken over the building, and the scholars no longer have the right to go about begging and singing ... *panem propter Dominum* (bread for God's sake) in the streets. Several features from the school can be recognised in the Cathedral, and the square forms a unit.

It was Hansen's pupil, Peder Malling, who built the university on the square seven years later and broke with the pure neo-classicism his master had borrowed from Rome and Greece. Malling, on the other hand, found his inspiration in the Middle Ages and provided the University with some pointed Gothic arches. And he went even further in his daring. The next important building went right over the top into the historicism that Malling had just embarked on: The University Library from 1861 dropped the whole of the neo-classical inheritance by being built in red brick, something that immediately created a fashion and made the neo-classical white or grey plastered houses old fashioned. So on Frue Plads we can see the radical development that took place over no more than three decades: the Cathedral and the Metropolitan School are neo-classicism, which dominated totally during the first half of the 19th century. The University represents the transition to the new style of historicism, in which the Library is built. There, architects took what they wanted from the historical architecture of any country and any time. A rule of thumb: the older the building looks, the more recent it is.

The library with its lancet windows is a pure Disneyland medieval fantasy. It is like walking into a cathedral. The columns are of cast iron, for this place *must* not burn down. Previous to this the library had been housed in the loft above Trinitatis Kirke for 200 years, and there it was burned lock stock and barrel – stacks of irreplaceable books and manuscripts – in the first Copenhagen fire in 1728.

The distinguished men of the Church, the canons, used to live in large houses with courtyards in Store Kannikestræde ("Great Canon Street"). That meant they were close to the Cathedral. During the Reformation they were gingerly tipped out of their homes. Some were allowed to remain in them until they died, but university professors gradually moved into them all. They also had to accustom themselves to not being Catholic any longer and to training clergy for the new Church. There were 11 canons' houses in the street, which were turned into residences for the professors and in time also emptied of them. Holberg's chestnut tree stood with its top leaning out across Fiolstræde. It was felled in 1950 and a new one planted. Holberg's chestnut is more a concept than a tree and forms part of the immortal romanticism of the Latin Quarter. Like buildings and churches, chestnuts can also be replaced.

In Store Kannikestræde, students lived and still live in three old halls of residence, built by good, wealthy men, each with its beautiful garden: the most prestigious hall of residence in Denmark, Regensen from 1618, then Borchs Kollegium from 1690 and Elers Kollegium from 1705. Store Kannikestræde links the Cathedral and University at one end with Trinitatis Kirke, the Round Tower and Regensen at the other. All for the sake of the students. It is their church, their observatory at the top of the tower and their hall of residence – a gift from Christian IV, who had the bright idea of combining the church, observatory and university library in a single building, erected between 1637 and 1642. That combination is not found anywhere else. The library was in the church loft, and borrowers sat and read in the niches in the tower if they couldn't wait to get home. The sole aim of the Round Tower is to form a solid foundation for the little observatory at the top, whence the astronomers could study the stars until the lights in the city became too much of a nuisance. In 1861 the observatory was moved to a new site in the Botanical Gardens. Here, too, light quickly caught up with it.

Today, the actual cylinder and the ramp leading to the top have become the most important features. You bury yourself in the structure, dive down into it "like a tiny creature in a shell", in the words of the author Flemming Bergsøe, who also had the impression of being in an unbelievably huge turbine *and* in a delightful, slightly smaller mountain – perhaps something like an elfin mound. It is difficult to say what the Round Tower is like. It is at all events mysterious. The enormous rebus outside is not the least bit mysterious. Connoisseurs of coded language assert that it is clumsy and simple. A mixture of Latin, Hebrew and figure language: Guide learning and justice (a sword), Jehova in the heart of the crowned king Christian IV (a heart). That is to say: Dear God, ensure that the king is wise and just.

The remarkable thing about the tower is that the 209-metre-long spiral ramp serves no purpose. It was not used for anything, not even in the king's own day. Only the Russian Tsar Peter the Great rode to the top, while his wife drove up in a carriage. Some scholars believe that the rather less than eight turns represent the spheres in the Ptolemaic system, which sees the Earth as standing still and as the centre of the universe. Others are convinced that the turns symbolise an ascent through the seven chakras of Hinduism and Buddhism, which are the psychic centres of energy along the human spine, not to mention the seven categories in the cabalistic tree of life and so on and so forth. The Round Tower is our pyramid for which no mystical interpretation is too mystical: If you placed the tower four times on top of itself, the height would be that of the Egyptian Cheops pyramid. A more down-to-earth story is that in 1880 a choirboy fell all the way down through the hollow cylinder at the centre and survived. It was necessary to remove a few stones at the bottom to pull him out. For the rest of his life he was the one who fell through the tower. Even in his obituary.

What can a tower like this be used for? For many years Copenhageners used it to commit suicide. One of Flemming Bergsøe's ancestors, the statistician Adolf Bergsøe, was married in Trinitatis Kirke. He was an important man in the city, and his bride was young, beautiful and the daughter of a very rich man. It was a marriage of convenience; her parents married her off. But a young man was also in love with her, and it was he whom she loved. The rejected suitor went to the top of the Round Tower, and as the wedding coach drove from the church far below, he threw himself off the tower just in front of the carriage.

The bride fainted; she went mad and hated her husband for the rest of her life. She tormented and plagued him so much that in the end he also put an end to his life.

It became fashionable to throw yourself off the tower, and the cartoonist Fritz Jürgensen could allow himself to laugh a little at it. His maimed suicide is seen lying in the street while a helpful gentleman shouts: "Heavens. Did you hurt yourself?" Finally, in the 1880s the authorities erected an extra high enclosure around the original railings.

Trinitatis means trinity in Latin – God, Jesus and the Holy Spirit. For Christian IV the colossus also became a collection of the three most important elements relating to the University – the Church, the Library and the Observatory.

The unique winding ramp in the Round Tower is 200 metres long and twists round a hollow cylinder down through which a choirboy once fell and survived.

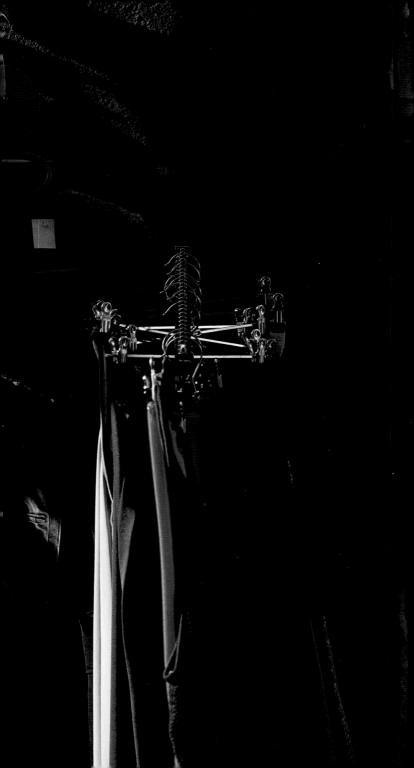

Around Pisserenden

The author Morten Sabroe slept in the last brothel in Teglgårdstræde in the 1970s. There was an iron bar under the bed with which to defend himself, for the prostitutes' pimps were very angry indeed. They had discovered which way the wind was blowing: the street was to be modernised, and they were to be thrown out. Sabroe was holding the fort in the brothel for a friend who had just bought the house to renovate it as the superannuated girls dropped out. "And what a house! The pros needed renovating as well; they were dolled up with mascara and powder and lipstick and wigs, waxwork figures from Madame Tussaud's Chamber of Horrors. They hung out of the windows from ten in the morning until five in the afternoon. They cackled like hens and displayed all their wares up on the window ledge so the street came to look like a scene from a Fellini film."

Most of those writing about the district were amazed at the age to which the girls could go on having clients: 16 a day – and already on a national pension! There was also room for homosexuals in these tolerant streets. They behaved discreetly in the 1950s and 60s, although Larsbjørnsstræde and the side streets off Strøget near Rådhuspladsen were also their province. Gays throughout Scandinavia knew that this was where to go.

"From doors and entrances to basements there issued a pungent stench of urine after visitors to the many pubs and bars. Here, for the first time, I saw very masculine women disporting a clear growth of morning beard, staggering home on heels that were far too high for them. In the entrance there were regularly two men passionately kissing each other goodbye after a good night." Such was the 1964 experience of the 15-year-old Allan Mylius Thomsen. Later, he moved into the district and wrote its history. By then the National Association of Gays and Lesbians had moved into Teglgårdstræde, and they were no longer discreet. "During the night, or rather on Fridays and Saturdays, the gays took over Pisserenden. The residents could hear their characteristic howls of jealousy as they fought," he writes in Nørre Kvarters Krønike (1997). Since the 1920s they have constantly been going to and fro between the local bars and the Ørsted Park.

Throughout almost the entire 20th century, Teglgårdstræde, Larsbjørnsstræde and to some extent Sankt Peders Stræde were

the red light area and the lowest of the low in town, though this had not previously been the case. Until 1900, these streets had been impoverished, but "clean", because there were worse places after all. But when the rough slum streets around Vandkunsten were redeveloped or simply demolished around 1905, that was where the girls went because that was where there were small cheap apartments to be had. Many moved their businesses out to Vesterbro. And when the turn came to the slums in Borgergade and Adelgade still more girls crowded into Pisserenden, the place famous not for having the prettiest girls, but rather the oldest, sitting in their windows and beckoning their clients up to them.

On account of the importunate professional women in the district, Adelaide Husmann refused to allow any women unaccompanied by gentlemen into her wine bar on the corner of Larsbjørnsstræde and Vestergade. She would not have its good reputation spoiled, and in general she preferred to feel she belonged to the respectable Vestergade. This ban was enforced from 1907 to 1981, but then the American President's wife, Hillary Clinton was allowed to have a proper man's lunch served to her in the still existing Husmanns Vinstue.

During the 1990s, the very last remnants of prostitutes, louts, rent boys, drunks and junkies, pimps and pub pianists, once the

The poor district surrounding Larslejsstræde, Teglgårdstræde, Larsbjørnsstræde and Sankt Peders Stræde is unofficially known as Pisserenden ("The Piss Duct") after the stench that once enveloped the place.

unchallenged rulers of the place, moved out. All the low pubs had disappeared and been replaced by vegetarian restaurants and juice bars. Some of the old inhabitants miss the girls. Some even miss the loafers, so Pisserenden is experiencing the same divisions as Vesterbro and Christianshavn and all the other districts that are on their way to becoming the home of well-dressed people with swipe cards to open their doors. That happened long ago in most of the old town. The five main streets – Sankt Peders Stræde, Studiestræde, Larsbjørnsstræde (Pisserenden), Teglgårdstræde and Larslejsstræde – have become too expensive for losers.

In fact, the whole of the old town has become too expensive.

"When I was a child in the 1920s and went from my home in Nørregade across to Teglgårdstræde, they were two profoundly different worlds. Nørregade was the home of high-ranking officials, well-known doctors and businessmen; they were mostly artisans in Sankt Peders Stræde, while Teglgårdstræde and Larsbjørnsstræde lived on open, vulgar prostitution. A striking change is that the old town has become respectable over the years since then. The social divisions here have disappeared," says Henning Palludan.

Details from the district where, to the intense irritation of some of the old residents, the colourful and occasionally beery street life has given way to safety locks and withdrawal into apartments.

Until recently, Teglgårdstræde was the place for cheap pieds-à-terre and women who unashamedly sat at the windows and beckoned to their clients.

Teglgårdstræde has become ... delightful! There it stands, powdery green, blue, yellow, red and apricot, and you can buy designer spectacles costing a fortune. The street is unrecognisable. Christianshavn and Pisserenden share the same fate in this respect: Both were originally humble districts. Later, they became colourful, left-wing refuges for the figures of '68 and their local patriotism. Those people love their own districts so dearly that only people like themselves and their close relatives are allowed to live there. The people of Christianshavn drove the stylish designer-couple Margit and Erik Brandt's café out. The inhabitants of Pisserenden forced one shop to stop selling the multinational Frisko Ice and drove Scientology out of a back yard.

During the 1990s, however, both districts were taken over by a new kind of resident –pseudo-sophisticates and hippies – whom the pace-setting rebels from the 60s view suspiciously because the newcomers complain at the regular drunkenness, noise and disorder in the place and because they don't mix with the locals. They bring their own friends with them and they have enough in themselves, say the local patriots, but they have abandoned all thought of getting rid of them. Conversely, those who criticise the place have the same feelings about Pisserenden as about Christianshavn: they feel excluded by a self-satisfied view of what is right. Residents reside in the hub of the Universe and are blessed with a quite special attitude: "A special sort of hippie respectability and an invariable demand for it to be colourful", as a woman from a different and more reserved part of town puts it.

Larsbjørnsstræde perhaps clings to the Latin Quarter by the extreme tips of its fingers, but it has never had anything directly to do with the University or the Cathedral. It used to be on the outskirts of the city, out against the ramparts, which lay where

Ørstedsparken now lies. Streets such as this on the edge of the city often housed the poor, for they would be the first to be attacked in the case of war. Together with Teglgårdstræde and Larslejsstræde, it rarely figures in the official history of Copenhagen. It is associated with no prominent houses or residents, but small plots, modest circumstances, no-frills housing, an ominous nickname and a tendency to be the back door of the rather finer Vestergade.

The 20th century was its century of fame, when Copenhageners well knew that street: Undisguised lechery, procuring and drink throughout the century until the 1990s, but with a period of overlap in the 1960s, 70s and 80s, when the old world was slowly slipping away and the new taking over in the form of hippies and activists, underground, butt and collectives. Expensive shops and restaurants replaced the butchers and bakers and dairies. An old-fashioned rowdy pub has over the years been transformed into a Japanese soup kitchen, and a quite ordinary Danish coffee bar has turned into the over-French L'Education Nationale with frogs' legs on the menu. Alongside stands the Floss bar, still the prey of black 1980s paranoia.

At one time this was the home of the most go-ahead clothes shops and good-as-new shops. The first leathersmiths raised some eyebrows, as, too, did Superlove's mixture of American rock and Che Guevara. The reputation of Flipmachine's second-hand American shirts and darned worn jeans with stars on made its way into the most distant province. People flocked to the street looking for cowboy boots and to the Roger clothes shop for hand-tailored appliquéd velour jackets. Now, the disloyal trendsetters say that the street is at a standstill. The avant garde goes off to Nørrebro and Vesterbro, but Kronprinsensgade attracts elegant people who do elegant things. People call it Tennis Street, and slender women there show off their hollow thighs and high heels. Larsbjørnsstræde is not so designed, minimalist and expensive. There is still something of the Third World and turquoise jewellery and Janus about it.

The history of the district becomes a little finer only when we come to the ancient village street of Vestergade, which still curves as it did when it had to go round the village pond. The broad middle classes are at home in Vestergade. Once, not so very long ago, it was Copenhagen's main street. It led into the city from the west, in to Gammeltorv, where the town hall stood until the new one on Rådhuspladsen was taken into use at the beginning of the 20th century. And so there stood one roomy hostelry after another on Vestergade, just like the hotels now behind the Central Station, because it was the most important approach. In that sense, Vestergade has been deprived of any significance. Its simple, dignified buildings still stand in the gentle curve. On the other hand it has acquired a post-modern significance in the Café Krasnapolsky phenomenon, which opened in 1984 and was immediately interpreted as a sign of the times, just as Tivoli and all other new and epoch-making places of entertainment have always been. Krasnapolsky was doomed to be the meeting place of the pseudo-intellectual narcissists, where people displayed themselves behind panorama windows and stared unrestrainedly at others.

"They run on melancholy", "they spend their time on the cold", "cold and sickly, an ominous symptom of the next generation".

The café was founded on all the unashamed rabble that Adelaide Husmann refused to have in her wine bar further down the road. Too modern for cultural pessimists and country bumpkins to be able to take. Now Krasnapolsky is just a café like all the others.

The Gammel Strand area

The gently curving street along the canal is open, light and beautiful. In Gammel Strand you live as though you were in the front row of a theatre. In ancient times, there was a sheltered beach here, where the fishermen drew their boats up on the shore. This was the village harbour, where they landed the fat herring to which Copenhagen owes its existence.

Behind it, the medieval town's finest streets fan out. This is the centre of the town, with a vast sky above. Strand Kvarter (The Strand District) has always been the home of prominent citizens. The cars have disappeared from the little square where they used to park in serried ranks until the 1990s.There are no men here with bags of beer bottles, no beery taverns, no sausage stalls, but a row of pavement restaurants serving classic Caesar salad and oysters and white wine in coolers. A decorative and expensive flea market, the Fine Arts Association and elegant fabric parasols. At the end of the square, in a palatial baroque building from 1729 there is the city's old pawnshop, now transformed into the Ministry of Culture. The place has been renovated from end to end, pampered and cultured.

This is new. Gammel Strand has always been a good address. Close to the king when he lived at Christiansborg, close to the seat of power, but never so consistently charming as now. Right up into the 1950s it was called the fishmarket, and the fishwives who sat there and sold fish from their stalls were legendary for their repartee. It was a rare occasion on which they didn't make use of their tongues: "... last Thursday there wasn't a fight at Gammel Strand all day, and not a bit abusive language was heard for half an hour," notes one surprised newspaper in 1774.

Fishing smacks and small sailing boats blocked the canal. The live fish swam around in well boxes in its murky waters or in enormous stone tanks in the various fish cellars in the district, for instance in nos. 4, 5, 6 and 8 Snaregade. Wholesale fish merchants and ship's chandlers were ranged side by side along the canal and in the sidestreets together with the fishermen's taverns. They hung their nets and sacks to dry. There was a smell of the sea and tar and urine from the pissoir on the square. Bjarne Tuxen has frequented the square since he was a boy in the 1940s. His father had a wine merchant's shop in Bredgade, and

Lunch by the Gammel Strand fishwife.

Snaregade, high, dark, and old. Erland Jonssøn Snare moved into the street in 1501. At that time, his large house was situated very close to the water

Luxury flea market at Gammel Strand. The stench and the fishwives' repartee have gone.
There is only one fishwife left, and she is delightful. The statue is by Svend Wiig Hansen.

father and son fetched spirits from De Danske Spritfabrikker in Snaregade. Drays would load and unload at the wooden ramp, the fishwives shouted their wares down on Gammel Strand, and the public houses were full.

"Now the old town has become like Nyhavn, which is no longer Nyhavn but is more like an English street full of pubs. The people who made this district have gone, for they couldn't afford to live in the newly renovated apartments. The new people own them. They expect something different from the old ones – order and service. Many of the owner-occupied apartments have been turned into small rest homes, for both young and old are pampered and spoiled." One fishwife remains – "the doughty and pretty Doris Marx," as Tuxen calls her.

Gammel Strand continued along the canal to one of the oldest streets Copenhagen can boast of – Nybrogade with its gable houses and attics. "Overlooking the canal along Nybrogade there is an old district that is one of the most remarkable in Copenhagen because it gives an almost complete miniature picture of the city from Holberg's day, a brief impression of a late baroque Copenhagen. A happy fate has arranged things so that at one place in Copenhagen it is possible to continue to enjoy an architectonic relic from what is called a good age," writes the art historian Christian Elling. Miraculously, the gable houses escaped the devastating fire in 1795, which otherwise razed Gammel Strand. These houses are from the 1730s and are directly facing the ochre walls of Thorvaldsens Museum.

At the bottom end of Gammel Strand, we come to a bit of the oldest surviving part of Copenhagen, narrow Snaregade with its tall houses, where, in 1515, Alderman Snare and his wife leased a large house with a courtyard stretching down to the water. And then there is Magstræde. These are two cobbled, murky and unusual places, where we can catch a glimpse of how Copenhagen looked in Holberg's day at the beginning of the 18th century. The style is baroque with a high roof and broad attics below. In those days people painted their houses red, pink, yellow or brown. The two streets "only" had one side turned to ashes by the 1795 fire. The flames didn't cross the street. So a few of the small number of half-timbered houses left in Copenhagen still stand on the left-hand side when you come from Gammel Strand. It was not considered fine enough to build in clay and wood, and consequently people tried to hide the half timbering with paint and plaster to make it look like the brick-built housing the king wanted for safety reasons after the first fire in 1728. He didn't have his way, for most people couldn't afford houses like that.

The outermost streets were built out into the Sound, founded on a slowly developing landfill made up of general rubbish and filth. The word "Mag" in Magstræde means "privy". It was the town's public lavatory and rested on poles out over the water. And there people sat beside each other. Slowly, the canal opposite the royal palace on Slotsholmen became filled up, and entire streets of houses and courtyards were built on top of it. Finally, it became too much for the king, and there is in fact still a strip of water left between the town and the little island that is the seat of power.

Nearby Hyskenstræde is a popular distortion of the German "das Häuschen" – the little house, another word for privy. The street led down to a collection of "little houses" by the shore. They were not indoors in those days. In the parallel Badstuestræde, men and women enjoyed a common sauna, but that was closed down in the 16th century because in addition to eating and drinking in the saunas people were also infecting each other with venereal diseases.

Nowadays, these same side streets are a place where connoisseurs go to find a quieter life than in Strøget and to seek different shops. Everything here is on a small scale and very special, and even hairdressers and delicatessens are vaguely redolent of spirit. The shops dissociate themselves from the general public and cater for a more exclusive one, people who know better. Virtually no immigrants live in the old city, and neither do they have any shops out here. People live close to each other in old houses

Gammel Strand, the Old Shore, is the logical name for the old Copenhagen fishing village and harbour. A protected coast behind a couple of islets such as Slotsholmen opposite.

where sound travels. They are wakened at night by groups of men singing and shouting and occasionally also sliding their hands down over the buttons of the entry phones. The dustbin men come in the mornings, and on Saturday mornings you can hear mounted police riding through the streets while there are still muffled sounds of drumming from the discotheques. "We are easygoing," says one resident. "And we are fortunate." These are film-makers, surgeons, advertising agents, pensioners from the suburbs, translators, IT folk, designers, stockbrokers and authors. Most without children or after the children have left home.

The streets behind Gammel Strand are outstanding examples of the subdued style that came after the 1795 fire. Hyskenstræde, Badstuestræde, Knabrostræde, Brolæggerstræde and Kompagnistræde are all genuine neo-classical streets. Simply to mention the most obvious ones. Copenhagen is a young city because it has burned down so many times, and so street after street stands there in the style that is so typical of the city: smooth, plaster-covered houses without decorations but with lots of windows in the front. All the same height. Oblique corners. The ordinary burghers' houses are never particularly wide, and so the rhythm of the streets becomes varied and fast. You don't tramp along one never-ending façade. "The streets are lively enough, the houses tall, simply full of windows," notes an aristocratic Swedish lady on a visit in 1872.

The curious thing is that the new houses were built in the winding medieval network of streets. These curve slightly and have a completely different effect from straight streets. You can see a long way and are confronted with a splendid sight when the street presents itself in this way. In a straight street you only have a clear view of the nearest house.

Near Nikolaj Plads

"A young man drove along with a harlot in a landau and stopped outside a house of ill repute in Dybensgade. I hurried across and spoke to him of his mother and the Saviour. The harlot was furious, heaped abuse on me, struck me twice across the face and arm with a stick. She then went off with him. But I went ahead of them, looked sadly into the young man's eyes and spoke to him from the bottom of my heart, while calling on the Lord. Suddenly, he broke away from the harlot, mumbled 'Thanks', hid his face in his hands and drove quickly from the street." So writes a street missionary from the Home Mission movement in 1885.

These missionaries went hunting for "slaves of sin" in the terrible city of temptations, and in the district around Nikolaj, St Nicholas' Church, they could always get bite. This is where the public brothels stood side by side, so close to each other that sailors from all over the world knew the area and visited it when they came to Copenhagen. Women like Scurvy Laura, Anna Nine-Fingers, Pasty Sofie, Go-Kirsten, Wooden Cow and The Flagpole hung out of the windows or accosted men on the pavement.

Holmensgade was a "meeting ground for indecency in its most degrading form".

As a boy, Hans Christian Andersen came in from the darkest countryside and moved into this district, living in the home of one of the most notorious women of the time without discovering what was going on. She just regretted he was not a girl.

Of the 13 streets in the town where brothels were permitted by the municipal corporation, three were here: Dybensgade, Hummergade and Holmensgade. All had a scandalous reputation, but Holmensgade was world famous and was too close to the fashionable part of Strøget, Østergade, and to Kongens Nytorv. Respectable citizens protested and collected signatures for decades, but the prostitution was not stopped until the 1930s, when the street was simply knocked down and replaced by a wide street known as Bremerholm. *That* took care of the ladies after 300 years' service. Now, the district has been so well done up that the old harbour and prostitute districts have disappeared. Regeneration and poor people can never be combined. The artists' taverns and the Nikolaj bohemia that came afterwards have also gone.

"If there is any question at all of a district in Copenhagen corresponding to the Parisian Montparnasse, it must be the old area around Nikolaj Kirke," wrote a journalist at the end of the 1930s. He looks into Nick's, where beautiful models are dancing "for all the world like a Parisian Apache dance" and shouting, "Fill the glasses, Nick! We're going to drink ourselves to death before the sun rises." That was in the 1930s, 40s and 50s. More cafés and crowds of inquisitive strangers came to the district where Copenhagen's artists and their friends spent their time. "Nice little shop assistants and office girls arrange to meet their boyfriends here and love to pretend they're in Paris with beer on the table and a cigarette between their lips".

It was known as the minefield, but now all is peace and quiet. Only two people live in a street such as Lille Kirkestræde. As in all the other historical places in central Copenhagen, the great indoor architect and connoisseur has also passed by with his paintbrush and pretty details – the right colours, the right windows and doors, the right cobbles, the right lamp posts. It has become charming. A quiet district in gentle colours. You can no longer get anything to eat, but there is plenty of wine, art and French kitchen utensils.

"The city works in a different way now. We used to have a couple of shops on each corner – a grocer, a dairy, a baker. They could live on the families here, but many of the houses have turned into offices, so there are very few people left," says the saddler Erik Hendriksen, who has worked in his father's riding gear business, Dahlmans Efterfølgere, since 1962.

Estate agents sell the large apartments in this part of town to couples in their fifties who want to come to town and go to the Royal Theatre, and the small apartments go to nervous parents whose children are leaving home. They don't want them out at Vesterbro or Nørrebro. "Their children might think its terribly hip to live in here, but it isn't. It's quite quiet in the evenings," says one estate agent. "Many people coming in from outside make the mistake of thinking that Copenhagen can only be Central Copenhagen. Most young people tend to move out towards the bridge districts, where they can afford to live. And they have taken a great deal of city life with them. To the middle aged, it's fashionable to live in the old town. The young people think it's boring." "Places in the old town appeal most to people from Jutland and very young people from the suburbs," says a musician from the nowadays very sophisticated Nørrebro, where the big DJ names are to be found.

Christian IV build small "booths" – houses – for sailors around Nikolaj Kirke. The streets were called after marine creatures and were named Laksegade (Salmon Street), Hummergade (Lobster Street), Delfinstræde (Dolphin Street), Ulkegade (Sculpin Street) and Størestræde (Sturgeon Street). When the king later had Nyboder (New Booths) built, the rows here became known as Old Booths, so as to distinguish between the two settlements for sailors. The church is dedicated to St Nicholas, the patron saint of sailors. And at the other end of Admiralgade there is a glimpse of Holmens Kirke, the naval church, which was used by the sailors from Nyboder.

In the *Copenhagen Guide* from 1748, a man living in the district has been keeping a close eye on his neighbours. He describes the houses and writes about the residents, especially the women. Does their hair curl in the nape of their necks? Do they have money? What about their figures? In Laksegade, he notes "Hans Jespersen, Messenger to the Exchequer. Door always closed", and further along: "A bawdy house, wife a whore". In Dybensgade there is a "... hostelry, said to be a bawdy house. A carpenter's plane above the door. Carpenter and wife died one after the other. On the ground floor a tea merchant. A single lady ". And in Store Kirkestræde an eating house: "The husband is called Hans Pedersen. The wife is a true devil. They kept an eating house for a long time." Then far rather: "... at countess Blum's a pretty girl. Waddles as she walks."

It's a modest district. It's full of lemon sellers, sailors, stokers, chair makers, skippers, washerwomen, whores and bakers. The

Evening in the district around Nikolaj Kirke. It is difficult to find anything quieter and more respectable in a large city.

Absalon in the setting sun on Højbro Plads. He was presented with the little village of Havn in 1167 as a reward for defending its lucrative herring market and the inhabitants against attack.

links between this place and the sea were maintained for a long time even if "Café Amerika" and "The Red Sea" disappeared. On his walks through the city, art historian and writer Broby-Johansen notes "the vibrant mark of a port". But you can't sense that any more. Now it's impossible to discover a single original type among the civil servants and financiers on their way to and from meetings in ministries and banks along Holmens Kanal.

All the old skippers' houses succumbed to the 1795 fire, and so the houses were all built at once in the following years. So we have yet another entirely neo-classical district with oblique corners and buildings of the same height. But it is nevertheless different, for while the other streets in the old town wind in and out because they were built on the natural road network from the Middle Ages, these are at right angles to each other in a typical modern square pattern. It is Christian IV's disciplined network of streets that forms the basis for this, as can also be

seen in Nyboder. And the place is also known as the mayonnaise district because the many fish and shellfish of the street names taste so good with mayonnaise. The city shipyard lay just round the corner, and it was here the catastrophic fire broke out in a timber store and then fell upon the rest of the city. It consumed 941 houses, Nikolaj Kirke and the town hall.

The shipyard extended across many of the tiny islets that lay off the coast in the Middle Ages. They were surrounded by water and well guarded. The city's criminals were "put in irons on Bremerholm" as slaves, some for life. They toiled in treadmills, partly to dig mud up from the harbour and to construct Christianshavn and Holmen, the naval dockyard, which was an extension of the original dockyard made because the city was overcrowded. In 1858, the city was so overcrowded and enclosed, while Bremerholm had room and to spare that the city authorities could not stand it any longer. The navy was perfectly well catered for out on Holmen, so the civil authorities took over the whole of the vast area in the middle of town.

It was a lovely place. Fortunate Copenhageners fetched fresh milk from grazing cows. Milk from second-floor cows in the stuffy back yards tasted different. The area was pure idyll with "yellow walls and glittering, tarred roofs. Tiny green gardens with huge timber scaffolding and rare old trees took up the space, and surrounding all this splendour the rough water, the fresh Sound, whose waves lapped so delightfully against wharves and slipways," wrote Peter Linde in 1945. The canal from Holmens Kirke to Kongens Nytorv was filled with earth and topped with a broad boulevard that was given a totally illogical name for a street: Holmens Kanal. And instead of the dockyard, there arose the compact Gammelholm district on the land behind the Royal Theatre, where it still is.

Holmens Kanal is Copenhagen's Wall Street and the main artery in an area dedicated to the power of money and politics. The parliament, Christiansborg, stands at the end of it. On one side of the broad boulevard towers the National Bank, and on the other side Danske Bank, which over the years has spread further and further into the small streets behind. In 1990, Den Danske Bank amalgamated with the neighbouring Handelsbanken. They knocked a big hole in the wall dividing the two buildings on Holmens Kanal and put a glass door in. On one side of the glass door everything is blue, the colour denoting Handelsbanken. On the other side, the carpets are red, for there we are on old Danske Bank territory.

The entire triangle between Holmens Kanal, Bremerholm and Vingårdstræde belongs to the bank, and here about 1300 people are distributed every day among the 33 new and old buildings. In this way, the streets have become unusually quiet. Business lunches take place in the bank; employees eat in two enormous canteens, and in the afternoon they all go home. The finance and banking district in the south-eastern corner of town is the one

with the smallest number of residents – under 500. In the Gammelholm district behind the Royal Theatre, which is about the same size, there are, for the sake of comparison, 1,800 residents.

The former port and red light district has more than any other become the financial district, with the Copenhagen Stock Exchange in Nikolaj Plads since 1974. Down on Højbro Plads space has been created for a couple of other banks as well as Danske Bank. This bank district started developing around 1900, based on the magnificent Erichsens Palæ on the corner of Kongens Nytorv and Holmens Kanal, an elegant building with six ambitious columns and a gable relief. The merchant by the name of Erichsen could not get closer to a royal palace when he had it built after the fire in 1795. The bank continues through several buildings along Holmens Kanal to the head office, which was also built by a rich merchant called Peschier. Both mansions were designed by the same architect, the neo-classical C.F. Harsdorff. Both merchants went bankrupt. The bank now owns all the buildings in the huge sweep down Bremerholm. From there, the office of the Public Trustee (The Ministry of Labour), the Ministry of Social Affairs and the Ministry of Defence take over the rest of the street in the direction of Christiansborg.

Towards the city, the Danske Bank occupies most of Laksegade, Asylgade, Dybensgade and Bremerholm. In a perfectly logical fashion, Hummergade has become Banktorvet (Bank Square) and the building that used to house the Skippers' Association has become offices. The sea is no longer of any significance.

In principle, the bank could be situated on the moon, because all business and communication is done electronically. But the proximity of the National Bank, the ministries and Christiansborg is symbolical and so valuable. The naughty streets – "the meeting ground for indecency in its most degrading form" – have been taken over by high finance, which has almost exaggeratedly renovated the neo-classical buildings. And they are constantly being repainted.

Strøget

Strøget winds its way through the medieval town and links the city's two great squares – the new Rådhusplads (Town Hall Square) and the old Kongens Nytorv (The King's New Square). One represents democracy, the other absolutism. One is associated with the cinema, the other with the theatre. One is chaotically awake in the evening, the other dozes off. Rådhuspladsen is young, no more than a hundred years old. It lives from hand to mouth without any distinguished history behind it. Kongens Nytorv is from 1670 and is royal from end to end. Rådhuspladsen has always wanted to be modern – lots of buildings have already been pulled down and replaced with something even more up to date. There is not a single building left from the time before the construction of Rådhuspladsen started. The buildings on Rådhuspladsen are in bare red brick, while those on Kongens Nytorv are plastered.

The modern centre of Denmark has the Central Station just round the corner and the American-inspired office district with tall buildings and a skyscraper on the first stretch of Vesterbrogade. All new. Rådhuspladsen is traffic, neon lights and opinion formers all the way round – the City Council, the headquarters of Danish industry, the newspapers. People gather on this great city stage to protest, and in one or more corners of the colossal square some little group of protesters with hand-written banners is always drowning. Some of them seem to be there permanently.

People with lunch boxes, people collecting bottles to cash in on the deposits, the five or six permanent vagrants, newly-married couples, tourists, Jutlanders and Copenhageners bump into each other here. The inevitable South American band is always playing, and people across by the sausage stall agree that the black bus terminal building is ugly. The pigeons gorge themselves on breadcrumbs and the rice thrown at the newly-married couples emerging from the registry office. There is a constant stream of people going backwards and forwards between Strøget and Vesterbro. The author Martin Andersen Nexø thought Strøget stuffy and bourgeois, an enclave to which Copenhagen life never gains access. But – "Rådhuspladsen! – where everything immediately unfolds and comes to life and grows expansive! Only here does one sense that Copenhagen is more than a collection of random buildings and gain the feeling of the mystique of a great city; the vast confusion that nevertheless all adds up; the thousands of remarkable faces that pop out of it and give us the glimpse of a new fate – and disappear into it again for ever." (1910).

Rådhuspladsen is an icon for Danishness and a place where people spontaneously gather when something is to be celebrated. In the Town Hall, immediately beneath the founder of the city, the Catholic and gilded Bishop Absalon, is the heroes' balcony where winners stand to receive people's homage. The statues in the square relate to Danish pride and idiosyncrasy – Hans Christian Andersen, the 19th-century soldier with the wounded trumpeter and the Vikings blowing the "lur", and the Town Hall bells that the entire country hears every day and on New Year's Eve. The Christmas tree is lit here. Rådhuspladsen is the symbolical centre of Denmark. In old Danish films the tower is always introduced to show very clearly that we are in Copenhagen now.

The actual Town Hall was finished in 1905 as something half way between a castle and an Italian royal palace. It is ready to defend itself with crossbows from the embrasures and from the tower's machicolations, whence you can pour boiling tar down over your enemy. The building is the last sigh of the old, embellished days before modernism arrived. The architect, Martin Nyrop, borrowed the battlements and the vertiginously tall square tower on the left from the town hall in Siena. He took the now slightly misshapen bowl-like shell from the Piazza del Campo in front of the same Tuscan town hall. Both town halls are built of reddish brown brick, but that in Siena is from the 13th century and was one of the first town halls in Europe. The Copenhagen town hall is a nostalgic building redolent of medieval romanticism and richly decorated. We can lose ourselves in its confusion of animals, human figures and fabulous monsters that stand still for a moment on the biggest façade in Copenhagen.

The Town Hall Square acts as a funnel that discharges people down into Strøget. Fundamentally, the same people ought to emerge at Kongens Nytorv. Only rather more than half of them go the whole distance. Strøget at one of these squares is not really the same as Strøget at the other. The entirely different histories of the two squares have an effect on their surroundings. Shops and shoppers rank according to them. It starts with food. 7-Eleven, Burger King, McDonald's, shawarma, kebab, Chinese. And discotheques and bars. Snatches of music escape them, which is unthinkable near Kongens Nytorv, where noise and the smell of food is tactless.

Two kilometres further on, Strøget comes to a subdued and expensive end. We have moved from Gøltrolls to Gucci, from the folksy to the royal. Every trace of popcorn and soft ice has been expunged from the air. Stalls have disappeared from the street at a stroke, and there are no prices on the clothes in the elegant shop windows. The crowds have thinned out, and people are no longer eating as they walk along. Shops and people have changed.

A woman who has worked in the underground toilets in Rådhuspladsen and at half way Amagertorv says that the clientele is completely different in the two places. People are very different, less respectable, but more fun at Rådhuspladsen. At Amagertorv they are thoroughly nice.

Strøget consists of Frederiksberggade, Nygade, Vimmelskaftet, Amagertorv and Østergade. Frederiksberggade is the youngest and shortest stretch of Strøget. "The street has always been too close to the noise of Vesterbro and the new lifestyle of Rådhuspladsen from the turn of the century," proclaims the authoritative book *København, før og nu – og aldrig*, Copenhagen then, now and never (1988). Frederiksberggade is the part of Strøget where something new can happen. Typically, that was where pornography and the youth culture were accepted. And typically, too, that part is teeming with life just at the time when the rest of Strøget is shutting shop. Gammeltorv (Old Square) is on the left and Nytorv (New Square) on the right.

The two squares were combined after the catastrophic fire in 1795 so as to act as a firebreak intended to prevent fire from

A demonstration in Rådhuspladsen, a rare event nowadays, for the square has now become a place for hero worship.

spreading further. This is the site of the oldest village, and Gammeltorv is the oldest meeting place – simply known as *the square* – where everything took place in the Middle Ages. The town hall was here until a desperate lack of space at the end of the 19th century led to the new one being built on what is now Rådhuspladsen just outside the ramparts.

But the old town hall stood with its façade looking out on Gammeltorv and Christian IV's fountain. Its back was turned towards Nytorv, where the city whipping post and scaffold stood. The whipping post was a tall, solid post to which people were

tied and lashed until the blood poured down them. The brothel keeper Anne Hattemagers was in 1723 whipped with a cat-o'-nine tails and then thrown out of the country. An execution was public entertainment. Between 1720 and 1730, for example, 14 people were executed in Copenhagen. According to Jan Møller in *Borger i Holbergs København, Citizen in Holberg's Copenhagen* (1982), most of them were poor women who had murdered their new-born babies. The last execution here – of two counterfeiters – took place in 1758, but branding and whipping went on for a further thirty years. None of all this came to an end, but it was simply moved

The Rådhuspladsen only became the centre of the city in the 20th century. It is dynamic and popular, whilst the Kongens Nytorv is exclusive and French.

elsewhere. The positions of the town hall and scaffold are marked in paler stone on the surface of the square.

The town hall burned down twice. Then they abandoned the position in the middle of the square and moved down to the corner. C.F. Hansen built the third town hall – combined with the law courts and prison – in the form of a stylish classical temple with soaring columns. Today it is the Copenhagen City Court.

In the Middle Ages, people lived by trading, and that was undertaken in the market squares. So the main streets in the city were the ones linking the various squares with each other and with the city gates and the harbour. From Vesterport (West Gate), people came in via Vestergade (West Street). From Nørreport (North Gate) they came via Nørregade (North Street). The two streets met at Gammeltorv, which was the centre.

Strøget continued to the busy Amagertorv, from which you could turn down to the Copenhagen harbour, Gammel Strand, or you could go on towards the city gate of Østerport (East Gate), which was near to Kongens Nytorv. For this reason, the oldest part of the old city around Strøget is referred to as the medieval city. The street network is from that time, but the buildings are much more recent. Only far later did the medieval street change into a place on which to stroll, spelt in French, *Routen*, where respectable people strolled back and forth as in Southern European countries. Everyone knew everyone else, and Martin Andersen Nexø felt claustrophobic and nauseated there in 1910:

"It is a quite ordinary sunny afternoon, on what is known as Strøget between four and five. You don't find it amusing here? Well, neither is it probably for the sake of amusement that the same people take this walk every day; they are the ones who *bear* the capital, let me tell you. These two rows of people going along at snail's pace, every day filing past an invisible *Castrum Doloris*, they *are* Copenhagen. They say it themselves – we and the world! Without them there would be no front rank.

We lack a daring smell of the million in all this correctness – and rags; why the devil don't they come in and duff up the stuck-up the eighteen-year-olds instead of standing scowling in the side streets? It would liven up this world of strolling shadows in which everyone knows the number of year rings on the other's horn – and his place in the tax register."

The author Otto Rung brings the regular time for a stroll an hour forward in his memoirs (1942): "At about the time for a stroll, between three and four, the wonderful Strøget, famous throughout Europe, was swarming with purely familiar faces. First and foremost the grandees of the Stock Exchange and industry with the obligatory top hat and impressive fur coat. Driving in his coach came the dapper little titular Privy Councillor Tietgen, and in his landau the martial, white-bearded Councillor Moresco. The top hats were raised in greeting from the pavements to the left and the right. But all on his own, leaning back in his light horse-drawn coach came the great patron of our capital city – Carl Jacobsen, the brewer himself – in a white waistcoat and with a full-blown rose dangling from his mouth."

Tietgen died in 1901, Moresco in 1906 and the Carlsberg brewer in 1914. But right up to the Second World War, Strøget acted as a meeting place for people who knew each other: "Strøget is Copenhagen's living *chronique scandaleuse*, which never seems to lack either good subjects or the desire to discuss them. 'I was told on Strøget yesterday' is a well-known turn of phrase when people want to repeat some more or less piquant piece of scandal without being more precise about the source. 'Seen together in Strøget' has the appearance of being discreet but is in fact an indiscreet piece of information that often puts the city on the track of a new love affair within the Copenhagen circles that are considered to be part of Society," wrote the journalist Carl Henrik Clemmensen in 1939.

Nytorv with the Law Courts on the right. The low platform in the cobblestones at the back of the square marks the spot where the city whipping post stood.

It's not like that today. When shocking numbers of Copenhageners moved from town to the "bridge districts" and the more distant suburbs, and because Copenhagen was to be *a City*, it was no longer possible for everyone to know everyone else on Strøget. No Copenhageners stroll there every afternoon now at a fixed time to see and be seen. The wealthy have moved north and no longer appear so self-assuredly in the streets as used to be the case.

"When I was a child in the 1920s, Copenhagen was a large provincial town, where people strolled up and down Strøget greeting each other, and the shop-owner himself stood behind the counter. My mother and I went to the egg market on Gammeltorv, to the Vegetable Market on Israels Plads and to Gammel Strand where the fishing cutters were moored side by side. The fishwives had live fish in the well boxes in the canal water and killed them as they were sold," says Henning Palludan. Today the market trade has disappeared; the shops are owned by large groups, and the town gossip is no longer heard.

To continue: "Amagertorv is the centre of Copenhagen. If you stand here, it isn't possible to go further into town," claimed the architects Jan Gehl and Lars Gemzøe *in Byens rum – byens liv, City Space – city life* (1996). Already by the 17th century, trade here was so brisk that it had to be regulated. Horses and carts blocked the entire square. This and Gammeltorv were the two major market squares in Copenhagen and they were quite inseparable. Medieval Copenhageners didn't use shops in the buildings, but stalls in the markets. Stalls selling clothing, shoes, salt and so on. Strøget today sells almost nothing but clothing. Food is limited to the basements of the department stores.

Amagertorv is simply a slight extension of the street, which here turns into a long, triangular ballroom with a finely patterned Renaissance floor and a host of entertainers and dancers to watch. It is obviously a place where people put in an appearance – also in the more implied sense, as can be seen in and from

the Café Norden and Café Europa. Both have panorama windows overlooking the real attraction of the place: other people.

The stork fountain has been deserted by 1960-hippies and the troublemakers who for months were the cause of chaos, "nocturnal orgies" and mass fights in 1894 when the then scandalous fountain was installed. The art critics poured scorn on it, and Copenhageners turned it into part of the city entertainment. People dived or fished in it; one poured some blood-red dye into the water, and the police became touchy. "Yesterday at noon one could see an officer chasing people away when they were standing looking at the fountain peacefully and quietly," wrote one newspaper. And a couple of weeks later: "Yesterday evening, between four and five thousand people gathered beneath the stork's wings. 20 police officers had difficulty in keeping them calm. Wild and warlike shouts were heard now and again. By midnight, 12 arrests had been made. The young people had to remain at the station for the night. After midnight, 20 young people formed a chain and gradually persuaded a couple of thousand onlookers to join them. They presumably wanted to see what would happen." Two months later, railings fitted with iron spikes were set up round the fountain.

The trouble was that the fountain was a gift from the Society for the Beautification of the Capital. "The association whose name now stands as ridiculously presumptuous," fumed the art critic Emil Hannover. He had a more highly evolved view of art than that expressed in this piece of middle-class work. The critics thought it looked like a table decoration.

After Amagertorv comes Østergade and with it the transformation. The price levels rise slowly but surely in this section of Strøget containing the department stores and culminating in the stretch between Magasins Torv and Kongens Nytorv. Since 1800, Østergade has been the most exclusive row of shops in the capital and hence in the country. It was just here that the exclusive, international fashion houses settled in the 1990s, when Denmark had enough money to interest them: Gucci, Versace, Hermes, Chanel, Cerutti, Mulberry, Max Mara etc. They want to be only where the others are and feel safest in a crowd.

The effect is self-perpetuating and underlines the hierarchy in this world-famous stretch. Shops in the two extreme poles can't just change places. Strøget is not Strøget, but several, quite different streets each with its own character and customers. The status of Østergade has been stabilised by the arrival of the expensive shops.

"You magnificent swarm of Østergade plumes, you comely ladies and slender maidens," wrote Nobel-prized author Henrik Pontoppidan. Until not all that long ago, Strøget was always poetically associated with women. It was a place where you looked at the ladies: "All this shimmering life on Strøget, all these flirtations, these passions, these meetings, these glances and smiles, these stabs in your neighbour's back and the first more or less clumsy attempts at an approach to the one secretly adored, all is framed by the resplendent rows of shops all the way from the corners of Kongens Nytorv to where Frederiksberggade opens out on to the vast desert of Rådhuspladsen," wrote a journalist in 1939. That kind of description is more applicable today to Kronprinsensgade, where well-dressed people stroll around looking at designer clothing and each other.

Østergade became so fashionable at an early stage that Peder Madsens Gang, a wretched, narrow alleyway full of the sick and the poor, criminals and prostitutes, became completely unacceptable. It had been there since the Middle Ages. Access was through the gateway leading to a chemist's shop at no. 20 Østergade, and there it suddenly was: "It has always seemed terribly depressing to me at one side of the gateway to the Swan Apothecary to see a never-ending stream passing by representing everything we possess by way of luxury, refinement and wealth, while within the same gateway unhealthy dwellings, deprivation and affliction are close to decimating an unhappy population," wrote Dr. F.F. Ulrik (1818-1917), a dedicated man who wanted to make the public

aware that infant mortality in there stood at 75 per cent.

Once more, Tietgen, the bank director, passed by, bought the passageway and pulled it all down in 1875. In its place he established Ny Østergade with an impressive building on each corner and providing expensive apartments for a discerning public. Further down, he created a link to Kongens Nytorv via Hovedvagtsgade, where the Café Victor is situated on the corner, a beautiful coffee-house in the style of the time. Østergade's historical elegance derives from its proximity to Kongens Nytorv. Wealthy people have always come this way. Occasionally, a well-established old giant like the gentlemen's outfitters Brødrene Andersen (1850-2000) comes to a sticky end, but that doesn't alter the fine reputation of Østergade.

Kongens Nytorv is Copenhagen's first royal square, from 1670. The next was Amalienborg, 1749, which lies only a stone's throw away. A royal piazza established to pay tribute to a king; it has his statue at the centre. In Paris, Louis the Thirteenth paid tribute to himself with his Place Royal in 1630 (known as Place de Vosges since the Revolution), and Christian V (1646-99) fancied one like that for himself. He visited the *roi soleil* and followed the fashion of the French court down to the slightest detail.

The site chosen for the piazza was a splendid patch of mud used as a market place by farmers. Residents called it Hallandsåsen (the Halland Ridge) after the desolate stretches between Skåne and Halland in Sweden, but the king had it levelled and cobbled, and at the centre of the many-sided piazza he established a green garden of flowers and trees. He achieved his equestrian statue as well, so heavy and clumsy that it has insultingly never been known as anything but The Horse. Created by a French artist, *naturellement*. Then he compelled the nobility to build fitting residences all the way round. His half-brother built Charlottenborg here on a patch of bare field outside the city. And Nyhavn was dug in 1671 to create a link between the sea and the new royal square. Until the arrival of the car in 1900, Kongens Nytorv

Kongens Nytorv with winter illuminations. From the left: The Royal Theatre and Magasin. France has always been the Kongens Nytorv ideal.

was a delightful, peaceful oasis in an increasingly overcrowded city, enclosed behind high ramparts. As an unbelievable luxury, you could here feel the air and see the light, and there exist almost Utopian idyllic pictures of people driving in sleighs across the broad, snow-covered square. Smoke is seen rising up from the chimneys in the elegant mansions encircling it.

Kongens Nytorv has been fortunate: It escaped the fires in 1728 and 1795 and came through the 1807 bombardment without damage. It is still beautiful with stylish, ostentatious buildings all the way round: after The Royal Academy Charlottenborg comes

the royal architect Harsdorff's white mansion with its temple façade, which became a model for several generations of architects who rebuilt the city after the 1795 fire.

The Royal Theatre is a glorious copy of the opera in Paris. And slightly withdrawn is yet another distinguished middle-class mansion, Erichsens Palæ. On the right side of the Palæ comes the colossal Parisian stucco palace of Magasin from 1894 with a flat Louvre dome. France is the constant ideal in this square, and the French embassy has quite logically set itself up here in a mansion from 1686 built by the naval hero Niels Juel over on the corner of Bredgade. Even the Hotel d'Angleterre, the English hotel, was given a French name in 1796.

Slotsholmen

Slotsholmen is something resembling a desert island at the centre of Copenhagen. It is linked to the city by eight bridges and to Christianshavn by the Knippelsbro bridge. There is water all round. Only a handful of people, their four dogs and the Queen's 20 horses actually live there. There are no children. There is not a single normal house on the entire island, but only monumental buildings of historical importance: Christiansborg Palace as the biggest and most important, the Royal Library, the Palace Chapel, Thorvaldsens Museum, the Exchange, the Riding Ground and Stables, the Court Theatre and half of all the ministries. Even the edges of the quays on Slotsholmen are higher than in the rest of the city.

There is no ordinary life here. At night, a very small number of lights are lit in this ghost town, for no one goes there. One man and his wife live in the Library garden, surrounded on all four sides by empty, historical buildings. The Speaker of the Folketing, the Danish Parliament, also has an apartment in Christiansborg, and politicians occasionally spend the night in their offices, even if that is not permitted. The royal court has a few official apartments on the Riding Ground, providing residences for the Lord Chamberlain, a lady-in-waiting, a couple of chauffeurs and a stableman. Only 30 years ago, Slotsholmen was home to almost a host of residents in relation to what there are now that the Folketing and the ministries have pushed everyone else out. Residences are removed as soon as possible in order to make room for more offices. The ministers refuse to be deported to Sjælland, so ten out of twenty ministries are packed tight together on the little island, and the rest are over on the opposite side of the waterway. The further away, the worse, unfortunately. Prestige decreases with every linear metre. The Prime Minister's Office is in the huge horseshoe of Christiansborg itself. The next most important – the Ministry of Finance – in the Red Building from 1720, the immediate neighbour to the palace.

Slotsholmen: The bridge house on the Knippelsbro bridge (so called after the bridgemaster Hans Knip, in post 1633-41), then Privatbanken, the Exchange and finally Christiansborg. Everything in beautiful verdigris copper.

The loneliest and most uninhabited place in Copenhagen is the country's brain. During the day, people pour into Christiansborg to exert power, to intrigue, love in secret, file papers and occasionally to give up. They make up a whole village every day. It represents a variety of occupations: 179 politicians and their appendages – bureaucrats, artisans, wise heads and journalists. Journalists coming in to observe village life immediately become part of it. So they start writing and transmitting on behalf of the village itself rather than for the community outside even though they swore they would never do that before they invaded the island. They are so much part of the set-up that people outside don't always understand the subtleties in what they say.

Occasionally, parts of the village move away from the island together with their appendages. That is when there's a conference, a regional meeting, a meeting of a summer group or perhaps simply a press meeting "out in town", as they put it. The city and the village are two different places. The main centre is the second floor, where most committee rooms and party rooms *and* access to the cafeteria *and* access to the Prime Minister's Department are to be found. One wing of the third floor, on the other hand, is known as Siberia. To have an office out in the endlessly long appendix known as the Riding Ground Wing is directly humiliating. "A place for backbenchers," is the way one political journalist puts it.

The formal centre of the village is the chamber of the Folketing, irrespective of the fact that there is often no one in it because the policies have been decided beforehand in the main area, in the ministries or in the corridors. But at least it is in the chamber that minutes are kept. The little community is run according to common, unwritten rules. For instance: If a journalist and a politician are talking in the main area, it's off record and names may not be quoted. If that rule is broken, the journalist is expelled.

As in other villages, the residents congregate every time anything exciting or unpleasant occurs. They push and shove each other, and the television cameras roll around them as they stand in small groups outside doors, waiting for news. Is help at hand? Will those in danger survive? And is it murder? In the evening, they all leave the island and go home to their parallel world. They settle in front of the television to watch what they have experienced in the Slotsholmen village that day. The eyes of the country are on them. Everyone who has ever been or tried to become something in the history of the country has spent some time on Slotsholmen: in Absalon's castle, in the royal palace, in the prison, in the Court Theatre, the Exchange, in the bank or in the parliament and ministries.

Christiansborg is fascinatingly and logically situated on top of Copenhagen's past. Everything that can be told about power is to be found in layer upon layer beneath the politicians of the 21st century.

Inside the mighty gateway giving access to Christiansborg, a narrow door leads down to the basement. Down there lie Copenhagen's roots – the foundations of Bishop Absalon's castle, which he built in 1167 after having received Copenhagen as a gift from Valdemar the Great.

The man had already been born with a massive golden spoon in his mouth, he had been in Paris to study, and then he received Copenhagen as a gift. It was the intention that he should defend the town against pirates and enemy attacks so that the merchants could trade in peace. And so he did. The merchants were given their defence in the form of a fortress filled with heavily armed men. In return, Absalon was given still more land and the right to dues when foreign merchants sought protection on his market places.

In Køpmannæhafn (merchants' harbour), as the village came to be called, the inhabitants scooped food up with their hands. Their boats became stuck in shoals of fat herring and couldn't progress further, so there was no need to use lines or hooks. Absalon built his castle on a low islet in the channel between Sjælland and Amager. He probably fixed the pirates' severed heads on posts

The royal horses are still trained in the Riding School on the Riding Ground. The building is a happy relic of the first Christiansborg, a splendid baroque palace that burnt down in 1794.

in front of the castle. At that time the island was only a third of its present size, and there were reeds growing on it.

Since his day, power has been centred on the island in various forms. Five castles or palaces on the same spot. When enemies demolished Absalon's castle two hundred years later, the then king immediately built the first Christiansborg Palace in its place. It burnt down. Then came the second Christiansborg. It burnt down. And now we have the third. There are remnants left from each castle or palace, which have been incorporated into the next edifice. Absalon's castle is in the cellar together with the remains of Copenhagen Castle.

From the first Christiansborg – in an international perspective a vainglorious baroque palace that burned down in 1794 – we have the Riding School with its colonnade, the Riding Stables and the Court Theatre with the stables beneath. The Riding School and the Theatre stand opposite each other each on its own side of the Riding Ground in two identical, tall, pale buildings. In one of them, horses train and appear. In the other, actors. Both places of entertainment had their period of greatness when the court was enjoying one of its own.

The stables on Slotsholmen peaked with a total of 270 horses in 1789 – the year of the French Revolution. They all had to be taken out every day. Today there are usually 20 horses in the splendid stables immediately below the theatre. They soften the appearance of the city, just as trees do, and they clatter through the streets, leaving behind them the feel of a different age.

The horses stand in a 60-metre-long luxury apartment, designed by the brilliant Niels Eigtved: light, high, airy and expensive. The stables were the only place in the first Christiansborg where genuine marble columns were introduced. There wasn't a bit of marble in a single one of the living rooms in the palace, but here in the stables, the vaulted roof is borne on black marble columns, the horses eat from marble cribs, and the lowest part of the walls is clad with marble. The stalls are divided by wooden columns with carved wooden vases at the top.

Every Monday, the sand in the Riding School is watered, and the clock is wound up. This hall, too, is dazzling. It is big and quite simple, 20 by 60 metres, and it stands as it did when it was built more than 250 years ago. The royal box is situated high up as the only surviving room from the burned-down luxury palace. Rococo is sometimes criticised for being over-elaborate, but the Riding School is strikingly plain.

On the way up the broad, straight stairs to the theatre, you can smell the horses. There is a quite unusual mixture of horse droppings and distinction about this entrance. The mad king, Christian VII, was born in the palace and a spectator at both the Riding School and the Theatre. He loved drama and personally acted in the Court Theatre during its brief period of greatness at the end of the 18th century. Some sources assert that it was built to keep the king away from the streets and brothels in town, where he was a regular visitor on the road to damnation and where he became increasingly mad. It might also be that he had to have his own theatre because the other kings and princes in Europe had theirs.

Others ruled the country for him while he developed schizophrenia. Alternately dull, furious, moody and frightened. He neither could nor would be a husband to his queen, the English Princess Caroline Mathilde, but his sympathetic and understanding doctor, Johann Friedrich Struensee, was quite willing to be.

The royal physician was the queen's lover from 1770. They had a daughter, and they hid nothing. They ought to have done. Struensee was so close to the king that he began to rule the country. In 1772 a coup was arranged and he was arrested one night after a masked ball in the court theatre. A few months later he was beheaded and quartered on the common, now Fælledparken, along with his friend the Minister of Culture, Enevold Brandt. The queen was exiled without ever seeing her children again. The boy she had with the king became the country's next king. Nothing happened to the daughter. There are relics of this drama inside the theatre – an entrance ticket to the masked ball

on 16 January 1772, when Struensee and the queen danced their last dance. They never saw each other again. The ticket is signed by their friend Enevold Brandt, who was also the Director of the Court Theatre. He was caught in the trap and executed because he had once romped about with the king and bitten his thumb. The theatre is a sultry pearl in vermilion and gold. When the mad king inaugurated it, it was cool, all white and blue. It is all made of wood and creaks as you walk about in it.

The second Christiansborg Palace was inaugurated in 1828, a humble age without money. The country was impoverished, and a national bankruptcy was declared. When the palace caught fire in 1884, the city fire brigade did all it could to save C.F. Hansen's Romanesque Palace Chapel, and they succeeded.

It was an embarrassingly long time before the third and present-day Christiansborg was built. Over 20 years passed during which Copenhageners were forced every day to behold the unpleasant sight of the walls of the burnt-down palace. 20 years with an enormous ruin standing in their midst. "The black, sooty, threatening embrasures in the old palace had for decades announced to residents and visitors that the city of Copenhagen had neither the means nor the determination to heal its own sores, but now everything had to be new. The palace was to be built up again; ashlars from all over the country were now transported to the capital and were later used for a most beautiful mosaic on the palace façade. Not everything needs to be as before," wrote Christian Raavig, born 1896, in his memoirs.

Not until 32 years after the fire was it possible to move into the new palace, but then, suddenly, Christian X refused. He didn't like it. There they were, with a vast array of royal halls, the Royal Gateway, the Prince's Courtyard and a spire adorned with the royal crown – all of them superfluous. The difficulty with the third Christiansborg was that it was to be both an old-fashioned royal palace and a building for the parliament for the young democracy, all under the same roof. That is to say the paradox of a people's royal palace. Both parties were self-assured, so the question was who was to dominate the building, and to whom did it most belong? A disagreement as to who should have most windows overlooking the Palace Courtyard is reminiscent of present-day hierarchy discussions in the State offices in town. At all events, heads of section, secretaries and heads of departments don't have the right to the same numbers.

The architect, Thorvald Jørgensen, drew a line right through the middle of the massive building. The king was to live on the right, democracy on the left. It was an obvious condition for the whole of this expensive and difficult structure with a throne room, great hall and much more of the kind that the king would move in. And he did indeed inspect all the rooms, but preferred to remain in Amalienborg in one of the four wonderful, manageable rococo palaces. He had good taste. The royal part of Christiansborg is now used for formal occasions when the queen receives ambassadors and hosts state banquets.

Christian IV lived in his curious circular Copenhagen Castle on Slotsholmen, and he had plans relating to power. He built a mighty naval harbour where we now find the grass, roses and benches of the Royal Library Gardens. In the wall at the end of the gardens, you can still see mooring rings. So that the diplomats and spies of foreign countries in Copenhagen should not know everything about what the country's fleet was equipped with, it was possible to tow warships into the Armoury Harbour via a narrow canal and there fill them with weapons and provi-

sions, well away from inquisitive eyes. There was room for a couple of ships at a time. Beside the garden/harbour lies the Provision Yard and the Armoury, from which the ships were loaded. The king built the Brew House overlooking Frederiksholms Kanal as a powerful corner bastion with walls 2 metres thick. It is like a red massif and has the same colossal, towering tiled roof as the Victualling Yard and Armoury.

Behind the Exchange, there was a canal in those days so that the merchants' ships could sail up to the glorified shopping centre on either side. The sea was the fastest, cheapest and safest way of travelling. The water was a bridge in itself, not something you built a bridge across, and Copenhagen lay very conveniently at the centre of the realm. In the 18th century, Denmark had the second biggest fleet in the world, coming only after Great Britain. The fleet was the symbol of Danish power, but when the British bombarded Copenhagen in 1807 and went off with the entire Danish fleet, that was the end of the seafaring nation of Denmark. The Armoury Harbour was filled in and left as a military rubbish dump for almost 50 years with tall grass and random paths. Now the gardens are a large, lush and enclosed garden surrounded by four walls.

The good thing about the garden is its peace and quiet in the midst of the noise from the city. It is a place where people can sit during their lunch break, imbibe the silence and then go out into the din again. The same was once true of the Royal Library at the back of the garden. But that peace is now a thing of the past. Groups of tourists chat quietly as they drift through the new extension, the Black Diamond. They stand up against the huge glass walls and study the researchers on the other side, or they look up to see Per Kirkeby's ceiling decoration. People come from outside to have lunch in the Søren K. restaurant, and there is too much disturbance, say the researchers, who can neither make themselves heard nor concentrate. The old institution has wakened up suddenly to the experience culture. It suddenly has to be a cultural centre. Only a third of the visitors borrow books

The philosopher Søren Kierkegaard in the Royal Library Gardens. These gardens were originally a harbour for Christian IV's warships. Readers of one of the major newspapers have chosen the beautiful gardens as the best place for kissing in Copenhagen.

or use the reading rooms; the rest are culture vultures coming for exhibitions, concerts and conferences and also tourists who just want to see the magnificent building, go up and down the travel-lators and have café au lait in the Café Øieblikket.

On Slotsholmen, the sculptor Bertel Thorvaldsen lies buried in the most incredible tomb in the country. That might well seem elitist. But his museum was the first museum in Denmark to be open to the public. Despite its beatification of a single person, this museum was a democratic institution. The opening in 1848 coincided with Denmark's being given a new constitution. Abso-lutism was at an end, the country was given a democratic govern-ment and celebrated a poor boy who had the world at his feet. He was born of alcoholic parents in Copenhagen in 1770, the same year as Struensee and his queen became lovers and started on their progress to catastrophe. Bertel progressed to international fame, great wealth and a tomb at the centre of power. Elegantly placed right up against the Palace Chapel and the parliament building. He started by helping his impossible father, who was a wood carver in the harbour, and suddenly the quality of the old man's work improved greatly. Thorvaldsen was admitted to the Academy – then an institution also offering training to artisans – at the tender age of eleven. He was awarded a gold medal, to which was attached a bursary for study in Rome, the city where you can see the genuine thing, the ancient monuments, which all artists in those days copied to the best of their ability.

Ever since the Middle Ages, right up through the Renaissance and until the middle of the 19th century, Classical Antiquity stood as a shining beacon for artists and scholars. They loved and admired it with a lack of reservation that is difficult for us to comprehend today. They knew their Antiquity. They *knew* their

Prins Jørgens Gård with the Supreme Court on the left and Thorvaldsens Museum. A bit of Ancient Rome.

Latin and what rules they were to follow to achieve the sublime. Thorvaldsen just managed to be buried in his mausoleum before the firm grip of Classical Antiquity was relaxed and Latin disap-peared as the examination language in the University.

Thorvaldsen remained in Rome for 40 years. And in direct contradiction of old habits, the Catholic Church asked the Dane – a Protestant! – to carve Pope Pius the Seventh in marble in St Peter's. He was the best; no one could compete, and he ran five workshops and 30 sculptors, masons, plasterers and sweepers at one time. His statues and busts of famous men and a few women are to be found all over Europe. He started wondering how it was all to end. What was to happen to all those original sculptures and drawings, to his huge collection of paintings, his artefacts from Antiquity and his own posthumous reputation?

Copenhagen offered him to build a museum for it all. In 1838, at the age of 68, he returned to his native city, where everyone was out to receive him with acclaim, music and flowers. The poor boy came home as a Romantic artist hero. The museum is a splash of colour in the midst of grey, neo-classical Copenhagen, a loud-mouthed advertisement for itself. It is also itself neo-clas-sical, but archaeologists had discovered that the buildings of Antiquity had been painted in many powerful colours. They were not only white. That discovery was just the thing for the archi-tect Gottlieb Bindesbøll. He broke with the long period of strict, discreet neo-classicism in Copenhagen and produced a consist-ent polychrome building. It was finished in 1848, four years after Thorvaldsen's death.

The danger of a one-man museum is that the one man on which it stands or falls becomes of no interest. That his works don't retain their significance, or that certain historical periods fail to appreciate him. And it's like that here. The 1950s and 1960s were an age of abstract painting, and that was a sad time for Thorvaldsen. In his day he was extremely influential and suited Slotsholmen well. The password to the island is power. Who has it, who once had it, who will achieve it.

New Copenhagen

Stand with your back to the lakes and look all the way up Gothersgade via Kongens Nytorv and on to Nyhavn. The axis is as straight as a dye right out to the harbour entrance and is the longest in Copenhagen. In an almost didactic manner it divides Copenhagen in two: the medieval town on the right, New Copenhagen with Frederiksstad on the left.

Christian IV was a man capable of great gestures, and he loved to impress. That couldn't be done in the capital city that was put at the disposal of the 19-year-old king in 1596. It was medieval, self-grown and unplanned, but Renaissance fashion dictated a completely different and grandiose town plan: a huge central square from which the streets radiated as from a sun. The king wanted one of these. He tried twice to have his will with two completely new districts where he could start from scratch: in Christianshavn and in New Copenhagen, but both places eventually ended up with straight streets in a criss-cross pattern like New York today.

King Christian IV is famous for his buildings, but he also created two large districts that are still alive and kicking – Chris-

tianshavn from 1618 and New Copenhagen from 1640. The Copenhagen boundary went where Gothersgade runs now. There were ramparts and a moat there. He bought agricultural land and gardens on the other side, right out to the Sankt Annæ redoubt, now known as Kastellet, the Citadel. And on the virgin land he placed his country seat, his park and the town he built for his mariners, Nyboder. Then he removed the old rampart and built Østervold with six bastions as a defensive arm encircling all the new developments. In this way, his Copenhagen doubled in size.

Rosenborg Castle

Rosenborg Castle is a dark treasure chest, packed to bursting point with the exquisite and bizarre belongings of kings and queens. The inventory shows what the most privileged people in the country chose to surround themselves with – and keep – over a period of 300 years. 5598 items are listed, one more bizarre than the next, for instance "carved stag's head with the antlers of the stag that on 28 December 1611, frightened by the advancing

Swedes, fled into the Danish district in Kalmar and thereby awoke the army", or the armchair from the same century, ingeniously constructed to grab a guest with hidden tentacles in the arms. The person so bound could then be subjected to running water pouring from a container in the backrest through tubes in the seat. When the victim was set free and got up, there was a blast from a trumpet hidden in the seat. Ha, ha.

Rosenborg is full to overflowing of pewter tankards, silver beakers, lidded tankards, drinking horns of rhinoceros horn, hunting cups, Venetian glass and epergnes, cups and statuettes of ivory, tortoise, coconut, ostrich eggs and amber. There is alchemist's gold and walking sticks turned from narwhal tusks or tortoise, heart-shaped vinaigrettes of gold, countless boxes and jewel cases, jewellery, canopies and a royal riding whip fitted with diamonds. Rooms and showcases are overflowing with curios. There is something of an old-fashioned kunstkammer about Rosenborg, from the time when kings collected everything – provided it was beautiful or idiosyncratic – and put things together in fantastic, theatrical displays without any objective coherence whatever.

Many rooms are in their original state: Christian IV's dark winter room with panels from floor to ceiling and a hundred inlaid Dutch paintings. Here he lay on his lit de parade, and here are his personal belongings – his chairs and stools, his table and astronomical clock. Plus his bloodstained jerkin from the Battle of Kolberger Heide, his bonnet of coloured silk with Tønder lace, all shot through, his bloodstained pillow. And earrings for his mistress – along with splinters from a blown-up Danish cannon and a Swedish bullet, picked out of the king's forehead and eye. In the writing room alongside, his son's queen, Sofie Amalie, had erected "a rising chair", an elevator. And so the next three generations left their royal and fashion-conscious fingerprints in the castle until it grew too small and impractical for the Oldenborg dynasty. Roughly speaking, Rosenborg was inhabited for a hundred years, hopelessly old-fashioned and forgotten for the next hundred years and has been a royal museum for the last 170

years. But the king's son, grandson and great-grandson stuck it out.

In Rosenborg Castle, Sofie Amalie had her portrait painted on the ceiling as the naked Hera, the mother of the Olympian gods. She had delicate and irreplaceable Chinese rooms installed in green lacquer and gold; Christian V came along with 12 gobelin tapestries, and Frederik IV with the daring looking-glass room with mirrors in the ceiling, walls and floor. In the small room alongside this there was the "rest bench" and His Majesty's collection of erotica. He loved Italy so much that he had Rosenborg whitewashed. Red brick was not fashionable in the South.

Christian IV's ideal city was Amsterdam, and his castle is built in the style of the Dutch Renaissance. Red brick with grey sandstone ornaments and curved cables. At first, it was out in the country. The king started building his country seat in 1606, and over the next almost 18 years it blossomed to become a perfect little castle that was finally called Rosenborg, "Rose Castle" situated in Kongens Have (The King's Garden), officially Rosenborg Have. Until recently, it was without electricity. A Copenhagen residence without electricity! It was avoided for fear of fire, and daylight was made to be sufficient, which made a visit on a blue-grey winter's day short and mysterious. A gloomy castle in the middle of a city is a rare experience: the *feel* of the castle is strong. The objects and artefacts, which can only be glimpsed in the twilight, fade into the background. Now the little castle has had electricity installed, so it is no longer quite itself, but has been brought into the modern world.

Kongens Have

Kongens Have is closed at night because it is so old and distinguished. Over its 400 years it has been a Renaissance park, a baroque park and now an English landscape park. Other parks are open round the clock, each with its own nightlife, but they only date from the 1870s or later and were created to be used and worn

Kongens Have – or Rosenborg Have, as the park is officially called – is flatter, more symmetrical and more stringent than the other parks in central Copenhagen. Stretching out on the grass is a new habit dating roughly from the 1960s.

down by the public. They have so far not once changed their style.

Kongens Have is laid out to suit the needs of a Renaissance prince – to demonstrate his strength, his good taste and to have something to eat. Towards Sølvgade there were three long fishponds, and at the far end of the park there was the large kitchen garden with asparagus, cabbages, figs, nuts, fruit, wine and spices. Even when Rosenborg and the garden became State property after the abolition of absolutism in 1849, the kitchen garden continued to provide the royal family with fresh vegetables until 1909. Christian IV's park was divided into square areas and there were also the two long parallel avenues, Kavalergangen (The Gentlemen's Walk) and Damegangen (The Ladies' Walk), which still exist today.

As the kings each made their mark on the castle, so they did, too, on the garden. Frederik IV proudly sailed Peter the Great around the fishpond in a Venetian gondola. The castle could just be made out in the background, for the king had had it whitewashed so as to be a bit like his beloved Italy – just a bit. To spare the Tsar the sight of the modest back gardens in Adelgade, the king hung a row of beautiful painted landscapes in front of them. The worst was Frederik VI (1768-1839), who was so indifferent to his castle and garden that he gave away a big stretch of Kongens Have. Where there so far had been a parterre garden with splashing fountains, pyramid-shaped yew trees and embroidery-patterned beds of low, pruned box hedges, the military established an endless gravel square – the drill ground, which is still there. A long, charming hothouse, which was originally an orangery and later filled with laurel bushes, he had rebuilt as a barracks.

Nyboder with the dome of the Marble Church in the background. Nyboder and Rosenborg were the first part Christian IV built of the enormous area he had bought and called New Copenhagen. It doubled the size of the city in the 17th century.

After the second great fire in Copenhagen, in 1795, the king cut out a chunk of the garden and gave it to Copenhagen. The money from the sale of the lovely new plots was used to purchase sites in the old town. In order to hinder a possible new major fire the authorities established squares and broader streets as firebreaks, and that cost money. In the new street actually created, Kronprinsessegade, the upper classes moved into a long row of beautiful, neo-classical houses.

In time, as the kings lost interest in the garden, Copenhageners became more and more interested in it. Struensee opened it to the public in 1771 just before he was brought down and executed. People loved and wrecked the garden, which became ever more worn down and untidy. The fishponds stank, the statues decayed, the military built a dreary, now demolished, building along Gothersgade, so that the view of Rosenborg disappeared. In 1833, space was created in the garden for a hydro where portly gentlemen imbibed mineral water as they repented their ways. Trees and bushes grew and took up too much space. A strong gale in the 1960s decided things. It blew down trees and brought light to the lawns, and people had the idea of sitting on the grass. It had now become an English *green* in the centre of town.

Nyboder

The maritime town of Nyboder had 6,000 inhabitants when at its peak. It was rather like a gigantic modern Japanese undertaking that takes care of its workers from cradle to grave in return for their everlasting loyalty and a whole life's work. The idea with Nyboder was the same.

Christian IV invented the corporate spirit. He wanted these people lock, stock and barrel – and he wanted to cut them off from the rest of Copenhagen. His mariners were to feel themselves as something special. They were given their own dwellings and lifelong security. They were given their own schools, orphanage and hospital, church, police and jurisdiction. Naval law

Christian IV wanted to have control over his navy from cradle to grave, and he achieved that with Nyboder.

applied not only to the men, but also to their wives and children. And the sons went straight into the system so that generation followed generation in the yellow rows of houses. In return, they had to be loyal to the king and available to the navy with their special knowledge. The author Johannes V. Jensen called Nyboder "Kristian IV's old slave town" and demanded that "the miserable, old, uninhabitable houses" should be demolished and a modern district built from scratch. The king's objective with the little community was quite simple: always to keep hold of his people and to ensure that their children took over. Each new move in the extensive game was intended to "influence, control and discipline", as Anette Vasström puts it in her book *Holmens by* (1985). Private life and working life were fused.

The husband's position in the naval command system could be physically read in the apartment placed at his disposal. The higher the rank, the greater the space. That was what it was like on the warships, and that was what it was like ashore. And for that reason people moved around hectically in the various sized dwellings in Nyboder as they were promoted and had more children. Some managed as many as ten different houses. In their old age, they were all given a little beginner's apartment irrespective of their former rank. The regular complement of the Royal Dockyard lived in a high-class slave institution – a total, closed community without any possible say in how their own days or lives were to be planned. Even when it came to marriage, they had to ask permission of the Nyboder Commandant.

"Marrying was not a simple matter, as was discovered by a young man whom the commandant's office considered too young and therefore refused him permission... In his desperation he found a way out. He adopted a serious expression and said that he had to admit to the commandant that the reason for his being so eager to marry was that the girl's good name and reputation would be destroyed if she were not married. That did it. The guardian of virtue and morality threw a devastating look at the miserable seducer and exclaimed, 'Oh, so that's how it is.

Send the girl to me tomorrow and let me see her.' The following day the girl presented herself suitably dressed for the occasion, received a lengthy sermon on virtue and good habits, but as she was otherwise extraordinarily neat and nice, she also received the much desired permission to marry," says Johannes E. Lous in *Nyboder* from 1929.

The State interfered in all areas of life. People were awakened in the morning by the sound of a bell, after which they went off in droves down to the Custom House and then across the water to the Royal Dockyard. In the evening the tattoo, a little procession of three watchmen and a drummer, marched through the streets to announce it was time for bed. And the authorities examined all homes once a year in something resembling a ward round. The children received free schooling, but that had to be repaid with 16-20 years of compulsory service. After confirmation, boys were sent to the Royal Dockyard without any idea of whether they were going to be sailors, artisans or gunners. They might be unusually gifted in some way, but that was of no significance. This enforced service was not brought to an end until 1856.

The Esplanade, Esplanaden, runs along one side of Nyboder, and at the end of this there is the Northern Custom House. From there it can be seen how close Nyboder and the Royal Dockyard are to each other. People only needed to cross the narrow strip of water and land at Nyvagt, the little building surmounted by the over-dimensioned crown. Esplanaden used to form part of Toldbodgade, the scene of abundant expressions of rivalry between members of the navy and the army. The navy used Danish as its language of command, and the officers were Danish or Norwegian. The language of the army was German well into the 19th century, and its officers were mainly German. The Guards were in barracks on Grønningen and they, too, would enter the affray.

This yellow town can be seen in many roles according to the surroundings' need for symbols. It can be an institution of slaves or an idyll ridiculous or heroic. The writer Ludvig Holberg was unkind when he dedicated his mock-heroic epic *Peder Paars* (1719)

to Nyboder. He found the residents inferior because of their fondness for reading broadside ballads. "Dear Friends! The great urge you have to read ballads has encouraged me to write this story of Peder Paars in verse." He was after them on other occasions as well. Everyone knew that the residents of Nyboder married early and had large numbers of children. In *The Fussy Man* he refers to a sailor's wife from there who had 32 children all at once without being fatter than an ordinary wife.

In those days in the 17th and 18th centuries, when the navy really meant something, Nyboder were not wrapped in sentimentality and mock comfort. That only came later. Holmen with the Royal Dockyard was the biggest employer in the country, and its employees all lived in a world of their own – Nyboder. They were more closely attached to the Royal Dockyard than to the city. Copenhageners were not keen on the belligerent folk in this first out-and-out working-class district, and they managed to establish a guard in there plus five iron collars and a sharpened trestle to sit astride on as a punishment. The lads from Nyboder went in to Copenhagen to cause trouble and then ran for home with the town watchman in pursuit. If they made it inside the limits of the naval town, he couldn't touch them.

After 1807, when the British bombarded Copenhagen and went off with the entire fleet plus cannon, cannonballs, gunpowder, rigging, sails, muskets – the whole lot – it was finished. Denmark started all over again and never quite achieved the same heights. Because the fleet had been so cut back, Nyboder was treated in the same way. And in step with the reductions, the collection of yellow houses was transformed into a symbol of the nation's fortitude.

In plays, novels and poems, the residents played the part of genuine and affable people with healthy interests – God, King

Nyboder was given its name in contrast to the old houses that were in the city around Nikolaj Kirke and which burned down long ago. They, too, were for mariners.

and Fatherland. The new industrial workers from the bridge districts were regarded as demanding and aggressive. The men from Nyboder were industrious, the women famously loyal and beautiful. Philosopher Søren Kierkegaard noticed them and preferred them to peasant girls, girls from Jutland, Funen or Bornholm (about whom he found something repulsive). "Now come the troops of the heart: the girls from Nyboder. Smaller of stature, plump, with ample, delicate skin, good humoured, happy, agile, a little coquettish and first and foremost bare-headed."

In his novel *Lucky Peter* (1898-1904), Henrik Pontoppidan lets his main character rent a room in Nyboder, as he himself had done for a number of years. He points out that Nyboder is cut off from the rest of Copenhagen by virtue of its esprit de corps, its rituals and the close-knit life the inhabitants share. Everything is so different there. He shows the old skipper Olufsen leaving the security of his home and walking off towards town. His wife proudly watches his well-groomed figure:

"The moment the skipper went past the Nyboder guardroom with the tall scaffolding in which the alarm bell hung, he moved his umbrella over into his right hand so as to be able return a greeting with the one on which he was wearing a glove if any members of the watch should give him a military salute – something he appreciated and always noted. Then he turned down Kamelgade and made for Amalienborg Palace Square, where he turned up every day for the moment the Guard marched up. When he had listened to the band for some time, he went back across Store Kongensgade, on through Borgergade and into town.

Here, outside the area where he had once had authority, where no one knew him as Skipper Olufsen who had been awarded the Order of Dannebrog by the King himself; where, in brief, he was a quite ordinary citizen walking along, a man whose elbow could be jolted without penalty – here, his back and his knees involuntarily became a little more bent, while he rather anxiously made his way forward on his tender feet among the people hurrying by. He never went further than Købmagergade.

What lay on the other side of that street was not Copenhagen proper, but a kind of suburb, so out of the way that he could not conceive of anyone wanting to live there."

When Christian IV ordered the construction of Nyboder in 1631, the houses were very avant garde: the architecture was quite unusual. The size of the apartments was unheard of, as much as 40 square metres. And the actual locality was so very far outside town. Nothing like this had ever been seen before. Christian IV wrote to the Admiral of the Fleet and asked for money. "As you are aware how important naval power is for this realm, you must take an interest in the men with whom you will fight today or tomorrow if it becomes necessary."

Nyboder is built in a simple, unadorned style in contrast to the rest of the king's Renaissance buildings. It is rare for ordinary people's houses from that time to have survived. They are usually simply pulled down, for they are nothing special. Houses belonging to the king and the nobility are impressive and therefore

they must be preserved in all their glory. Nyboder was built in three phases: There is only one row left of Christian IV's original houses. They are single-storey buildings, and among them now is the Nyboder museum, Nyboders Mindestue. The yellow rows with two storeys are from the 18th century, when the large 40-square-metre apartments were split up so that more people could be squeezed into them. This was in the boom period when trade was flourishing and the fleet growing. The most recent grey rows are in 19th-century brick. Some of the old houses were demolished so as to build bigger and better ones for the officers, while others were sold off.

The district was twice as big as it is now and was graced with far more names from the animal, plant and mineral kingdoms, for instance Tigergade, Pindsvinegade (Hedgehog Street) and Elsdyrgade (Elk Street), Leopardlængen (Leopard Street), Elefant-gade, and Bjørnegade (Bear Street), Timiangade (Thyme Street), Meriangade (Marjoram Street), Salviegade (Sage Street), and Hjertensfrydgade (Balm Street). And then there was the famous Enhjørningsgade (Unicorn Street). A certain Mr Krak turned up in the 1850s and changed all the wonderful names: "When streets form a single line, they must have the same name irrespective of whether they are crossed by transverse streets," he said and tidied up the mess.

The pompous monster Saint Paul's church has nothing to do with the naval enclave. The Nyboder residents attended Holmens Kirke (the Naval Church) and were buried in Holmens Kirkegård (the Naval Cemetery). The navy was to have had a round church, Sankt Annæ Rotonda, as Christian IV's Protestant counterpart to St Peter's, but the money ran out. Instead, they rebuilt an old anchor shop as Holmens Kirke.

At the beginning of the 1990s, the unthinkable occurred: The navy moved from Holmen to the town of Frederikshavn, and the

Amalienborg Palace Square. Rococo showpiece designed for the absolute monarchy in 1749.

navy's yellow town lost its significance after more than 350 years. What is left? Nyboder still belongs under the Ministry of Defence. The naval colleges are still in the Royal Dockyard, and all officers and non-commissioned officers go there at some time during their training. Then they live in Nyboder. But anyone can be put on a list for an apartment in the old naval town.

Frederiksstad

It is impossible to find a rye loaf, a piece of meat or a litre of milk anywhere in the Frederiksstad district surrounding Amalienborg, the Queen's home. The finest district in Copenhagen is true to its character and lives well on grand pianos and jewels, paintings and antiques. A little hand-made chocolate from Alida Mar-strand's cellar in Bredgade is the nearest you can get to buying food. The rest of the long street concentrates on fine homes and collectors, and with endless hammer blows, four auction houses ensure that the most coveted things in the country discreetly change hands.

The aristocracy has surrendered its mansions to business and commercial organisations. Men in white shirts leave their ship-ping offices, banks, insurance companies, lawyers' offices and embassies and fill the lunch restaurants in this carefully inte-grated, quiet part of the city. It is sand-coloured, pale grey, white and copper green. No colours are allowed to shout out. There is a faint smell of the sea here and a stench of lorries. So much so that the fine shops can't leave their doors open. A Sunday in the thinly populated Bredgade is one of the most imposing but deso-late sights in town.

Frederiksstad is a court district. The Queen lives just round the corner; the Lord Chamberlain's office is in Det Gule Palæ in Amaliegade, and many court officials live in 30 official residences in the Amalienborg complex. All the ceremonial is part of the Fre-deriksstad show. It infects the surroundings, where every other

Frederiksstad, an imposing detail from the buildings around the Marble Church. The residents of this district are and have always been wealthy. They have bought history, peace and quiet in this splendid district.

The architect Ferdinand Meldahl designed both the Marble Church and two semicircles of 80 luxury flats around it. This made it more worthwhile for the financier C.F. Tietgen, who paid for it all.

shop is by appointment to the royal court. Even the dry cleaners call themselves royal.

Until things went downhill for the nobility, they all had to have a mansion just here so that in the winter they could come in from their estates all over the country and be in the forefront when the season started. A mansion was simply a necessity. The closer to the court, the better. The last of the nobility's mansions was surrendered in Sankt Annæ Plads in the middle of the 1990s. Now only a single one of the Copenhagen mansions is occupied by the nobility – Det Vedelske Palæ in Frederiksholms Kanal. The conversion of entailed estates into fee simple in 1919, as a result of which the nobility had to give up a third of their capital and land, followed by the collapse of the Landmandsbank in 1922, did for them.

Frederiksstad is a precisely defined district, framed by Bredgade, Esplanaden, Toldbodgade and Sankt Annæ Plads. Store Kongensgade is the vaguely provincial shopping street in the area, where it is possible to buy something as mundane as food, but it lies outside Frederiksstad proper. There are only about 30 residences left in Amaliegade. The great change in the district is that it has been emptied of people living there.

The finest district in Copenhagen was created in one absolutist moment: Within ten years, the district was finished, almost as it is today. Frederik V laid the foundation stone in 1749 with one sole desire: to celebrate himself and the 300 years of the Oldenborg dynasty. So there were naturally 300 beds in the local hospital, Frederiks Hospital, now the Danish Museum of Decorative Art, and the first patient was admitted on the king's birthday in 1757. The initiative for the expansion of Copenhagen was originally civic and practical. It came from the wealthy merchants and timber merchants, whose premises lay beside the water at Toldbodgade, but the king's lord chamberlain and most powerful man in the country, Adam Gottlob Moltke, was bright enough to fuse the two interests. The king donated the land, which was already within the ramparts of New Copenhagen, to the city of Copenhagen. In return, the wealthy built magnificent mansions and houses on it.

The absolutist king called the new district after himself and was placed at its heart, in the middle of Amalienborg Plads, as a tunic-wearing Roman emperor on the bare back of the stallion, with bare sandaled feet and flowing cloak. He couldn't possibly be made more handsome, the equestrian statue couldn't possibly be made more expensive. It is the most costly piece of art Denmark has ever lashed out on.

Just as Christianshavn had been carefully designed as an ideal town with squares and streets running at right angles to each other a hundred years earlier, so Frederiksstad was now planned down to the finest detail. And just as happened in Christian IV's town on stilts, the king persuaded the new residents here to build. They were given 30 years freedom from land tax, and the nobles in the royal square were presented with the sites. The result was a superb rococo district, born of surplus wealth. A Sunday child such as architects and art historians queue up to kiss: "Buildings of the most superb architectonic quality," is the opinion of Tobias Faber, Professor of Architecture. He and other specialists put this part of Copenhagen on the same artistic level as the monumental buildings dating from the same period in Paris, Dresden, Berlin and Vienna.

"Frederiksstad was not a provincial event in a distant, Nordic country, but a fully valid example of outstanding European architecture," writes the art historian Claus M. Smidt in *Frederiksstaden 250 år* (1999).

The former Lord Mayor of Copenhagen, the Social Democrat Jens Kramer Mikkelsen, borrowed something of the aura for Ørestad, the new district being built on Amager, when he wrote:

"Ørestad will be a 'New Copenhagen', that will be the envy of those around us. A historical example of the best that Danish town planners and architects can achieve at the start of the 21st century".

Frederiksstad is the epitome of its epoch: absolutist, hierarchic and dictatorially governed from the top. The unique feature about the district is that one man planned and designed it according to his own ideas, and that man was not the king. He was the court architect, Niels Eigtved. Neither before nor since his day has an architect in Denmark had so much power. He was the absolute power in the new town and planned it all according to his own taste – bright, light and elegant rococo. A sophisticated, delicate and happy architecture that a stricter later age has sometimes considered superficial, decadent nonsense and an expression of 18th-century irresponsibility and frivolity.

In Denmark, the style was only in fashion for a few decades, but fortunately that brief period coincided exactly with the building of Frederiksstad and Eigtved's presence. The country was also enjoying a period of flourishing commercial life. There was wealth everywhere in this district. It is still like that today, except that business has taken the place of nobility. Among the news items in the local Frederiksstad newspaper there is the good story that no fewer than three families from Vesterbro have been rehoused in Frederiksstad after being displaced by urban regeneration. They like the new place with Langelinie just around the corner and a peaceful courtyard in which they have no need to fear drug addicts, but they can't afford to live there permanently.

Niels Eigtved stood on the bare marshy land and could start from scratch. He drew two intersecting axes – Amaliegade and Frederiksgade – which meet in an imposing royal piazza surrounded by beautiful mansions. The *point de vue* of the short Frederiksgade was to be the biggest and most splendid church in Copenhagen, built in honour of the king.

France was an irresistible ideal for fashion throughout the 18th century. First baroque, then rococo, then neo-classicism. Copenhagen built *hôtels* and *palais* with *cours d'honneur* in front and wondered whether the plans were at all *à la mode*. For safety's sake they were sent to Paris to be checked out. The whole urban plan and the idea of Amalienborg as a *place royale* is French, and although Eigtved never set foot in France, he had learnt what he needed at second hand through teachers and engravings. Outstanding French artists were brought to Denmark.

Niels Eigtved turned to his vision with incredible energy. Within a brief period he designed squares, churches, the four palaces on Amalienborg Plads, Frederiks Hospital and a whole series of mansions and houses. He had time and energy to go into details: If a builder came along with an unworkable design for the house he was planning in Amaliegade, Eigtved redesigned it. His requirement for Amaliegade was that all houses should be in the same colour and style, of the same height and with flush cornices and windows. He was ambitious and visionary. Everything went according to his excellent general plan, and that is why Frederiksstad is as generally acclaimed as it is. Its admirers today long for a similar firm, competent and wilful hand in developing new districts. There is a need for someone with taste who can bring it together; there is a need for an Eigtved.

The rococo town is still the home of discreet and very wealthy people who are not desperate to play a significant role in the local community. The district is conservative in attitude and thinking. "They are rich people who live there. They look for serious matters, perhaps historical. They can't be bothered with nonsense like criticisms of loos and news about cafés," says the editor of *Adresseavisen Frederiksstaden*, one of the most localised small newspapers in Denmark. "People from the offices also use the district. I would maintain that they are the same kind of people as those living there: lawyers, ship owners, stockbrokers, embassy staff, businesspeople. Amaliegade is the most distinguished street a solicitor's chambers can be situated in," he says.

Rather older people move in here when their children have

left their mansion in northern Sjælland. Frederiksstad is quiet and stylish and has large gardens and courtyards free from noise.

It was not intended that the king should reside in the new district, but that he should remain where kings had always resided – on Slotsholmen. So at first the noble families of Moltke, Levetzau, Brockdorff and Løvenskiold had the four splendid mansions at Amalienborg all to themselves. But the royal palace burnt down in 1794, so Christian VII and his family were homeless. They moved at short notice and temporarily into three of the mansions, but they never returned to Christiansborg. They preferred to remain in the octagonal Amalienborg Plads to their days' end. The square is not monumental in any unapproachable, overwhelming sense. It is not extensive and mighty, but rather intimate. The mansions are far from typical royal residences with all that goes with them. The Queen lives in Schacks Palæ – the one with the five chimneys.

"The middle-class way the Danish royal family has cultivated since Frederik VI, behaving as an ordinary family, recognisable to its people, has been supported by the architecture of Amalienborg," writes Thomas Kappel in 1796. København som kulturby (1996). "Perhaps the interplay between the self-understanding of royal power and the architecture of Amalienborg has been the very reason why monarchs have wanted to remain here despite the rebuilding of Christiansborg."

It is not a castle: You can see in through the windows. Cars drive across the palace yard as though it were a democratic crossroads. And all the things that go with a royal palace – stables, riding ground, chapel, theatre, state apartments – are absent here. They are all at Christiansborg.

This is the most exquisite rococo location in Denmark and Eigtved's pièce de résistance. So fine is it that the city's streetwalkers were expressly forbidden to approach the palace square. The heights of the buildings differ round the entire circle, the aspect of which is so varied that art historians and architects

actually talk of a "vigorous" impression. A sign of rococo is that a building doesn't just stand there like a single enormous block, but is divided up into larger and smaller structures. Eigtved maintained a fixed rhythm at Amalienborg: He first built a pavilion, then an intermediate building, a mansion, an intermediate building, a pavilion. And so on all round the square.

Another characteristic of rococo is that the eye is drawn towards the central section of the building, which is emphasised. This is certainly true of Amalienborg, where columns, balcony and the tall windows with basket handles are gathered at the centre. On the edge of the roof sits a large sculptural group of boys playing, vases, coats of arms and graceful women. The centre is decisive and is in focus.

A third characteristic is the decoration, both outside and inside. It breaks the symmetry and launches out into curving, elegant ornamentation. Stiffness and rigour are completely out. Rocaille is the fundamental motif in rococo, and some people believe that is where the term rococo comes from. It is a chaotic intertwining or mixture of all kinds of things – shells, laciniated and serrated acanthus leaves, palm branches, bands – which can be put everywhere. And so they were.

The deranged and unfortunate Christian VII, who all his life reigned as a marionette, lived in one mansion. The crown prince, who in reality ruled Denmark from the age of 16, lived next door and so was in constant need of his father's signature. They had to have easy twenty-four access to each other, and it was a terrible nuisance to take a carriage each time. Simply to walk across was unthinkable. The solution was an extension – the remarkable

The Marmorkirken (Frederik's Church) is the "oops" project of the area around Amalienborg. 145 years passed from the time when the king in his omnipotent majesty laid the foundation stone, till the church was consecrated. ▶

colonnade over Amaliegade, linking the two mansions. At first sight it only seems to consist of two rows of columns with four in each and joined by lintels, but hidden above this is a corridor with a 2.2-metre headroom, which the king and crown prince used.

But they were only living temporarily in Amalienborg, of course, and in spite of all they were rather thrifty, so for financial reasons the colonnade was made entirely of wood – columns, pillars, cassette loft, beams, walls and rafters. It was expected to last 10-12 years. The magnificent Ionic columns are made of wood and coated with sandstone-coloured oil paint. The last coat of wet paint was "bespattered with sand" so as better to resemble the genuine, costly thing.

"Marble church, silent and lone/ unfinished, mossy and empty/ in whose saint's niche the nervous boy/played games in plenty" wrote the poet Emil Aarestrup (1800-56). He was born nearby and so he played in the impetuous Frederikstad project, the unfinished church. The idea was that Frederik V should sit on his high bronze horse riding straight towards the gigantic domed church. Instead, there was a 19-metre-high ruin looking like something from ancient Rome. So he was riding aimlessly towards an ancient building site with free-standing marble columns, tall weeds and bleating sheep out to graze. Women used to put out their washing lines across it. And people stole the Norwegian marble.

The ruin stood as Amalienborg's neighbour for over 100 years. People decorated the railings around it and tried to ignore it. Some thought it was a disgrace – an insult to the succession of kings – but the Golden Age painter Eckersberg and all the others who missed Rome and some decent motifs, enthused about the

The gardens in Amaliegade are deep and full of trees and old buildings. This is Leprahuset behind the Museum of Medical History in Bredgade. The little building is full of diseased bones used for research.

ruin, which to their eyes was romantic. The sculptor Thorvaldsen was wildly enthusiastic about it and defended its right always simply to stand there and look picturesque.

145 years elapsed from the time when the king most graciously laid the first stone until the church was consecrated. Everything went wrong. First, there were plans for a pompous baroque church designed by Niels Eigtved himself, 35 metres higher than the present building and flanked by two free-standing towers. But Eigtved died. Afterwards, his rival Thurah made a vain attempt. Then came Nicolas-Henri Jardin up from France to approach it in the neo-classical style, which was now *à la mode* in France. He managed about 19 metres of the church before being stopped by Struensee in 1770 on account of a lack of money. Then 100 years passed. A host of suggestions were submitted, including churches in every conceivable style, a bath house, a gasometer, a burial ground or simple housing. The financier C.F. Tietgen had the last word: He paid for it; Ferdinand Meldahl designed it (with an eye to St Peter's in Rome), and one summer's day in 1894 the church, and thus Frederiksstad, was completely finished.

All the subdued elegance was too much for the writer and art historian Broby-Johansen. He was impressed, but found it a relief to step out into the neighbouring Toldbodgade: "When it is full of life with traffic from and to the quay and the warehouses on a busy working day, it is nevertheless gratifying to get out after the mouldy museum that is the bourgeois district." (*Det gamle København, The old Copenhagen*,1948). He relishes the curious fact that the Communist newspaper, Land & Folk, has moved into the elite Bredgade. Now the paper has gone, and the mansion has become a hotel with newly-rich tendencies. For the same political reasons, writer Martin Andersen Nexø hurries through the district on his way to Vesterbro with the words: "Bredgade belongs to the court and it is following of nobility, diplomacy and bourgeois fellow-travellers." At least, Frederiksstad has been faithful to its idea. So far for over 250 years.

Nyhavn

Tatoo Ole and Tatoo Svend are still to be found along the harbour. Cap Horn boasts go-go girls; men drink beer from early morning in the cellar; and Swedes buy cherry wine in Toldbodgade. But all that is really only shop window dressing.

The restaurant at the side of Cap Horn has 1952 vintage burgundy on its wine list and fried sweetbread with Serrano ham. The harbour has abandoned its old emigrants' and sailors' fascination with America and replaced it with French culture, turning into one of Copenhagen's main tourist attractions, coming just after Tivoli. In summer the quayside is a sea of human activity, through which you can only make slow progress while the sun is shining in your eyes. Nyhavn is entertainment. The clientele has changed, but that isn't because the sailors were driven out. There are simply not so many of them any longer, which has pulled the rug from under the pubs, lodging houses and the girls.

Swedes, Americans and Norwegians sit in basket chairs under white fabric parasols and read menus in two or three languages. The Danes sit on the quayside with a beer in their hand. And every Saturday and Sunday an Asian family comes in with a handcart, puts the old mother down somewhere on the quayside and collects bottles. There is a constant flow of beer lorries in the streets. Residents water their entrances and doors with Rodalon to take away the smell of urine. "We breathe a sigh of relief in the autumn. Now all is going to be peaceful once more, and the furniture has been taken inside, so we can see Nyhavn and the cobbles again. To stroll across Kongens Nytorv on a winter's day when the odd Christmas tree is being sold and the snow is falling – you feel you're in love even without a partner," says one resident from Lille Strandstræde. "In summer we're forced to share it with others. That's the price for living here."

Not a sailor to be seen. In former days it was common to be in port for a fortnight, but today the ships might perhaps not be there for more than eight hours. The Seamen's Union has lost half its members over the past 10-15 years, so that there are only about 3,000 sailors left. They have left some nostalgic traces behind in Nyhavn in the shape of sailor's menus, maritime antiques and two rows of wooden ships in the canal.

In the good old days, there would at any one time be 22,000

sailors from all around the world in Copenhagen – with money in their pockets. Blond Eva danced in Cap Horn surrounded by young men wearing caps, sailors' jerseys and dark blue baggy trousers held up by a tight leather belt. Out on the pavement, small groups of seamen and loafers would be drifting about waiting for something to happen. Music escaped from the small pubs in the basements, and policemen went on their beat two at a time just to be on the safe side. The street was – almost – paved with broken teeth.

From Nyhavn you could buy a new life in America. When the Danes started emigrating in earnest in the 1880s, the shipping companies opened ticket offices in Nyhavn, where 14 people were unfortunate enough to buy tickets for the Titanic's maiden voyage in 1912. Only two of them survived. Nyhavn was linked to the seven seas, thoughts of adventure and freedom. All romantic notions were more or less valid right until the 1950s and 60s. You could buy a stew of meat and vegetables in the early morning and start dancing in the late morning. Nyhavn was a place for mariners and naval ratings and so it was also full of tattoo artists, ships' chandlers, shipping offices, lodging houses, Christian missionaries and pubs named after distant places – Café Texas, Palermo, Shanghai, Mozambique, Cap Horn.

The girls were tied to specific pubs and drew the men in with them. Some had come ashore from the ships they were sailing on. Others without jobs lived in small hotels or rooms scattered around the district. The Nyhavn lasses were especially girls from the provinces who supplemented their wages as maids in town.

Some of them gave up their jobs as maids. They had regular boyfriends among the sailors who took it in turns to provide for them when they were ashore. The town's real, hard brothels were around Nikolaj Plads and in Pisserenden, and no poets have tried to romanticise them. But the Nyhavn girls were wrapped in a tender, amusing veil like this, the last verse in *Nu går våren gennem Nyhavn, Spring has come to Nyhavn*:

"Come my lovely Nyhavn lassie/ Let me love you tonight./ See a simple breakneck stair I have placed against the door to heaven./ I can smash all barriers/ I can break all bonds./ But this evening I'll be quiet/ if only you will hold my big hand." (Sigfred Pedersen, 1954). By then, the more professional prostitutes and their pimps have already moved into Nyhavn. In 1942, the Danish film *Afsporet, Derailed*, had its premiere. Preben Neergaard played the Stone Marten from Nyhavn, and piquant women rolled about screaming and fighting. The film marked the beginning of the appearance of inquisitive provincial visitors in Nyhavn. Perhaps the first. Everyone from outside was grouped together as tourists. Today, they have taken the place over.

Cap Horn started with jazz in the 1950s, and some people were opposed to it. So-called ordinary people didn't go into Nyhavn otherwise. They never lived there. The decline came in the 1970s and most of the 80s as it did in so many other parts of the threadbare city. The new public hadn't yet appeared. An exclusive French restaurant tried to establish itself in this dreadful street at the end of the 1930s, but it was far, far too soon. "To attract an eccentric public who think it an amusing idea to go to a menacing street to have a meal as good and expensive as in the leading luxury restaurants in the most elegant parts of town is possible in Soho in London," are the crabby words of a journalist of the time referring to the "perverse restaurant culture". It was not possible in Nyhavn, Denmark.

When Christian V established his new squares and ordered his equestrian statue, he also needed a new harbour: Kongens Nytorv and Nyhavn were both outside the old medieval town. The elegant square and the sea had to be connected, for trade must flourish and make Copenhagen and the king rich.

The 400-metre-long and three-metre-deep canal was dug in 1671 so that ships could sail in and dock by the quayside. And the merchants could live there. On the sunny side they built a canal street of 35 houses, and the incredible thing is that it is still there. It survived the great fires that destroyed so much of

Evening in Nyhavn. Sailors have been replaced by Swedes.

Copenhagen in 1728 and 1795 and the British bombardment in 1807. Behind the five-metre-broad belt of people eating there is a row of charming, narrow houses with their roots in the late 17th century. Some of them have been made taller or have been given new façades, but even so.... They hang delightfully together in a flickering row of red, ochre, black, blue, pink, green and white.

There were merchants there before the sailors. Nyhavn's first century belonged to them. Their own ships were moored outside their houses. In the deep plots towards Sankt Annæ Plads there was room for a labyrinth of warehouses, stables and gardens. And only on the far side of the square does Frederiksstad begin. The 18th century was what is referred to as the age of mercantilism, when Danish ships earned fortunes by sailing as neutral in a war-torn Europe.

All that came to a sudden end in 1807 when the British attacked Copenhagen and confiscated the entire fleet. And there they were left behind. Nyhavn became an anchorage for small boats plying regularly between Danish towns and a few routes to Norway, Sweden and Iceland. There was no longer a smell of the seven seas, but of survival and bustle. Goods and passengers were carried to and from the provinces, and several small hotels made their appearance in the streets behind and on the harbour. The seamen changed places with the merchants, and Nyhavn distanced itself mentally further and further from the elegant royal square at the other end, where the city jetset sat in their basket chairs under the awning on the Hotel d'Angleterre terraces with coffee and iced water.

The Nyhavn of the seamen slowly took shape. And in the 1980s it disappeared again when the enterprising Strecker brothers were the first people from outside to buy a cheap house on the quayside and make prices rise by 300% within a few years. Now the international public no longer sits up on Copenhagen's elegant square, but down along the quayside – still in basket chairs and still under a white awning.

Tivoli

People immediately become conservative in the magical gardens, for everything must look exactly as it did when they were children themselves. We go there every year with a critical eye: What have they changed now? Do the animals' heads still roar with their mouths wide open? It's more than enough that they've changed the old brown leather balls with rubber ones.

Any child with parents worthy of the name gets to know Tivoli from end to end before reaching puberty and will at any time protest against changes in the Tivoli of their childhood. Irrespective of how nice and amusing the new things are, we become upset on reaching the children's playground, for where on earth has that enormous suspended goldfish gone?

Certain things must quite simply last for ever – the scenic railway, the Tubs, Purgatory, the Balloon Swing, the Veteran Cars, the Boats and the Chinese Pagoda. Cross your fingers. Tivoli is the garden of memories so much that it almost hurts. It is the continuation of childhood in an illuminated, dark green fairy-tale forest in the centre of town. The reaction of the public to change in the garden is as much one of panic as that in a workplace manned by stick-in-the-muds when a dynamic new boss arrives: What is he going to do? And how can we stop him?

Our own children ought to try their skills on the same ancient amusements as we did ourselves. Tivoli knows its reactionaries and tries to strike a balance. The gardens keep one eye on their nostalgic visitors and their season ticket holders, and another on matter-of-fact families with children, a third on the unruly young people and a fourth on their unmentionable competitor at Holme Olstrup, out of town.

The next three elements in the belt of parks around Copenhagen – the Ørsted Park, the Botanical Gardens and Østre Anlæg – all came into being in the 1870s, but the lights were lit in Tivoli three decades earlier. To the surprise of everyone, a 27-year-old hyperactive son of a diplomat was given the king's permission to open the elegant amusement park on a piece of the actual fortress around Copenhagen. It was the best site in town and a place sacred to the military, but Georg Carstensen (1812-1857) managed to lease this otherwise untouchable site because he promised

From left to right The Chinese Pagoda from 1900, more Chinese than China. Oriental/Moorish/Tivoli Nimb from 1909. Columbine in the Pantomime Theatre, designed by the same architect as the Royal Theatre, Vilhelm Dahlerup. Pierrot came to Denmark in 1800 with an Italian group and became a symbol of the unchanging nature of Tivoli. Right from the start, Tivoli has been wild about things exotic.

to erect only low, wooden buildings that could immediately be pulled down if an enemy approached. Enemy soldiers should not to be given a chance to hide behind anything.

In August 1843, Carstensen erected some plain wooden gates for the public, and with that the greatest attraction in the country was in full swing. It was a success from the first day. Carstensen had seen various versions of Vauxhalls and Tivolis abroad, and at home he had seen how hopelessly undernourished Copenhagen was in the way of entertainment. People had to go right out to Dyrehavsbakken or to Frederiksberg to have fun, and the establishments were so small and primitive that there were plenty of challenges for a man of the world on whom

no limits had been imposed. Carstensen simply introduced European public entertainment habits to Denmark.

The idea with a Tivoli or a Vauxhall was to take a rural, romantic garden and fill it with surprises – grottoes, statues, temples, aviaries and pavilions – just like the aristocracy did. Now he added music, refreshments, illuminations, fireworks and amusements to the gardens. It was a something for the ordinary people. And then he charged entrance.

Carstensen was given a luxurious and undulating site with water and views and an elegant avenue consisting of three rows of trees in a zig-zag pattern reflecting the breaks in the ramparts. The place was brilliant, for everything was there already. The

novelty in his establishment when compared to others was especially based on three things: the size, the locality and the elegance. He went for them all, and also sought to attract an elegant public. So there were no "itinerant salesmen or entertainers, no barkers, no booths, no dirty songs, no frog-swallowers, no disharmonious barrel-organ music or visible indecency," writes Luise Skak-Nielsen in *Tivoli og verden udenfor, Tivoli and the world outside* (2000). There was Lumbye's happy dance music, Strauss and music for brass band.

Tivoli was summery, light-hearted and lightly constructed with painted wooden pavilions in Greek, Roman, Arab, Turkish, Tuscan or Chinese styles. Anyone in the world was welcome to join the decorators, especially in the 1870s when the rest of Copenhagen was going mad on the architecture of foreign countries and times past. At the same time, the ramparts in Tivoli were levelled to the ground, and the moat was filled in. The landscape disappeared, and the place was slowly surrounded by buildings. In the 1890s, Martin Nyrop built the Town Hall alongside, and Tivoli suddenly found itself in the midst of the new centre. It is quite unusual for a city to be so wonderfully unconcerned about costly space in its midst. The Town Hall bells and Tivoli are intimately linked.

The oldest building in Tivoli is the Pantomime Theatre, from 1874, built by Vilhelm Dahlerup, who at the same time was busy

A winter tree in Tivoli. The founder of Tivoli, Georg Carstensen, had two brilliant and happy ideas – illuminations and fireworks.

building the Royal Theatre in the Italian Renaissance style and with the Paris Opéra as his model. Masked comedy, commedia dell'arte from 16th-century Italy is performed in the Pantomime Theatre, a mixture of styles, history and traditions typical of Tivoli.

The theatre is more Chinese than China, but every colour has its correct ritual significance. The bearer elements are red to symbolise masculine strength and *joie de vivre*, while the supported elements are painted in the female colours, blue and yellow. The dragons guard the building against fire and sickness. The Chinese characters above the stage mean "with the people the same pleasure" or "pleasure in common with the people" (*København før og nu – og aldrig, Copenhagen then, now – and never*, 1990). The Chinese Pagoda was erected in 1900, designed by the gardens' director for 40 years, Knud Arne-Petersen, who fortunately was also an imaginative architect and able to draw inspiration from the warm lands. Not until the cultural radicalism of the 1940s,

50s and 60s did Tivoli's architects and the rest of Copenhagen give historicism a rest. It went out of fashion, but even that produced something good: the gardens are full of poetical modernism. This was an age without historical stylistic plagiarism. It doesn't sound particularly romantic, but that is what it nevertheless is in Tivoli. A simple and open style with abstract elements. The concert hall is brilliant.

The dramatist Kjeld Abell was director from 1940 to 1950 and started by going underground during the German occupation, while what were known as the blackout pilots guided visitors round a darkened Tivoli. He persuaded the architect Poul Henningsen to come inside, and together with the groundbreaking garden artist Gudmund Nyeland Brandt, he created the Parterre Garden in 1943 and thus one of the most wonderful things in Tivoli. The garden is at the Lake end nearest the main entrance and consists of a large number of small fountains in low wooden tubs, surrounded by benches and flowers and just as delicious

and meditative as the gardens belonging to a Moorish sultan's palace in Andalusia. The Parterre Garden was made according to Poul Henningsen's ideas: subdued, asymmetrical, intimate and in human dimensions.

The 50s were a time of increasing affluence, when things were on the way up, and one piece of dark undergrowth after another in Tivoli disappeared to be replanted, illuminated and made magical. Every spot was ploughed up and used, and the tourists came in their thousands. So many of the most beautiful and festive attractions date from an age that people are otherwise quick to accuse of lacking in taste. Most of the good things were the responsibility of Poul Henningsen's son, Simon. He said that Tivoli was not to be burdened with real architecture, but to have open, light pavilions in beautiful colours. Along with the artist Erik Christensen, he had a wonderful time. That, at least, is how it looks. Christensen invented the glittering dragonflies on the lake – and that must be sufficient proof.

Now the terrifying artistic challenge is to change the gardens radically without changing them at all. The fairytale gardens used to think they could live on flowers, light, music and nostalgic visitors who were becoming too old for mechanised entertainment. But neither used there to be so much going on in Copenhagen as there is now: "The 90s created new conditions in the battle for people's time and money. Competition from the city of Copenhagen continued with new growth areas and attractions in the harbour area, on Holmen, at Vesterbro etc. That is where the new things are happening, that is where it is *snowballing*," writes Luise Skak-Nielsen in her authoritative *Tivoli og verden udenfor.*

There is nothing to suggest that Copenhagen has any intention of becoming boring again, so Tivoli must continue its hyper-attentive metamorphosis on the heels of people's changing visions and needs. The gardens have always done that, however incredible that may sound, for they still give the impression of being unchanged.

The Park Belt

Copenhageners ought every day to kneel in gratitude to one man. He was melancholy, jealous of his honour and sometimes hated by his contemporaries. But luckily he was also clever. He managed to get the parks established.

The architect and town planner Ferdinand Meldahl (1827-1908) was a brilliant political strategist. When the State gave up protecting Copenhagen behind ramparts and moats, he applied all his energy to getting the huge green fortification terrain out of the hands of the Ministry of War, who wanted to see the land used for building. Instead, Meldahl envisioned a row of beautiful parks, and he forced his will through. Thanks to him, the ramparts have been replaced with a long and beautiful belt of parks extend-

Ørstedsparken seen from Nørre Farimagsgade. The park was laid out on the site of the ramparts. The lake is a piece of camouflaged moat. The row of houses marks the start of what was once all Copenhagen. The old city gates of Vesterport, Nørreport and Østerport were removed in 1856. The ramparts were levelled in the 1870s.

ing from Kastellet, the Citadel, via Østre Anlæg, Botanisk Have, Ørstedsparken to Tivoli. The lakes in all these parks are remnants of the ancient moat. The rises are more or less refashioned ramparts.

The whole of this lush, extensive, glorious stretch could just as well have been built on with stuccoed blocks, and the Citadel could have been levelled, as was proposed by the Ministry of War demolition commission in 1865. Too much space sacrificed for parks would be "a loss to the Exchequer" and would cut Copenhagen in two so that people would be forced to live in the suburbs, for instance right out in Nørrebro. We can hardly today imagine abandoning excellent large residential districts just to make a new park. Parks must be there from the start. Fortunately, the influential Professor Meldahl was on the city council and made a great fuss because of the demolition commission's plans. He drummed up support from other critics, and now people delight in their parks every day. Without them, the city would shut them in.

Meldahl believed that Copenhagen should be a modern city and the Paris of the North. For no less than 40 years, from about

1860 to 1900 he devoted all his energies to this objective. Østre Anlæg, Botanisk Have and Ørstedsparken all opened in the 1870s. Meldahl was Copenhagen's less drastic answer to General Haussmann, who created a new fashionable Paris in the 1850s by forcing down a vast network of broad boulevards and squares on to the city's old winding streets, many of which he demolished.

Although Meldahl built a large number of grandiose buildings such as the Marble Church and Søtorvet near Dronning Louises Bro, his great achievement is the parks and the little things: "I took the initiative to provide music in public places. Swans and boats on the lakes," he notes in his diary.

Ørstedsparken

The Ørsted Park is first and foremost notorious for its nightlife. It belongs to the gays at night. Everyone knows this, even international tourist guides, which refer to it. During the day there is a rush into and out of the men's toilets, where sex explodes at lightning speed. During the night, men court each other on the gravelled paths. Rent boys keep to special patches of shrubbery and are visited by closet gays and married men taking erotic risks. Others avoid the park at night.

Gays think they have won so much right to the place, that they opened "their" park to the public during the Culture Night some years ago and offered "safe cruising" with a guide. "You have to behave rather like in a wildlife reserve – tread carefully and don't overdo it, for otherwise the original quality will be spoiled. One guided tour a year in this reserve is just acceptable," explained one arranger.

Historically, Ørstedsparken was a spontaneous meeting place for men, even before it was a park at all but simply a few bastions. When the military surrendered the ramparts in the 1850s and therefore stopped patrolling, it quickly became a haven – "A playground for all kinds of disorder" – where men who had not known each other beforehand could meet every evening and night "for sexual encounters", as Wilhelm von Rosen put it in *Månens kulør. Studier i dansk bøssehistorie 1626-1912, The colour of the moon. Studies in Danish gay history 1626-1912* (1993).

The police heard rumours to the effect that various men turned up on the ramparts late in the evening and sat down on a bench in order to "pursue intercourse contrary to nature". Constable no. 108 Jacobsen lay in wait on 5 May 1865 close to this bench and in the moonlight saw two men "kissing and caressing each other with such great passion" as he had never "seen a man and woman show to each other". The passionate couple were the 43-year-old waiter Peter A.V. Hansen and the 39-year-old cap maker Lars Hansen, and the trap closed on them. One of them was married, the father of seven children and lived in Gothersgade. The other had had relations with many other men over a number of years.

Since then, the place has had an unbroken history as the meeting place for gays. When the rampart was turned into a park and so closed at night, they clambered over the hedge. When it was reopened in the 1970s, they went in straight through the main gate. The same determination can be observed in Paris, where since the 18th century gays have met on the same corner of the Tuileries.

But there are limits, and they were decided by the Copenhagen politicians under the leadership of a conservative member of the city council during the spring of 2001, when, to the fury of the gays, the shrubbery on the most popular night spot was removed by the park gardeners. Where they had previously been able to hide, it was now light and airy. Unknown perpetrators replied by tearing down the hedge around the newly sown grass, and the relationship between gays and the authorities has since been very tense.

A satyr with the legs of a goat in Ørstedsparken. A meeting place for men at night.

Ørstedsparken is situated on the site of the old rampart and moat that encircled Copenhagen and was in danger of suffocating it for lack of space. The ramparts were the favourite place for Copenhageners to stroll. The British attacks on the city in 1801 and 1807 showed that the fortifications were hopelessly out of date.

The café's first lessee herself believed she was bringing new life to the park, so that it would gain a reputation for being something other than "a forbidding and lawless gay park". The present lessee is one of Copenhagen's most hip clubs, and some of its hip public must have gone out there to sit in the sunshine as well. Events in Ørstedsparken are exclusive and sub-cultural. And there isn't a sausage stall or a soft ice vendor for miles around. People here drink iced coffee with maple syrup.

The phenomenon Master Fatman celebrates a cosmic, fond and ironic 1st of May here. And thousands of visitors lie in the grass, listing to ambient and techno music on special occasions. So loudspeakers are fixed in the trees all over the park, and cool DJ's stand in Israels Plads and mix the music. The park's regular drop-outs sit on the sun-drenched benches along the lake as though they owned the place. And if they get up early enough or simply spend the night in the park, they can watch the tai chi folk doing their incredibly slow exercises on the other side, at the top of the steep slopes. Young back-packers lie fast asleep in the grass in their polar sleeping bags, and joggers groan as they round the kidney-shaped lake.

"Ørstedsparken makes no demands," said the author and critic Erik Thygesen in an essay. "Of course there is Botanisk Have and Kongens Have, but despite their names, they are not parks in the same way. You have to take care of Botanisk Have; it isn't at all robust – mostly to be admired. And Kongens Have is far too demanding; the great flat lawns, the straight rows of trees; the important sculptures demand respect and submission."

The park behind the iron railings and solid sandstone pillars opened as a park in which the more respectable middle classes could go for a stroll, people who constantly and willingly bumped into each other on the intersecting paths. Park keepers ensured peace and quiet and locked the park at night. Down-at-the-heel types were thrown out and children were mercilessly chased if they trod on the grass or made too much noise. Ørstedsparken

was and is a splendid park with rare and costly trees, while Østre Anlæg was filled with cheap elm trees. And Ørstedsparken is still the fine park, well kept and weeded, with rockeries and herbaceous borders that are meticulously tended in contrast to Østre Anlæg, which is typecast as an untamed park.

The lake is crossed by a listed iron bridge. It was brought to the new park from a gap in the ramparts left when the Nørreport city gate was taken down. Frederik VII was upset that the rhythm of his rides along the top of the ramparts was destroyed by the resulting gap, and so the bridge was placed across it. Delightful couples walked arm in arm and were surprised by splendid tableaux, peacocks, flowerbeds and views. The brewer Carl Jacobsen filled the park with casts of ancient statues and ordinary mortals in splendid confusion. The industrial age of casts and reproductions had just started. Ørstedsparken is an artistic lumber-room, an outdoor extension of the over-filled Victorian homes that sprang up along the park on Nørre Farimagsgade. Ørstedsparken can reasonably be thought of in that way – as an affluent home from the first years of industrialisation. And there are many things in it.

Botanisk Have, the Botanical Gardens

While Ørstedsparken is a distinguished park, Botanisk Have is a ballroom that you enter with a certain reverence. In this neat and learned park, Copenhagen University rules supreme – for instance, you are not allowed to walk on the grass, and the garden closes on Mondays in the winter because there are not sufficient funds to keep it open. The grants made to the university depend on student numbers, and there are falling numbers of students of science. That is felt right down to the most humble levels.

Botanisk Have refuses under any circumstances *merely* to be an urban park. It is a *university* park in which every blade of grass has been entered into a computer. The public comes in third place after research and teaching. Until 1960 most of the garden was closed for half the day so that professors and students could work undisturbed. There is still a sense of a quiet old-fashioned park life: no dogs, no bicycles, no joggers or topless visitors, no beers or noise, but there are 27 gardeners with their bottoms in the air and an attentive and admiring public.

The perfect green lawns are kept free of people for aesthetic reasons. Here, it is the plants that decide, all of them having been entered into a book of acquisitions since the 18th century and each of them having been given its personal number. At that time no one thought of giving human beings similar numbers. This is a living metropolis of strange plants, as the writer Ebbe Kløvedal Reich says. You are in a museum here, and all the objects exhibited have small green signs in front of them, so you can see whether they are striped snapdragons, bulbous buttercups, mountain chickweed or pyramid bugle. The collection is one of the biggest in Europe. The amazing thing about the little park is that it contains 13,000 species, more than all Europe combined, where there are only 11,000. Landscapes from all over the world are packed tightly together on an absurdly small space: a far-off forest, mountains, bubbling brooks, cute rose beds and wild natural areas, banana jungles and meat-eating plants, coffee and tea.

You can go from the deepest, steaming jungle to Greenland, Siberia and Alaska in two minutes, and you can feel it physically as well. Large refrigerators make sure the temperature is that of Thule. A small dune needs to have sand added all the time, for otherwise its matt green vegetation of sea holly, sea kale and galea will disappear. The gardeners are subtle enough to recreate acceptable conditions for palms from the tropical rain forests, citrus trees from the sub-tropics, rhododendron from the Himalayas, lilies from the steppes of Asia, cactus from America, sunflower trees from Galapagos and saxifrage from Greenland. Some live in dunes, others in snow and cold on high peaks, and others again on heaths, in limestone mountains or on areas of sour humus. But all this must be possible here in Danish soil, in a capital city that is rumbling all around.

The good thing about placing the gardens on the old rampart terrain in 1874 was the dizzy heights that they acquired free of charge along with a bit of the moat that is now dressed up as a lake. The remainder was filled in with soil by endless rows of men with spades and wheelbarrows. Everything was raised or lowered, 1.6 metres on average, so that this park, too, could be in the English landscape style with some axes providing views – one down towards the lake and one transversely. It must have been a huge task even if some of the old things could be used: the rock garden in the middle of the park is on the remains of a redoubt, that is to say an enclosed defensive work from which it is possible to fire in all directions.

The concept of a botanical garden varies from one century to the next. This location is the garden's fourth and is by far the largest because there was finally room in town. Christian IV and the doctor Ole Worm set up the first in 1600, a medical herb garden in the Italian style in Skidenstræde ("Shit Street"), which later changed its name to one with the contrasting connotation of Krystalgade ("Crystal Street"). The botanical gardens were later at the side of Frederiks Hospital, and finally behind Charlottenborg near Nyhavn.

Christian IV and his time were most interested in the healing properties of the plants. Later, in the colonial age, minds turned to those there was money in – rubber, cocoa, cotton, coffee and tea. Then came the turn of decorative plants from foreign lands, and now the task is to preserve threatened species. In this way, the modern botanical gardens are more reminiscent of the zoological gardens. The most valuable plants are in a new, theft-proof hothouse with electronic surveillance. Threatened species are maintained partly in a seed bank, partly in a tissue bank. The seeds are dried and kept at a temperature below freezing point. Some can last for several hundred years if they are kept in liquid nitrogen at minus 196 degrees. They can both live and germinate afterwards. Species that cannot be kept as seeds are cultivated in test tubes on artificially created nutrient plants.

Botanisk Have, the Botanical Gardens – sand dunes, marsh, forest, jungle, mountains, ornamental gardens, desert and Greenland gathered together on a very limited space and surrounded by city on all sides.

High up on a hill in Botanisk Have opposite Rosenborg Castle lies Det Astronomiske Observatorium, the Astronomical Observatory, which is unknown to most people. It opened in 1861 because the observatory at the top of the Round Tower had become too small, while light and dust were spoiling the view. And astronomers believed that the tower shook a little on account of the increasing amount of traffic in Købmagergade. We are talking of horse-drawn carts.

So the university was enabled by one of the great men of the kingdom, the Royal Inspector of Listed State Buildings, Christian Hansen, to design a new observatory. He had worked as an architect in Athens for 17 years and built churches, the University and the Royal Mint in the Greek capital. So in Copenhagen it was quite natural that he should choose a model of a Greek Byzantine church, built in the shape of a Greek cross with a dome in the middle. Instead of the altar, the telescope was at the heart of the building. At the same time Hansen also erected one of the biggest building complexes Copenhagen had ever seen: the Municipal Hospital, with an enormous verdigris dome in Øster Farimags-gade. There, he placed a chapel under the dome, and below that – the operating theatre. The two related buildings can see each other across the park. This was a lovely idea, but even then it was foolish.

The observatory had moved less than a kilometre. It was still in town, when it ought to have been out in the country, but the authorities refused to pay for a professor's frequent journeys out to darker and clearer surroundings. In addition, the university believed that it was necessary to have him and his students in town. Even in his day, the astronomer Ole Rømer (1644-1710) was more ambitious. He thought there was far too much light and smoke in Copenhagen for him to be able to see properly, and so he built his own observatory at Vridsløsemagle far outside the city.

The statue of Tycho Brahe stands at the centre of a flower-bed in the square outside the observatory. He died in 1601, and Galileo took the first telescope into use in 1609. Irritating. So

Tycho Brahe was the last of the great astronomers not to have a telescope at his disposal. He never saw a telescope, but he could think. Roughly speaking, he discovered two things: First, that the traditional tables relating to the movements of the sun, moon, planets and stars were not accurate when he went out and tested them with simple instruments. And secondly: one day in 1572 he saw a supernova in the sky with his naked eye. It was an amazing event at that time, for the sky was thought to be eternally unchanging. And suddenly there was a big, new, radiant star. He couldn't believe his own eyes and called his servants. They confirmed the sight, and this started him on his systematic and critical task – of exploding the dogma that the firmament is immutable.

The Astronomical Observatory is from the time when observatories were appearing all over Europe in the middle of the 19th century. You enter a lofty, circular room with a colossal bricked column in the middle. That is intended to stabilise the telescope up in the dome and it reaches far down into the ground. All in all, it is as high as Rundetårn except that it is partly underground. The observatory is in a way Rundetårn number two. A third of the million bricks used on he building are down there. So the guns on the Rosenborg drill ground could be fired without vibrating the telescope. A winding staircase makes its way alongside the wall up into space. At the top, a door is opened in the roof, and you can pop your head into the actual copper-clad dome, where the astronomical telescope is fixed. Right at the heart of the building. The room is painted black and coke grey so as not to provide the enemy – light – with an opportunity.

Østre Anlæg

Østre Anlæg manages on its own. It is less tamed and more natural than the city's fine parks, and less frequently used, less smart and less beery than Ørstedsparken. It is full of dandelions, stinging nettles and ground elder. Apart from the rose garden

In Østre Anlæg, the old fortifications can still clearly be seen. This is how high
the ramparts stood around Copenhagen.

Østre Anlæg is typecast as the untamed bit of the park belt. No herbaceous borders here.

and the rhododendron bed, it very largely looks after itself. It is used by local people from the fine Stockholmsgade, its schools and the surrounding district. That is what it has always been like.

Whereas Ørstedsparken was excavated and the earth moved around in the grand style, Østre Anlæg was only slightly changed. It was planted on the cheap with elm trees, while Ørstedsparken was given the more expensive kinds. There is more of the old Copenhagen here than in the gentle, undulating "English" parks, which were fundamentally filled with plants and trees bought for the purpose. This park seems more robust than the others. Here, you can walk up on the flat area of the high, sharp-profiled rampart and feel how huge and brutal the defences were. The dark lake, surrounded by reeds, is in a clear zig-zag pattern and shows what it derives from: the old, laboriously excavated moat surrounding the city, 30-35 metres across, two or three metres deep and in those days so full of fish that the military could sell the fishing rights.

There are extensive playing fields and playgrounds on moats that have been filled in. Copenhagen's first playground opened here, which a photograph from 1891 shows to be a piece of completely bare ground without any equipment at all, where the children could simply play as best they could. They should be grateful. Nowhere else are you allowed to walk on the grass.

The elm trees are dead everywhere and stand naked on the slopes down to the lake. A few have collapsed and fallen across each other or out into the water. The sight is splendid and mysterious, but unusually chaotic for a park, which is normally a carefully controlled area. People using the park in the old days would immediately have demanded that they should be cleared away. In an ecological sense it is entirely in keeping with new thinking to leave them: some insects and beetles only survive in dead trees. But the motive is money. It will cost a fortune to take them out. Copenhagen no longer plants elm trees. Before the fungal elm disease, 25 per cent of the 18,000 trees lining the streets of Copenhagen were elm. Now there are none. In other parts of

Østre Anlæg, artist Jørn Rønnau has fashioned the dead trees into sculptures. Almost entirely hidden by bushes, there is a smooth skull down by the side of the lake. The elm tree trunk has been carved in the shape of a long femur. In front of Statens Museum for Kunst, a tortoise is crawling along, and further in the park there is a naked trunk, now transformed into a high-rise block with a gilded roof and holes holding perches for the starlings to land on. The sculptures will be allowed to stand there until they can't hang together any longer.

The Stucco District

Although Ferdinand Meldahl and his parks took a big bite out of the promising new terrain between the ramparts and the lakes, he also did keep something for houses. They stand there unchanged and well preserved to this day, but art historians and architects are not exactly ecstatic about them. People who know about such things find them superficial, false and overdone. They maintain that the distinctive character of this period is that it has no distinctive character. But the interesting and special feature in the district along the parks is that it was built during the same, ultra-short hectic period, the 1870s and 80s. And it was built to great acclaim.

No one has touched this district since, and it is not mixed up with building from various different periods. It was made in one fell swoop. Street after street is perfect in its way. So you can walk along Nørre Farimagsgade, along Frederiksborggade down to the lakes and in around Israels Plads and see exactly what they dreamt of in Copenhagen in the bustling period after the fall of the ramparts. It is all a clear demonstration of the slogan: "Long live liberalism! We'll show them what we can do."

The stucco building properties make up one collective manifestation crying, "Long live liberalism! Now we'll see what we are able to do".

One half of the symmetrical French Søtorv seen from Dronning Louises Bro. This is what Paris in Copenhagen looked like in the 1870s, when the architect Ferdinand Meldahl went in for a grandiose international style.

A glance down along the five-storeyed houses reveals a profile that bounds to and fro because they are all strewn with knick-knacks and thingummies. The façades are "gnarled" and are dominated by long, horizontal bands and cornices. There is a triangular gable or semicircle over every window. All over the place there are flower-adorned goddesses or goats to smile at us, and on either side of the window there are flat columns and capitals. "What we lack in Copenhagen is relief in our façades, something that can create light and shade," said Meldahl in 1878. People were tired of the smooth facades of neo-classicism.

The decorations go on ad infinitum on all storeys. Industrially produced strong men and graceful women in cement hold up the balconies, where garlands of flowers, bunches of grapes, cherubs and roaring, bearded men fight for a place alongside shells, lions and decorative heads in the limited space available. They were all ordered from German catalogues. The imposing houses form a complete contrast to the simple, bare and smooth houses in the centre, where the builder would at the most lash out on a narrow Greek key border between the first and second floors. But times were different. That was a quiet period of thrift after the second great fire in 1795. An interpretation of the over-ornate houses is that the new ruling class, the bourgeoisie, had no symbols of its own and so had to invent them by borrowing from other countries and from other times. The background to the buildings is liberalism and individualism. The older houses in town are based on a foundation of absolutism and humility.

The novelist Herman Bang's world of stucco is in Nørre Farimagsgade. Bang used stucco (a mortar of plaster and lime) as the symbol of the superficiality and pretentiousness of the newly rich Copenhagen of the time. The great builder Hellig-Hansen was the model for Martens, the builder in the novel, a man without training who slaps as much decoration on his ambitious and impressive buildings as is technically possible. Hansen himself lived in the corner house between Turesensgade and Nørre Farimagsgade, the house with the round corner tower, caryatids, balcony, balustrade and columns. It looks like a wedding cake.

In Rømersgade and Ahlefeldtsgade Hansen also built in the international Parisian and boulevard style. Hans Hansen (1849-1923) was so meticulous and distinguished in appearance, so perfect in his language that he was never called anything but Hellig-Hansen (Holy Hansen). Herman Bang knew him personally and visited him in his home. Hansen built theatres and houses like mad without being able to keep check on what he was doing, for he ended as a pauper in the General Hospital in Nørre Allé without a penny to his name, unable to speak and walking with a stoop. And he died forgotten by all.

There were other new features in the district as well. The workers' movement collected money and surreptitiously bought a site in Rømersgade, where it built its first meeting hall for the new trade unions. The evangelical Home Mission came to town and settled in Bethesda on Israels Plads. Copenhageners found the new architecture splendid, magnificent and grand, and an architect wrote that the recently constructed extension of Frederiksborggade between Nørreport and the lakes was borne by artistic energy: "Seen from the street, the place looks like the palaces of a former age, indeed even more sumptuous. The Renaissance has reached us – finally! What rows of columns and pilasters, what infinity of artistic ornaments. That is the opinion even of cultured people, as though the great Italian masters have given a hand, or at any rate whispered in their disciples' ears and guided their hands."

In those days it was not embarrassing to copy others, in fact it was rather fine. You borrowed from the new Paris, which in its turn borrowed from the French and Italian Renaissance – a chapter in architectural history that belonged far in the past. These architects were called "Europeans" because they looked abroad for inspiration and Parisian elegance. But there was also another "national" movement in which attempts were made to resemble old Denmark with battlements on red brick buildings. They borrowed from Denmark instead of foreign countries.

Right down by the Lakes, opposite Dronning Louises Bro (Queen Louise's Bridge) we find the greatest triumph of the "Europeans" – Søtorvet from 1876, built in the style of the Louvre with zinc towers and symmetry above all. With a bit of luck you can picture the lakes as the Seine. On either side of the bridge there is a reclining naked, bearded male figure. One is the god of the Nile with 16 children, the other the Tiber.

Nansensgade

Round in the back streets things are far more sober. The long Nansensgade was a working-class street. Its history in brief is that there were once 35 pubs in it. Now it has two sushi bars, several fancy cafés and a wine bar where you can taste vintage wines and eat tapas. One pub has survived the changing times. That is the only place where you can hear real beery shouting and unimaginable songs like this: "Now we're off to Nødebo, home to Pastor Blicher. All the people there they say that he's a pussy licker."

The other 34 taverns have been exchanged for designer clothes, drawing offices, booksellers, publishers, flowers, modern Italian furniture, American ditto by the Eameses, classical Danish furniture from the 1950s, Italian wines, vintage balsamic vinegar, chocolates, vintage scarves from the leading French fashion houses and Versace stilettos at 2,500 kroner a pair. The Chinese from the China Grill have sold the business, including the rancid frying oil, and gone home to China. Their successor is typical of the district: Yet another stylish take-away for all those who can't be bothered making their own food. They couldn't dream

Café in Nansensgade. The poor back street has become a street for bohemians.

of putting their teeth into half a grilled chicken with chips, but perhaps into lime chicken with lemongrass and ginger.

Estate agents call it central Copenhagen's bohemian street. But it could just as well be Bobo Street, a combination of bourgeois and boheme, a new category of younger citizens with an idiosyncratic mixture of money, higher education, informal but precise taste and an anti-establishment attitude. Especially in the 1990s, Nansensgade lurched away from social groups four and five. Now it has become somewhat expensive, and it's difficult to find a place to live there, as almost all the flats are in co-operative housing associations with long waiting lists. Entrance doors and lampposts are adorned with fluttering appeals from people who would give their right arm to be able to move into this atmospheric, "creative" street. The public is youthful.

The street has been transformed since it was put together in only five years between 1870 and 1875 on the boggy meadows down by Peblingesøen, a pale copy of the stately buildings in Nørre Farimagsgade.

Working-class families lived one on top of the other in a labyrinth of buildings in the courtyards behind the houses of the elite, and in Nansensgade. One group of apartments was called Siberia, "this infamous and tightly packed enclave of about 180 apartments, each of about 35 square metres, in some of which lived a father, mother and eight children. This chasm provided shelter for about 800 persons who had to share 20 dustbins and 19 privies. Until 1936, the light was always turned off in the stairs leading up, so you had to have a torch or a candle if you wanted to go down to the privy – and of course a stick to keep the rats at bay," writes Wiggo Jedich, known as Black Wiggo. Siberia has today been replaced by a nine-storey block of offices. Another group of apartments was known as Morocco, and the fire brigade regarded the families in both blocks as doomed. They could not be saved in a fire because some of the back yards were so narrow that it was impossible to spread out a blanket to catch them if they jumped.

Nansensgade was not in the least bit Parisian in the fashionable Ferdinand Meldahl boulevard sense, but perhaps more appropriately as a concentration of Parisian atmosphere – "the raw, but also warm smell of living people, *le peuple*, the likes of which you have to seek in the Paris districts of *Menilmontant* or *Porte des Lilas*, wrote Erik Wassard as late as 1990 in *København før og nu – og aldrig*. That doesn't ring quite true today, when   has been crowded out of the street. This is happening in all the central districts.

Of course, the workers must all have a church. The street is part of the parish of Saint Andrew, Sankt Andreas, the church with the slender verdigris spire on the corner of Øster Farimagsgade and Gothersgade. It is only just 100 years old and already threatened with closure because the congregation has become sparse and sophisticated. It is impossible to drum up a full parish council in the now de-siberianised, de-moroccanised Nansensgade. When the church was built in 1901, Nansensgade was one of the most densely populated in Copenhagen. There were 25,000 residents in the parish, who were baptised, married and buried and even went to the occasional church service. The church had something to do in those days. Now there are only 3,000 residents, young, busy and as indifferent as the rest of town.

In the old back yards, the back buildings, privies, sheds, garages and workshops have been pulled down and replaced with soft lawns, deckchairs, herbaceous borders and ecological herb beds. The trees have gradually grown so tall that they must be severely cut back every year to let the sun shine on the residents' dinner tables and the children's sandpits. A peaceful, lazy garden life unfolds there, a green life, which cars driving too fast down Nørre Farimagsgade don't dream exists in the middle of Hellig-Hansen's stucco massifs. At night, people fall asleep to the sound of the town hall bells, and in the morning they wake to the song of the blackbird in the courtyard.

The corner of Nørre Farimagsgade and Schacksgade in snowy weather. The district was built in record time in the 1870s and has not been altered since. So it has what architects call "a harmonious, cohesive appearance".

Christianshavn

All those people who live in Christianshavn and say expressly they are Christianshavners hold left-wing views, asserts one young man who lives in this town on stilts established by Christian IV. A town within the town – planned for rich people, taken over by poor people, and now *radical chic*.

The soul of this part of Copenhagen is demonstratively on the left, just as that in Frederiksberg is on the right. Local patriotism in Christianshavn is red, at least for the time being, for new kinds of people are moving into the expensive residences on Holmen and around Christians Kirke. Real Christianshavners read the national newspaper Information and the local paper Christianshavneren; they boycotted and drove out the fashionable Margit and Erik Brandt's café at the end of the 80s and protested loudly at the first 7-Eleven in the 90s. They see themselves as bohemian, alternative and the children of 1968. They are against the State, against the local authorities, against everything, but *for* Christianshavn. And they go in constant fear of the "nyhavnisation" of their beloved district.

Whether you are an underdog or an architect, both are convinced that Christianshavn is better than anywhere else in the country. And people who have never set foot out there also think it's ever so charming. That's what they have heard, and that's what they believe. The positive reputation of this part of Copenhagen is self-perpetuating. People quite exceptionally vote for the Social Democrats, the left-wing Socialist People's Party or the more left-wing Unity Party in view of the price of houses. And people here are more vociferously opposed to the EU than any other part of Copenhagen except the impoverished Kongens Enghave.

"On election days you can see Christianshavners queuing up to vote in the school and looking forward to giving the EU a drubbing. I don't think there is anyone who votes right of centre in Christianshavn," says the same young man, and it looks as though he is right. On the surface the left-wing cultural elite sees to entertainment, while their friends from the residents' association, the local council and the local paper give voice to local opinion. But that is only on the surface. The non-socialist parties have got hold of a third of the votes.

The Canal Café in Torvegade. Tourists sail past and are envious – or so the people of Christianshavn believe.

Christianshavn was built for East Indiamen, merchants and whalers and has been taken over by left-wing academics and others.

And even if the *real Christianshavners* managed to close down the trendy café, a whole lot of others of the same kind opened soon afterwards. The restaurant Era Ora moved into the old morning tavern, Bodega Den Røde Lygte, and was given a star in the Michelin guide. And 7-Eleven goes on as before.

There is a strong feeling in Christianshavn of "them and us", as they say in the university. *Them* are the affluent newcomers from the 1980s and 90s, who are not considered to be real Christianshavners because they own expensive flats, especially in Strandgade, Wildersgade and Sankt Annæ Gade; they vote non-socialist, own cars, play no part in local affairs, force the prices up, are never at home, behave with an air of reserve and complain that there are a few sots sitting on the Square drinking beer. They might even enter into an alliance with the system – the police – to get rid of them. And that is not done in Christianshavn.

The others are *us* – the real Christianhavners, who were either born in the place or moved there in the 1960s and 1970 as impoverished students. They see themselves as a threatened original population. They use specific pubs, drink beer from bottles and love Christianshavn, its sots, its boat people and its artists. They think the others are stylish and so a threat to the variety, that they spent too much time in restaurants and make their houses and courtyards look too nice. Individually, the real Christianshavners feel that as a team they give expression to the attitudes of a whole group. The others don't.

In Hanne Møller's book *Christianshavn, en bydel i forvandling, Christianshavn, an area undergoing change* from 1996, Bjarne provides a description of the others: "We sit down by the harbour in the summer and have a beer and say hello to each other and talk about this and that. They don't sit down there, do they? Like hell they do. If they sit down there, they're on their own, and then they'll have a couple of deckchairs and a barbecue. And they're not far from putting a fence round them so the rest of us can't get near. They are very different indeed from the people I've

known over all the years I've lived here. There are some who've understood how to adapt. But there are others who can't. They're insulted if they happen to tread in a piece of dog shit."

Bjarne and others of like mind have the *Christianshavneren* newspaper as their mouthpiece, and they see their district as a unit, in which people are, or ought to be, more or less the same. So the paper can disapprovingly note that the architect Henning Larsen has been awarded a prize for his beautiful, almost floating bank in Christianshavn, for people don't like it. Over 9000 people live out there, but they are not all included under the heading of Christianshavners.

Those who do call themselves Christianshavners came from elsewhere not all that long ago. They came to a dilapidated little slum miracle, the carefree, perfect remains of Christian IV's fine trading centre, which had survived both the first Copenhagen fire in 1728, when most of the medieval town plus six churches disappeared in the flames, and the second in 1795, which razed almost the rest of the colourful old buildings to the ground. Copenhagen arose again in a simple neo-classical style in white and grey, but Christianshavn was still over there, untouched. When the British waged their war of terror on Copenhagen in 1807 and killed 1600 Copenhageners, the centre of the city burnt again, but nothing on the other side of the Knippelsbro bridge. So Christianshavn has an incredible number of houses of a ripe old age. There are ordinary burghers' houses here from before the introduction of absolutism into Denmark in 1660. They are not exactly ten a penny elsewhere. And when the ramparts around Copenhagen were levelled in the middle of the 19th century and transformed into parks or new residential districts, Christianshavn kept its zigzagging ramparts and moats.

The town the first academics and students of architecture discovered in the 1960s and 1970s was a village that had it all. Some bought entire rows of tumbledown historical houses and renovated them. The hoarding around the barracks in Bådsmandsstræde were knocked down and Christiania arose. Communes were set up. People took action and occupied, wrote, sang and demonstrated in the anti-authoritarian 60s and the political 70s. At some stage they graduated and found work. Their houses became ever more beautiful and more expensive. But their old distrust of the authorities went on. Naturally the long-defunct Left Socialist Party celebrated its 25th birthday in the Christianshavn Residents' Centre.

Together with Nyhavn, Christianshavn is an outstanding example of what is known as "gentrification", a nice turn of phrase that means turning a worn-down working-class district into a fashionable place taken over by a new and affluent public. They do up the houses so that prices rise, and the original residents are forced out. It is still happening over most of Copenhagen, most recently in Vesterbro.

The faded, down-at-heels Amagergade, where the television series *Huset på Christianshavn* was filmed with a jovial removals man in the main role, is unrecognisable. It has become charming and radiant in yellow, red, ochre and white. Every centimetre in the previously dirty, palid and overcrowded working-class road has been twisted and turned and kissed and painted. There is a wonderfully luxuriant courtyard garden behind the blocks, with paths, trees and flowers, benches and peaceful sunny corners. "Lord, incomprehensible are Thy judgements and past understanding Thy ways, anno 1765" is the prophetic inscription on one of the houses.

"The district was probably not more run down than many other places in town, but the most remarkable thing about Amagergade was the gutter planks, which as it were made the road shabbier," says Karl Persson, born 1897, in *Københavnere fortæller, Copenhageners' tales* (1972). "Two square notches had been cut in the thick planks covering the gutters along the pavement so that it was possible to lift them up if necessary. The rats made use of these holes and popped up and down. I once saw a rat attack a 14-year-old boy. It jumped up at him; he knocked it back down; it sprang up at him again, and he knocked it down again,

but involuntarily took a step backwards. It turned out he had been standing on the hole in the gutter plank that the rat wanted to go down, and there it disappeared." Persson was his parents' twelfth child; eight of them had died as infants from "this here consumption", his mother explained. The father was a navvy, and she was a charwoman. Only 80 years later, this foul street with its tenements and nasty narrow back yards is a much sought-after idyllic oasis in the metropolis.

Sociologists talk of gentrification in three stages. In the first stage, the pioneers move into a run-down district in the old town. Artists and people with an unconventional life style. They can live cheaply here and do their own places up. In the second phase more ordinary people from the middle classes move in, for now it is no longer dangerous to live there and invest in the district, but rather interesting and fashionable. For there are also artists living there. Prices are on their way up. Contractors buy cheap, renovate and sell expensively. In the third phase, things really start to move. The district is now fashionable and taken over by people with money. Now, the original residents are forced out, both because the prices are sky high and also because the newcomers want a district that is respectable from end to end. A string of expensive flats, trendy cafés, restaurants and specialist shops follow in their wake.

Christianshavn is in the third phase. Holmen, the royal dockyard, and the new residential district on the old B&W site are full to overflowing with seriously affluent, absolutely self-assured middle-class Christianshavners with a tendency to remain private. A third of the new apartments have been sold to Danes living abroad, something that annoys Social Democrat politicians in the town hall. On his stretch of the bulwark facing the canal, the developer has placed large notices bearing the message: "No mooring. Private."

So it is quite certain that the life on the quayside, on the basis of which the flats were originally sold, will not be achieved.

The district's upper class of doctors, architects, journalists

and actors live in the former aristocratic area of Strandgade and along the canal. The upper crust has lived here throughout the almost 400 years Christianshavn has existed.

Christian IV wanted a new town as a military buffer to Copenhagen, and it might just as well be inhabited by the aristocracy and wealthy merchants, especially Dutch and others with international capital. In 1617 he asked the Dutchman Johan Semp to design his new town on the flat, marshy beaches off the coast of Amager. The following year, work started in the Dutch fashion with canals where ships could tie up just outside the warehouses near the wealthy merchants' premises. The thoroughly unusual feature about Christianshavn is precisely that it was planned. It was drawn with a ruler; it was thought out and didn't simply arise of its own accord. Copenhagen itself was and is one big mess in relation to this – chaotic, self-sown, convoluted and in no way planned as a whole.

The Dutchman's first proposal resembled a star with a marketplace in the middle, and the streets going out from it like the rays of a sun. That was how the preferred town plan looked during the Renaissance, but it could not be done in Christianshavn as these radial streets were not a practical possibility, and the individual sites would acquire some peculiar, small dimensions. So Kemp designed a town with a chessboard network of streets (like New York), and that turned into Christianshavn – still with a central square but with long, parallel streets and side streets at right angles to each other. The town is divided by the canal into the upper town, closest to Amager, and a lower town, closest to Copenhagen. Torvegade cuts transversely across the two, so Christianshavn consists of four quarters, which meet where Torvegade crosses the canal.

The king twisted the arms of many good men to persuade

Christianshavn was drawn up using a ruler which puts it apart from the crocked, self-grown mesh of streets in the oldest part of the city.

them to move out into the marshland. He promised them market town privileges, independence and twelve years free from tax, and he gave them the sites free of charge, if only they would drain them and built fine houses on them. They were not keen, for there were plots to be bought elsewhere, and they already had good houses, some with courtyards, some without, in town, so why on earth should they move out there? The king's new town developed into a long-lasting problem. The mayor of Copenhagen, Mikkel Vibe, couldn't refuse, so he built the first two houses there, 30 and 32 Strandgade, in red brick and with curved gable attics like those on Rosenborg Castle. They are still there, minus the gables and one storey taller, but they are still there. And you can live in them. The painter Vilhelm Hammershøi lived in number 30 from 1899 to 1909 and it was here he painted his pictures of ascetic, empty rooms with windows and doors and dust dancing in the sun.

Whalers, traders and ship owners followed the mayor and built in Strandgade, but as late as 1680 a third of the plots in the new port stood there desolate and undeveloped.

As its name suggests, Strandgade was right by the shore in those days. People had jetties and gardens stretching down to the water. The closer you lived to Copenhagen the finer it was, so the houses reduce in status as you move out towards Amager. Although the developers along the transverse canal also knew how to make their mark, they were not in the same class as Strandgade. And even by the canal, the finest houses were on the Copenhagen side, that is to say Overgaden neden vandet.

Trade and shipping blossomed again. Christian just managed to inaugurate the biggest baroque church in the country out there in 1696, before the start of the new century. The whole of

So lovely that it hurts. The slum of Christianshavn has been transformed into the opposite in under 40 years.

Christianshavn is Dutch in inspiration, and this includes its long awaited first church. The architect Lambert van Haven gave it the appearance of the mighty baroque churches in Amsterdam in hard-fired red/lilac brick. The brilliant, twisting spire was not added until half a century later.

Christianshavn expanded and earned fortunes in its heyday – the breathtaking 18th century. Merchants built enormous warehouses; private individuals erected sumptuous houses; and the fleet established a deeply admired technical miracle of a dry dock that was used without interruption for 150 years and then given the name of Gammel Dok (Old Dock) because a new one had been built out on Dokøen in the royal dockyard. The timber merchant Andreas Bjørn was allowed to take up a huge area at the end of Strandgade and in the 1730s extended his vast shipbuilding business across what are now Wilders Plads, Krøyers Plads and Grønlandske Handels Plads. The man added almost six acres of land to Christianshavn and linked his shipyard island to the main island by means of a small bridge.

And the extremely energetic English rope maker, Peter Appelby, came to town and occupied a large wet tract up at the other end of Christianshavn – the area behind Christians Kirke and the Sugar Factory's large triangle along Langebrogade. These were big men with big ideas, and everything smelt of the sea: shipbuilding and trade. The dynamic period of mercantilism began in 1755, when Danish shipping and trade enjoyed an enormous boost because of international prosperity and because Britain and France were at war. The war created a vacuum which neutral Denmark exploited and profited from. The flourishing trade lasted for about fifty years – until 1807, when the British sailed off with the entire Danish fleet. That forced Denmark into the war on Napoleon's side, and for the next seven war years there was no overseas trade under the Danish flag.

But during the good years before this, Asiatisk Kompagni settled on Asiatisk Plads in Christianshavn to trade from here with India and China. In the case of Denmark, the period was almost exclusively a Copenhagen phenomenon, and it resulted in serious affluence. Copenhagen merchants were major shareholders in the company, and Christianshavn had got a foot inside the economic miracle.

"Asiatisk Kompagni came laden with costly silks and fine porcelain, and the arrival of a vessel from China attracted all the finer part of Copenhagen out on to the square to see and admire and buy. And if you looked in on the merchants, preferably on a day of festivities, it could be seen the solid, opulent furniture, the table setting with the heavy silver candlesticks and the Chinese porcelain. There were houses where the porcelain had crossed the Equator three times before landing where it was intended. It was ordered in China, brought home by the customer's own ships after the initial firing, painted and decorated here in Denmark, sent off to be fired a second time and brought back to Christianshavn." (Bering Liisberg, *Christianshavn*, 1918). The king also drove across the bridge to see monkeys and parrots from the distant, exotic places.

In 1738 the Dutch-born architect Philip de Lange built for the company the first of two fine baroque mansions with identical facades facing Strandgade. At the back, it can be seen that the second of them, built in 1781, was in reality only a warehouse. Niels Eigtved designed a much bigger one alongside it, for goods were pouring in. And later, another one rose at right angles to the site as Eigtved had dictated that his should, and with which the new Ministry of Foreign Affairs conformed 200 years later. In Christianshavn, warehouses stand transversely. They don't over on the Copenhagen side of the inner harbour.

The absolutely outermost and hindmost warehouse – just opposite Nyhavn – is from 1766 and was built to store skins, whale oil and dried fish. This was the home of the Royal Greenland Trading Company for over 200 years until it moved in the 1980s. The large ships bound for Greenland tied up in the harbour basin, and a host of dockworkers boiled oil and made barrels, loaded and unloaded. Many Greenlanders came to Christians-

Christians Kirke with Henning Larsen's bank buildings in front. A new affluent district is emerging around the church, irrespective of how much fuss the "original" Christianshavners make.

Asiatisk Plads with Eigtved's warehouse from 1750 on the left. In the profitable old days – the 18th century – whalers and wealthy merchants lived in Strandgade, while the warehouses were over-flowing with goods from all over the world.

havn, and many stayed there. Up on the marketplace there are three Greenlandic sculptures with motifs from everyday life in Greenland, and around them a small company of Greenlandic men drink deep. This part of the town has to this day a relatively large Greenlandic community, and embassies and offices from the North Atlantic countries, Greenland, The Faroe Islands and Iceland, have taken over the colossal, deserted warehouse.

Ships came and ships went in the generous 18th century. Flags, pennants and sails fluttered, and the salt air came in from the sea. The huge warehouses and merchants' mansions still stand as reminders of the vibrant period when this port and trading city was awash with trading companies, seamen and new money. Asiatisk Kompagni even donated the extremely expensive equestrian statue of Frederik V on Amalienborg Slotsplads as a gift to the king. Jacques-François-Joseph Saly's statue is one of the finest made in 18th-century Europe.

So far, so good. When the British took away the fleet, the fairy tale was finished. Take for instance Andreas Buntzen, an extremely wealthy Christianshavner with a large merchant's house on the corner between Overgaden oven Vandet and Bådsmandsstræde. His ships sailed all the seas in the world, and goods from Iceland were stored in his warehouses side by side with products from the East Indies and Africa. His ships, laden with riches, were taken one by one by the British during the war. And the few that escaped were wrecked. Come 1826, Buntzen went bankrupt, and he was not the only one. In 1843 Asiatisk Kompagni wound itself up and sold the buildings in Christianshavn. The port that had once been so filled with noise and bustle suddenly fell silent.

The philosopher Søren Kierkegaard remarked in 1845 that "here you feel deserted and imprisoned in the silence that isolates you," and he strolled on down streets so empty that you could hear your own footsteps. The big warehouses contained nothing and gave nothing. "In the districts where people actually live, life is far from being extinguished but far from being noisy,

it is like a subdued sound of people that at least on me makes a similar impression to the hum during the summer which by its mere presence suggests the silence out there in the countryside. One becomes melancholy as soon as one enters Christianshavn, for the memory out there is melancholy among the empty store rooms, and melancholy is the sight of the over-populated streets, where the eye can only discover an idyll of poverty and misery." Kierkegaard feels as though he is in an impoverished market town: "The quiet noise of people, the fact that everyone knows everyone else, that there is some poor devil who at least every other day does service as a drunk, and there is a lunatic who, known to all, looks after himself."

The history of Christianshavn in the 19th century is roughly that it remained uniquely impoverished and squalid. In most other districts of Copenhagen rich and poor still lived one beside the other, in the sense that the haves lived in large, light apartments at the front of the building, while the have-nots were grouped in cellars and attics, in back buildings and side streets in a rigid hierarchy.

In Christianshavn, on the other hand, there were no haves in most streets, just as there were no have-nots in Frederiksstad around Amalienborg.

The author Johannes Jørgensen (1866-1956) spent his years as a student in that strange place called Christianshavn, which reminded him of an ancient German woodcut. Like Kierkegaard, he comments on the silence: "Many an evening I have spent wandering through the modest crowds in Torvegade; through the long and desolate Strandgade, whose rows of fine old houses lead you like the wings in a theatre to the backdrop architecture of the German Church (now: Christians Kirke); along the dark canals of Overgade, where Burmeister's factories blaze in the night; and through small, winding, badly lit streets whose old houses and narrow courtyards are full of poverty and stench. I have wandered in the twilight across the great squares and past the tall, old warehouses that fill the extremities of Christianshavn. During the daytime, these places stand there in a singular – if one dare use the word – *still* silence."

People lived extremely close together: 3.5 persons per 100 square *alen*, that is to say four people to an area of 26 square metres. Poverty in itself was nothing new, but suddenly its extent was enormous. Mass poverty spread because the agricultural workers were moving into town to find work in the new industries.

In the old houses in Christianshavn the situation was so horrific that it was discovered further up the social ladder: "Put a man or woman who loves orderliness and cleanliness in an apartment where the light is dim in the middle of the day, where the air stinks, where the stove produces smoke instead of heat, where the ceiling and walls compete in wear and dirt, where there are huge holes in the floor while all the cracks are teeming with vermin, how long does it take you to forget cleanliness and order? Is it surprising in these circumstances if the husband prefers the pub to his home and if the wife becomes slovenly and indifferent, the children unhealthy and miserable? Do not make the objection that this picture is too dark, that such apartments are not to be found; after eighteen months working in Christianshavn we know better: there are hundreds of people out here who live in surroundings like this every day," reports Pastor Vilhelm Munck, curate at Vor Frelsers Kirke, in 1867.

But there is an odd highlight. Jules Verne came this way in 1861 and climbed the tower of Vor Frelsers Kirke, Our Saviour's Church. Three years later, he used the experience in *A Journey to the Centre of the Earth* as an antidote to his young nephew's vertigo. The poor boy felt the spire sway in the wind and became weak at the knees. He was soon crawling on all fours, and then on his stomach. The professor forced him to open his eyes: "Through a veil of smoke I could make out the houses, which looked quite flat, as though they had been flattened by falling out from up here. Flakes of clouds were floating by above my head, and thanks to an optical illusion it seemed to me that it was they that were

standing still, while the spire, the ball and I myself were rushing along at a great pace. The green fields spread out further on one side, and on the other side the sea was sparkling in the rays from the sun. The Sound stretched right up to Elsinore, and some white sails out there looked exactly like the wings of gulls. In the mist towards the east you could glimpse the almost erased Swedish coast. All this vast view swirled around in front of my eyes."

Otherwise there was no fresh air to be had. Christianshavn had become a destitute part of town, but in spite of everything with enough middle class citizens to set up the first organisation in Copenhagen offering support to its needy citizens. The association took the reader along on visits to the poor. This was something new. From the 1870s, refuges for the needy came to public notice, writes Karin Lützen in *Byen tæmmes, Taming the city* (1998). Especially one property in Overgaden oven Vandet became famous and infamous. –The Jew House, owned by a grocer by the name of Levy. Several people were sent out to visit it and produced some shocking reports.

The journalist Axel Sørensen from the weekly Nutiden also went out visiting the slums: "Far out in Christianshavn, in a dirty, forbidding alleyway, there stands a house with a very suspicious appearance. If you glance into the back yard and have overcome the first paralysing stench from the rotting filth lying across the cobbles, you will catch sight of five oblong holes in the wall. Indeed, you cannot really call these entrances anything but holes, for there are no doors or any other means of closing them. And filthy, rickety ladders lead up to them, in some of which a few rungs are missing here and there."

The people in the darkness were wrapped in stinking rags, drunk out of mind, and very, very hungry. But alongside the Jew

Sought-after row of houses along the canal. The king twisted the arm of many a good man to make him move into the swamp.

Rowing on the canal. Businesspeople eating lunch.

Christianshavners are afraid that the canal might become a second Nyhavn. "We don't want it to become any smarter," they say each time something new appears.

House and the tenements people also lived a normal life, where the children could toboggan on the ramparts and skate on the moat in the winter. Gerda Rendtorff lived in Torvegade as a child in the 1890s: "In those days Christianshavn was like a town on its own. When you had crossed Knippelsbrobridge you immediately felt at home, you knew almost everyone, for the same families had lived there for generations." She lived in a big house with a courtyard round four wings, one of which was only low; this was used as a hay loft, where the straw and the corn were stored, and a large numbers of carts came into the courtyard all day long:

"A vet lived there as well; he was used by most people living on Amager. He had a stable and a coach house in the yard, and occasionally, mostly on Sunday mornings, his patients would be horses having their teeth filed. One day a week he marked pigs. They had a metal tag fitted in the ear cartilage, and this was naturally done to the accompaniment of screaming and

Christianshavn Canal divides the district diagonally into the lower town – nearest Copenhagen – and the upper town. The lower town has always been the finer of the two.

howling. During the day, the vet went out into the country in a large-wheeled gig for a single person. He had a medicine chest mounted on the back, and when his son wasn't at school, he always sat on the chest."

Poverty took a firm hold in the following century. The poet Halfdan Rasmussen, born in 1915, grew up in Christianshavn. His father worked in the royal shipyard, while his mother looked after a mangle business, in the dark floorboards of which her feet wore "a relief that encompasses the eternity of a hard life". By the 1920s, Copenhagen wanted to redevelop, that is to say to demolish old Christianshavn because some of the city's worst slums were situated there. Luckily nothing came of this. After avoiding the two great Copenhagen fires plus the bombardment in 1807, that *would* happen of course.

But in the 1930s the council couldn't contain itself any longer. They pulled down the whole of one side of Torvegade to put five enormous blocks of flats along the street, which was now twice as wide as before. A new, broad and wind-swept entrance to the best preserved part of the capital city.

"When I moved to Christianshavn with my parents, I was scarcely a week old. At that time, in 1968, Christianshavn was still a working-class district with B&W as the dominant firm. Directly opposite our apartment in Overgaden oven Vandet there were some B&W buildings from which you could see great flashes of light when they were working. Below the apartment there were some small fishing cutters in which the fishermen sailed out early in the morning and came home during the forenoon. The courtyard was originally a proper back yard. But they pulled the back building down while I was quite small," recounts Rachid El Mousti in *Barndomsbyer, Cities of childhood* (1998).

He was born and grew up in Christianshavn in the transitional period between the old and the new life there. Christianshavn was the part of town whose industry had the greatest number of workers per factory. And however crazy it might have sounded back in the 1950s and 1960s, when the shipyard was the biggest employer in the country, with over 8,000 employees, Christianshavn survived its closure and bankruptcy. The navy's move from Holmen also went miraculously, and industry has now once and for all moved out of the old harbour and working-class town.

The Social Democratic core voters, who had worked in industry, also moved out and surrendered their part of town to the left-wing academics. The dominant group today consists of senior and leading public employees. The new residents earn more than the Copenhagen average now, but the Christianshavners' income was below average in the 1960s and 1970s. A large group of people do *not* live in Christianshavn – immigrants. The foreign citizens in this part of Copenhagen are from the rest of Scandinavia, the USA and the EU countries, while people from Turkey, Pakistan, the former Yugoslavia and Africa generally speaking are not to be found there.

Christiania

Just under a thousand of the nine thousand Christianshavners live in the world-famous, or infamous, "free town" of Christiania, where there are guided tours in English or Danish for interested visitors every Sunday. Speechless tourists turn up to get an explanation of this unusual – and in most countries unthinkable – experiment.

The main entrance in Prinsessegade leads directly into the Prairie, which used to be a completely open, bare drill ground in the Bådsmandsstræde barracks. This was constructed in the 1830s as Christianshavn's third barracks. The first two were both closed down in the 1920s, but this third one, by far the largest, was left there long enough for it to be invaded and occupied by the '68 generation. It stands there as a palpable result of the youth rebel-

The small town of Christiania is just as much split up in good and bad areas as are all other towns.

Three residents of the mini-state of Christiania. Hated by the middle classes and the third biggest tourist attraction in Copenhagen.

The "Dolmen" in Christiania, seen from the town moat. In the background the chimneys on Refshaleøen, yet another artificially extended island.

lion, flying its own flag: three yellow dots on a red ground, one for each "i" in Christiania.

Dogs big and small are running about in the street, which in atmosphere is rather like a frontier town in the Wild West. This is Christiania City, a large, square area where almost all the enterprises, pubs and shops are situated. Further out to the north, in the *expensive*, green and peaceful districts with a view of the ramparts, town turns into country and forest. Out there, you can walk among the trees and forget Copenhagen.

The guide proudly shows the finest attractions of the little town – the cinema, the grocer, Carl Madsens Plads, the children's theatre, Martin Nyrop's enormous Riding School, now called the Grey Hall, the Women's Workshop, the Health Centre, the German travelling journeymen's banana house, the coast road, the horses' enclosure, the impressive DIY centre in an enormous mili-

tary Riding School and an indoor skateboard rink constructed with generous help from the pushers.

Following the closure of Pusher Street and thus the hash market in 2004, Christiania has got money troubles. There are markedly fewer customers in the shops and pubs of the Free City, and one member of staff in Christiania's financial office says, "We are under pressure all around. Psychologically and moneywise. It is difficult to say how long we can hold out".

On 7 November 1971 a small group of squatters, all of them men, wrote down their aims with the new community: "To build up a self-regulating community in which every individual has total personal freedom as long as the community is respected. This community shall be able to support itself financially as a demonstration that psychological and physiological pollution can be avoided by a common effort. Devised by Sven, Kim, Kim, Ole

The houses in Christiania range from miserable shacks to beautiful, large detached houses with their own bathing jetties down by the rampart. Some residents live on cash benefits, while others have funds. Nevertheless, all pay the same amount every month towards common expenses.

and Jakob, with the right to improvements." In financial terms, the experiment didn't work: half of the residents at any one time are living on social security. And Christiania doesn't pay rents, only direct expenses. It is a place of meetings, and over the years these large general meetings have decided on certain prohibitions that determine the extreme limits to this minimal state of Christiania: No hard drugs. No insignias on the back. No violence. No weapons. No trade in buildings or dwellings.

Most of these extreme prohibitions are breached without any action being taken. There is both violence and weapons in Christiania. But there is also the gentle side, which turns its back on brutality. People who toil day and night to fulfil the old experiment. A little notice in the Grøn Plan house says: "Respect each other's peculiarities. No disparaging comments."

All permanent residents pay the same amount, 1,300 kroner a month at the moment, for electricity, water, sewerage and other communal benefits. They pay nothing to the Ministry of Defence, which in law is the responsible owner. Christiania is run collectively through the meetings, which many of the residents find incredibly boring: "Some people are enormously concerned with one thing, others with something else, and they go on until they have persuaded each other," says one young woman, who keeps away from them. The guide also avoids these common meetings: "They are a long drawn out process. People talk and talk. I can't be bothered. The common meetings are so confused." There are no votes, and people discuss until they agree, so that in principle everyone takes part in all decisions. If there is no dominant feeling in favour or against, the meeting can't reach a decision. The

next stage down is area meetings, and then house meetings or corridor meetings.

"I feel safest here. The lovely thing about Christiania is the nature, and then there are no cars here. In everyday life when I go down to the bath house or out to buy fuel, I don't feel the stress I feel the moment I step out into Prinsessegade," says one woman. "We talk together in the sauna. You don't do that in the public swimming baths. And in the bathhouse later in the day I meet the postman who delivers my letters. The greatest and most important thing we have in common is freedom. Freedom to be who you are. We are not bothered about what others think of us. You can live and paint your own house here as you want: I know some people who bought a big, expensive terraced house in Albertslund. They worked hard and saved up for it, but they are not even allowed to paint their own house. It must be in one of two colours, and they are not allowed to erect a different fence. Around their own house!"

Another young woman, who has left Christiania, says: "I was very keen on it. You could go about in rubber boots and a nightdress and feel quite comfortable. It was a bit like travelling in some exotic place all the time. When you went into the Health Centre it was like entering an old hippie film; it worked well. There is a great amount of diversity. The place is full of women with flowers in their hair, and then there is someone going to the dogs on a bench alongside.

Some live in dream houses by the water, others in sheds. Some talk of *my* house and *my* garden. Others are so generous that even in their tiny houses they can find room for some mentally sick person to move in. Just imagine how much time the active residents devote to this. For some it has been a relief to give up that dream and use their energies on something else."

Power in Christiania is diffuse. Who makes the decisions when you are discussing everything at the Common Meeting? That's a personal matter. Some people's voices carry more weight than

others', and there is always silence when they are speaking. Insiders say that things are run by some powerful but coarse women who apply a harsh tone. There is a power structure and some hierarchies that it takes years to see through. And if you want to have something done, you have to go out and get others to back your idea and discover what arguments work on whom. On the rare occasions when a house falls vacant and people are queuing up to get hold of it, it is the neighbours who decide who is to have it. The system is diffuse. What do they ask for a house when they don't take money?

"Fundamentally, it's a question of who you like. We know most of them already, for they have started in a shed somewhere else in Christiania," says a former resident. "It's bloody difficult. You have to go in and argue your case. Some told me to hurry up and go to yoga, do my shopping in Christiania and make sure I'm seen by as many people as possible. You're dependent on something but you don't know what it is. Perhaps the next-door neighbour

has someone else he'd rather have in."

The decision-making process is complicated: Perhaps the neighbours want to keep some nice sub-tenants on the basis of the argument that "We know them, and they're prepared to do something. If we don't take them, we'll get this guy that plays music too loud, and we don't want him because we've got small children. Or the guy that's on drugs, and we won't share a loo with him." And perhaps they would simply rather look at her than him.

One resident says, "It's not necessarily fair to take the ones we know and get on well with instead of working on the basis of a random housing list, meaning that any Tom, Dick or Harry can end up next door. Our way of doing it is more 'natural' in relation to people's needs. If someone has been applying for five years, lives in a shed and puts in a lot of effort out here, it is fair that he should have a house. It's discussed while people themselves are present so that they can hear the arguments as to why

they shouldn't have it. And then he can go away and think that it's reasonable enough that the woman with the three children should have it."

The residents of Christiania are getting on for 50 years old. There are televisions and computers in the homes, and the Peace Ark is having a charity party to get money for a new roof. "Loppen" has ended on the budget as a regional location for amateur music, and what corresponds to the local authority Department of Roads and Parks works well. Good people work hard and are stressed. But the main arteries out into the general community are closed. That was in the old days, and the good stories from the old days have become part of local mythology: The time they broke down the hoarding over 30 years ago. The time when Tine Schmedes was elected to the municipal council as the representative of Christiania and breast-fed her baby in there. When the Father Christmas from Solvognen distributed free gifts in the major department stores. When 30,000 Danes demonstrated in favour of Christiania in front of Christiansborg Palace. And the best story, which is told time after time – also by the tourist guide: When heroin almost brought about the collapse of Christiania, and Christiania set up guards and photographers at all the entrances, threw out the hard stuff and sent people to dry out. That was the last real common action, and that was at the beginning of the 1980s.

Today, the little town is divided into good and bad districts just as much as any other town. Just as in the rest of Christianshavn, there is an element of losers, yuppies and artists living here – or the mire, the liberals and the saved, as the groups were already called in a book long ago. Only one of four newspapers has survived, and there are only three communes left. Christiania mirrors life outside, but the picture is slightly delayed. Today there is talk of throwing out those who owe money to the com-

Figurehead. The navy had 300 years on Holmen, which for most of the time was the biggest employer in Copenhagen.

mon purse. They talk about those who *piss* on the community and use too much electric current without paying more than the others. They ought to be punished with individual electricity meters so they can pay according to what they use, says one proposal repeatedly made. The rest of society has gone over to that a long time ago for precisely the same reason.

Holmen

The first of the five islands constituting Holmen, the Royal Dockyard, is 80 years younger than Christianshavn. It is built on mud that convicts using treadmills dug up from the channel between Copenhagen and Amager. They walked like hamsters inside the driving wheels and established one island after another from 1690 and for most of the next century. Then the authorities took pity on them and invented a dredger that could be drawn by horses.

The Royal Dockyard consists of a series of linked islands: Furthest away from Christianshavn lies the oldest of them, Nyholm. Then come Dokøen and Frederiksholm, then Arsenaløen and Christiansholm. All this colossal work was carried out exclusively for the sake of the navy: 700,000 square metres of new land, 400 buildings, sheds and minor buildings from three centuries, and over six kilometres of quays. A well-functioning ideal military city just opposite Copenhagen, which the navy naturally found it difficult to give up, considering that all its history was encapsulated there in stone and water, quays and barracks, stores and schools, slipways, docks, offices and workshops. Nyholm was developed because the naval dockyard on Gammelholm in the city had become too small, the water too shallow and the ships bigger and bigger. They often developed such speed on being launched that it was impossible to stop them before they ran into the quay opposite.

The workers walked from their homes in Nyboder, down Esplanaden and took the boat or the floating bridge across to the other side. The wives were allowed over when the husbands' wages were to be paid – often in foul natural produce. At times, 6,000 people worked there, and for a couple of centuries Holmen was the second biggest workplace in the country. During the plague at the beginning of the 18th century, temporary huts were built for the dockyard workers and the naval crews so these "workers so important in times of war" could be kept away from the city as it suffered from the epidemic. Nyholm still belongs to the navy and is a place where they still stand on ceremony. Different rules apply here from elsewhere. The guns on the Sixtus bastion are fired here in salute, and medals are distributed for loyal service here. Nyholm is a treasure trove of unique buildings: some of the oldest artisan-crafted buildings in Denmark are there – Spanteloftbygningen (The Mould Loft Building) from 1743 is situated right out by the canal with open gates. Full-size templates were made in the loft here before the real frame timbers were made from heavy oak beams.

Østre and Vestre Takkeladshuse (the East and West Tackle Sheds) from the 1720s are the oldest. They are two long, low, yellow half-timbered buildings constructed no more than 30 years after Nyholm was filled in, when the dockyard moved more and more jobs out here from Gammelholm. They were stores containing everything for rigging a ship. They face on to a canal, where the bollards for tying up ships are sunken cannon, only a quarter of which projects above ground. When the frigate Jylland was to be turned into a museum ship at Ebeltoft, its cannons were hacked out of the asphalt here.

More maritime recycling: The furthermost piece of land jutting out into the water, right out by the Sixtus Battery, is known as the Elephant because the warship Elefanten is buried under the cobblestones. New terrain was established by sinking a run-down old ship, filling it with boulders and driving piles into the seabed around it.

The Dutch-born architect Philip de Lange (1700-66) is a great and important man in Holmen, where he designed a great number of simple, beautiful buildings. The 30-metre-high walled-in rigging sheers with its baroque decorations is his work. If the brickwork is removed, the construction will remain standing. It is made of wood without the use of nails because it extends the life of the wood when wood and iron are not mixed: a mast would be lifted to the top and slowly lowered down into the opening for a mast on the ship. De Lange also designed the small building beneath the heavy crown, Hovedvagten, the guardhouse, quite understandably referred to as "Under the Crown".

The flag flies right out on the point. It was never captured. Not during the Battle of Copenhagen in 1801 and not during the Second World War, when, in 1943, Vice Admiral Vedel gave the fleet the order to scuttle itself so that it should not fall into German hands.

In 1924, Commander T.A. Topsøe-Jensen described this unknown region in this way: "How beautiful and varied it is; islands and islets with beautiful trees and shrubbery, separated by canals that remind us of a Dutch landscape, all framed by the beautiful old rampart. And on seeing the buildings, we are amazed at the architectonic sophistication, especially in the oldest and in most of the more recent buildings, where modest means have been used by way of workshops and stores to create a harmonious picture. It is no wonder that architects, painters and all others whose eyes are open to natural beauty and architecture have delighted at the treasure we possess in the naval dockyard and hope that it may be preserved for coming generations."

The Royal Dockyard has even saved Madeira wine! At all events, vines from Madeira grow up the east façade of the Arsenal building. Tradition has it that a Danish ship took cuttings from the island on its way to the Danish trading post of Tranquebar south of Madras, and planted them in pots during the journey. When they arrived home, they planted the vines in various places on Holmen, where they still thrive. But the most heroic piece of the story is that when Madeira was struck by phylloxera in 1861 and all the vines were destroyed, the poor folk discovered that the

The naval barracks on Nyholm, the oldest of the islands. All the islands were created bit by bit as the need came. Piles were driven into the seabed and filled in with soil and mud from the entrance to the harbour.

A lovely unpolished corner of the Holmen. They are getting increasingly rare.

Royal Dockyard had a stock of healthy plants. And so they were given some cuttings back, and these were grafted on to Australian vines. And so in this way, Madeira actually derives from Holmen. And despite the cold up here, quite rare species of South American monkey trees grow in large numbers on Holmen.

The navy and the naval dockyard had three hundred years on Holmen and left it in 1993. The navy is still present in a drastically reduced form on Nyholm, now a so-called naval station. The surrounding area was closed during the Kosovo crisis because Denmark was officially at war. In relation to the rest of Holmen, which is now under civilian control, certain rules still apply here: Access to the public from sunrise to sunset, no cars, packed food or fizzy drinks, but punctuality, quiet, order and compulsory salutes between officers and ratings, as is demanded by naval etiquette. An old press officer says that it gives him quite a start when he catches sight of a sausage stall over on the civilian part of Holmen. "Many of us still think it's ours," he says apologetically.

A new town is emerging on the other, civilian, islands. The same is happening in Frihavnen, the Free Port, which has also been deserted by its original masters and officials. The two new towns can see each other across the water and mirror themselves in each other. They are extremely wealthy and unavailable to people with ordinary incomes, but they are not identical: The view of those who have studied the subject is that the difference between them is that Holmen has gained a reputation as the "good guy" – the good, mixed and creative town – while the Free Port simply has money.

Holmen is filled with young people who leave mountains of bicycles behind while they go to classes in the schools of art – the school of architecture, the film school, the theatre school, the Rhythmic Music Conservatory or the School of Modern Dance – but they can't afford to live there. The new town is not that mixed.

In the afternoons, the students have to cycle home to the bridge districts or take the water bus across to the other side, but

The Mould Loft Building from 1743.

Houseboats on Holmen. There is a feeling of a lazy port about Holmen. In the background the naval barracks on Nyholm.

their presence on Holmen enables estate agents to label this as the place for "life and creativity". People living on Holmen have to go in to Christianshavn to do their shopping and must pass Christiania, which estate agents call the undoubtedly major negative about Holmen. Many wealthy clients from North Sjælland or abroad will feel repelled and prefer the security, peace and quiet in Copenhagen North Harbour in Østerbro. There is a certain raw quality about Holmen, which is worth its weight in gold in the right circles. Advertisers and media representatives constitute a kind of labile group who like to be in unconventional surroundings and are able to find them.

They can't exist in an ordinary office block and persuade people that they are creative. And so they always look for places where things are changing: where subcultures or ethnic groups or outsiders come up against what is normal. But they don't want any of them in their pure form. They want to be in the places where the two meet, and when these new places have been absorbed into normality, they go elsewhere. Holmen attracts IT people. The Free Port has attracted a different clientele of solicitors and financial services along the quays.

There is fresh air, lots of room, views, a constant sense of and proximity to the sea, fine buildings, beautiful avenues, workshops and Parisian axes on Holmen. Monumental, solemn buildings alternate with wooden sheds, workshops and halls in a green landscape of tall, old trees. This varying scale between high and low, distinguished and business-like is the special quality of Holmen. "That's how you could build a new town today," says the architect Jens Kvorning from the school of architecture, which

Experimental, spacious water house. In the background the rigging sheers on Nyholm.

The cannon boat sheds on Frederiksholm. Listed buildings fitted out as offices.

The Opera at the Holmen is a gift from the wealthiest man in Denmark, ship-owner Mærsk Mc-Kinney Møller.

Firing the daily salute from Sixtus when the flag is raised or lowered. Of the five islands comprising Holmen, Nyholm still belongs to the navy. In the background a glimpse of the rigging sheers from 1749, designed by the Dutch-born architect Philip de Lange, who was fortunately responsible for many of the buildings on Holmen.

Nyholm: The Sixtus bastion with the flag. The crown rises ponderously above Nyholm Guardhouse from 1745, also by Philip de Lange. The large building in the background is the barracks.

has moved into some of the best buildings on Holmen, including Philip de Lange's simple main store from the 18th century.

After having been an area out of bounds to the Copenhagen population for 300 years, Holmen opened as a vast and unpolished area that has still to become neat and well groomed. There are not many places left like this. Copenhageners regard and use Holmen as a place for day trips, as something new very and different.

The splendours, untidiness and rawness are what meet the people who rent apartments in Philip de Lange's 18th-century South Store for 40,000 kroner a month. You can also buy the odd one with or without an attic window. They cost an average of nine million kroner. But at that price, they also want to have some of Holmen for themselves. So now the ordinary public is holding its breath, for if anything can destroy Holmen it is privatising the place with tidy hedges and fences. Its great quality is that you can go everywhere on it.

But now, Holmen is already more closed and private than during the transition period and is being criticised for it. "The old naval part of town has ended up like a doubtful copy of the Ballerup housing scheme from the 1960s. Blocks of flats with vast windows like a fish tank facing public roads, so-called recreational areas following the Rødovre scheme - who is gong to plant a tree here?" asked Henrik Sten Møller, the architectural critic. And young architect Bjarke Ingels from Plot (a firm of architects) is just as angry because of what he calls 'a suburban biopsy' in the capital: "Now look at Holmen in Copenhagen for instance. There you see an example of what happens with the arrival of the so-called 'grey gold generation', who live in the suburbs and want to move into town because they want to go to the Royal Theatre and the opera. I do not know whether it is the fault of the 'im-

migrants' or the investors, but what has happened is more or less that Birkerød has been moved to Holmen, especially in one location where there are terraced houses with front gardens surrounded by a hedge, and then a miserable three-storey provincial town on the other side of the canal - and thus the qualities which are already there have been erased completely", he said to *Byplan Nyt*.

In the sloping black wooden houses down towards Erdkehlgraven, the so-called gunboat sheds from the 1830s, advertising agencies, media advisers and the others transformed the simple, uninsulated houses into lovely, warm offices with parquet flooring, skylights and plateaux in which employees don't have to sit on sloping floors. They have terraces right down to the water, and they don't like people to walk down there.

Critics are hard on this suburban biopsy *inside the capital.*

Vesterbro

The sharp taste of the dark green rucola salad is no longer the correct yardstick for how smart a district and its inhabitants have become. It's to be had everywhere. You have to go out to the extremes to test where a district is fixed on the fashion scale: Can you get cold-pressed, organic thistle oil? Do they have Max Havelaar bananas, cockles, fresh baked durum bread, chocolate with a high cocoa content, decent cigars, designer clothes and minimalist Italian lamps? They can all be found in Vesterbro now. Everything moved there within a couple of years.

An exclusive supermarket has moved into the main street with its rippling, water-spraying system and fresh fish beneath crushed ice, French cheeses, expensive wines, unique service and lots of room. And then the ultimate sign: a notice by the entrance forbidding the use of mobile phones in the shop. Manifest dependence on and use of a mobile is passé in cultured circles. Next door there is a high-ceilinged wine bar with a large open window façade overlooking Vesterbrogade. A wine bar? If the shops in a street are really its barometer, its temperature has risen here, and the street has simply become a different one over a couple of years. All-night shops and greengrocers are disappearing as the rents rise in the first part of the street. Pubs are closing all over the country, but nowhere as quickly as in Vesterbro. They are being replaced with cafés offering lean food and better coffee. The billiard sharks from Vesterbros Torv left their regular pub when it was sold and turned into a café with service on the pavement. The Chinese grill bars are languishing and dying. International chains are buying up the hotels, and the few private apartments there are going up and up in price.

In Istedgade, an organic bakery has painted large, child-like sunflowers and a blue sky on its façade. The other new arrivals are not quite so romantic. They know that they are in a city – and in particular a district with a rough reputation – and they call the shops in which they offer tailor-made clothing or haircuts Asfalt, Mania or Shunt. There is still something "dangerous" about Vesterbro, and at the far end of the street, where the trendy new shops are setting up, the danger is actually quite out of danger. The rough and *honest* has come into fashion, but there must be a limit.

Halmtorvet is the most tainted address in the entire country. Everyone knows what the name stands for. It is redolent of guilt and shame and wretchedness, for this is the patch permanently occupied by street walkers and drug addicts. Or rather, it was. They have moved out of the elongated square, where fountains and pétanque pitches have taken their place, and where the replacement for the morning pub – the café serving brunch – has already opened. There is plenty of light. The old brown meat market and the new white one are on one side of it, and they don't shade the sun.

Vesterbro is changing its appearance and its residents. People talk openly about the old and the new Vesterbro. The right one and the wrong one. They are worried and enthusiastic. This part of Copenhagen is doing an enormous somersault that began in 1998 and is proceeding in step with the urban regeneration.

Estate agents are new to the streets here, and they have generally speaking not been very evident in this district before. Peter Norvig, a well known estate agent and specialist in Frederiksberg and the expensive areas to the north of Copenhagen has opened an office in Enghave Plads, which he has justified by saying that "quite a lot has happened here". This man couldn't conceivably have been on this site even as recently as the 1980s and 1990s, for things were very different then.

Now Vesterbro is selling in respectable circles. Værnedamsvej is the best address; Westend in the English style with pompous wrought iron balconies is rather similar. Vesterbrogade possesses colossal apartments, but it is also noisy. Since 1995, prices in Vesterbro have risen more than anywhere else in the country. And of the 19,000 apartments in this district, only about ten percent are owner-occupied – the lowest percentage in the whole of Copenhagen.

Within a few years, the estate agents reckon on selling good big flats to wealthy elderly clients who are tired of living in their nice suburban houses. At the moment, they are selling to the children of these people – the new Vesterbro residents. Prices have gone so high that the students themselves can't afford to buy an apartment here. They have to go out to the northwestern suburbs, Valby or Vanløse if they themselves are to be able to afford a one-bedroom flat. So their parents buy and rent them out to their children.

Estate agents encourage them to park their cars and walk around the streets to see how safe they are. The parents were brought up with all the old Vesterbro associations of sin, shame and squalor. In the special language used by estate agents, Vesterbro has graduated to "charming". This covers tall, narrow streets with parti-coloured façades, and "atmosphere" means street life. The opposite is "classic" and "quiet" – or a combination of the two in the "embassy district". The old working-class district has become an area where students live, over half of them between 18 and 34 years old. In the rest of the city only 37 per cent are that age. Half of the congregation in Sankt Matthæus Kirke are about 30, whereas the average only twenty years ago was 60-70.

Roughly speaking, the history of the residents looks like this: At first, when Vesterbro was built in a wave of liberal enthusiasm between 1870 and 1900, the workers lived cheek by jowl in all the tiny apartments. Then they moved out into small houses at Rødovre and elsewhere in the 1960s and 70s, and the unmarried, unskilled worker living on social security stayed behind with his big dog in Copenhagen's cheapest flat without bath or toilet. He had grown up here or in Nørrebro, voted for a left-wing party, said no to the EEC/EU and drank beer. Vesterbro became more and more of a slum up to the 1990s, when Northern Europe's most extensive urban regeneration scheme was launched and gave the district a much more attractive appearance and higher

Vesterbro is no longer a typical working-class district, for workers constitute only about 28 per cent as against 62 per cent in 1970 and even more before that. The new residents are students. Their taste is different from that of the old residents. For instance, they like their coffee.

rents. The new resident is a young woman with her high school leaving examination on her way to something better. She eats organic food, cycles and lives in a two-room flat with bath and toilet costing about twice as much as it cost the old man on social security. She didn't grow up in the district, and perhaps she won't stay there when she has children. You find traces of her everywhere, for she wants something different from what he wanted, and she can afford it, too.

They still live side by side in this bridge district, the strength and attraction of which is precisely its mixture. You won't find any Vesterbro resident who doesn't mention that first of all. It's not just one kind of person living here. It hasn't been decided which of the two – the old or the new resident – is going to run the district, or whether it is possible for them both to live there at once together with nursery school teachers, office workers, social workers, advertising specialists and bohemians. In the on-going discussion concerning the old and the new Vesterbro, the male represents trouble, solidarity, unity, magnanimity and breadth, while the female comes along with order, profit, sophistication and perhaps also children if the district behaves itself.

It's something new in Vesterbro when a couple dares to go on living there with children. They used to move out, and with them went two thirds of all children before they reached the age of ten. The immigrants stayed. Now the Danish families in their good new flats also stay and they demand organic food, outdoor areas, entertainment, dance and role play in the nursery, where they have already been christened *the new parents*. In the olden days the children were simply to be kept there. Now the parents want more, say the nursery school teachers. Much more. Crèches and nurseries are allowed to keep the children a little longer than the six to twelve months it usually took their parents to get away from the district. It was in and out again all the time.

Those who love the old Vesterbro warn against its *suburbanisation*, in which the town becomes nice and boring, and where all the closed-down pubs send people home to sit in front of the television with their bags full of beer bottles. And where the new residents don't understand that they are living in a town full of noise and with lots of people close by, but would prefer organic vegetable gardens, plenty of space around them, peace and security. In short, the feared culture of the middle classes. Be careful of the nostalgia and slum romanticism, say the others. It wasn't all that much fun with miserable tiny apartments and an entire district without children. The slum was a place where the privileged young people passed through and prostitutes and drug addicts ended up. The new situation is that the strong ones stay there. They don't always move up in the Copenhagen hierarchy with their new education and new money.

In Vesterbro, people – or at least some of them – pay tribute to the scavengers, half-wits and maladjusted lives. A policeman believes there is actually a special moral code in the place. "I've worked in all parts of Copenhagen, but I've never experienced the same moral code as in Vesterbro. In fact I've never known a district have a moral code. In other parts of Copenhagen, the moral code changes from place to place, from pub to pub, but it is implicit all over Vesterbro. This is how we do things, and this is how we don't do things," says Jørgen Larsen in *Vesterbro* (2001). "When I was looking for a culprit and made enquiries in this district, I was always met with the question: What is it about? If it was grievous bodily harm I could always get help, but if it was about the theft of material things, well, I had to work it out for myself."

The district's capaciousness is held out as its greatest asset and quality, and people compare themselves with the completely alien Frederiksberg just over on the other side of the street – scarcely to the advantage of Frederiksberg. The parish priest in Sankt Matthæus Kirke has said that the distance from Vesterbro to Frederiksberg is greater than from Vesterbro to Calcutta, for in Calcutta magnanimity and helpfulness thrive along with misery. Apart from a little cross-border shopping on Vesterbrogade, there are not many classical Frederiksberg ladies who move further into Vesterbro. Nor does the opposite happen. The two districts divide precisely and also in political terms at Værnedamsvej and at the other border crossings without any soft areas and no-man's land. They are like day and night, like a villa garden and a backyard, like cat and dog, and they don't love each other.

People who can't stand petit bourgeois respectability, small dogs and social aspirations thrive in Vesterbro. The district itself thinks it's a kind of Montmartre with room for all and plenty going on. A district of *characters* and a district that doesn't work in offices. Perhaps some do, but that's not the idea with Vesterbro. You encounter an enormous curiosity there, which newcomers have to get used to. People stare openly and address you directly. They comment on each other and interfere. A woman says that the very day she moved in, a woman from the fifth floor knocked on the door and welcomed her and then immediately told her about all the others on the staircase. A couple of days later, a friend rang the bell by the street door, at which another woman stuck her head out further up and shouted that the person she was looking for never got up before ten o'clock.

The famous anonymity of the big city doesn't do well here. You quickly get to know other people and vice versa. You belong, and to some this is a great personal sense of security. It's very difficult to find people who are nervous about living there, but they do exist for instance in Sundevedsgade, Sommerstedgade and Skelbækgade, where many residents are fed up with the stream of prostitutes, pimps and clients. But they are not always a problem: "I love to walk down Istedgade. There are lots of police, and you are on nodding terms with the streetwalkers. They know you live there and have given up any idea of selling you anything," says a man from Oehlenschlægersgade. There are no street gangs or street riots in Vesterbro, but drug addicts and a special provincial sense of warmth alongside the city profile.

The district has always been famous for its nightlife and all its pubs. Nørrebro was seen as a working class district without much to offer in the way of entertainment, Vesterbro as as place of work and pleasure. Tom Kristensen's novel *Hærværk, Wilful damage* (1930) about a self-destructive journalist is centred on this district, where gambling dens, women, bars and traffic are bathed in petrol fumes and neon lights. His drunken main character, Jastrau, is erotically excited merely by setting foot in Vesterbro.

The writer Jacob Paludan didn't really like this sinful district, but nevertheless: "It pulsated with life here, and the female world was not quite so dissociative; there were conmen here and hall porters, long cars and sleeping unemployed, the raw atmosphere of a city," he writes in 1940.

Now the pubs are dying out one by one. They simply can't exist any longer. Although the number of licences is rising, the number of pubs is falling. Throughout the country as a whole, Vesterbro's share of licences has fallen by 45 per cent in only five years. They are closing around the regulars, who angrily blame the cafés – this superficial, post-modern cappuccino syndrome that is replacing the original, very Danish beer-drinking environment with an artificial import. The ethnographer Maiken Rude Nørup, the author of *Det Københavnske værtshusliv, Life in Copenhagen's pubs* (1999), rejects the idea that cafés are the direct cause of the pubs closing. It's the new customers who are doing that. The composition of residents is changing: new types are coming and others are moving out, and the new ones have a different taste and way of life. At first, the new residents only came to central Copenhagen, and as a result we saw the opening of Café Sommersko in 1976 and later Dan Turéll, Victor, Krasnapolsky. Then the cafés slowly spread out into other districts. They reached Nørrebro before Vesterbro, where there was only a single one in the district in 1990. Now it is difficult to keep count.

People go to a café for the sake of the food or the coffee, not for the beer. The café has to keep up with the various small dishes and can't start offering chili con carne or tunamousse ten years too late. French, Italian, tapas, Thai, Japanese – the sequence is not a matter of indifference. In the café, conversation and the newspaper are important. Some take their work with them, do homework or write postcards. There is a sense of restlessness and energy in the room. It is difficult to sit there alone without doing something. The people under the ethnographer's observation told her that they somehow felt naked otherwise. You have no contact with anyone, but you are nevertheless part of something. That's how most people want it. It is unheard of to interfere in other people's discussions in the café; you mind your own business. At least during the day. In the pub, they all know each other well and have done so for years, but many of the regulars would never dream of meeting outside or inviting each other home. They know when to expect the ones they are used to talking to, and so they themselves turn up at the same time.

The host and the waiters play a much more important part than in the café, where the waiters are typically students or someone going through some transitional period in life. To continue there as a waiter is a defeat. In the pub, they keep the good ones; they are worth their weight in gold. They mean stability; they must be there and ask how things are going, and they know what the customers usually have to drink. If very little is going on in a pub, it is the waiter's task to start something off around the bar, especially to start a conversation. He reads the newspaper so as to be able to talk about football matches he has not seen. A good waiter is a great social personality who knows people's lives and who observes the seal of silence. The café waiter doesn't care and is a bird of passage.

A good waiter can take his customers with him to his next job, and a good host invites his guests to a Christmas lunch on the house. He arranges billiard matches and harvest festivals. His regulars expect him to pay back in some way or other, with more than ordinary good service, and that he does. Guests celebrate birthdays, weddings and funerals there.

In pubs, people are curious when new guests come in. Anyone can talk around the bar, and you are allowed to break into other's conversations or to speak to someone reading a newspaper. You don't go there to talk quietly and privately. That takes place at the tables, where the unwritten rule is that you can be left alone. Conversely, the café consists almost exclusively of small tables that invite intimate conversation. The bar is full of muffins and croissants and coffee machines, and the bartender isn't interested in always having someone around. The café must maintain a good standard in the kitchen, be organic, change, arrange poetry readings and exhibitions and keep ahead of the field. A pub mustn't change too much or too quickly, for it is the regulars' living room.

A café is a light, open and "healthy" place looking out on the world and informing customers about cultural offerings in brochures and posters, a female space with freshly pressed juice. But a the pub is darker, inward looking and cosy, encouraging you to talk to someone while you are there. The decoration is homely, witty and offbeat – notices with amusing texts, postcards from the regulars, snap frames with pictures of the guests. Pubs look like they did twenty or thirty years ago. A café would not survive for long if it had the same attitude or even if it had too many lamps from the 1980s.

When Vesterbro was built at lightning speed in the 1880s like Chinese boxes filled with front buildings, side buildings, back buildings, sheds and workshops, every twelfth resident in Copenhagen had been born abroad. They didn't just work at random, but formed groups within the various trades. For instance, 59 per cent of the men employed as tailors by gentlemen's outfitters were born in Sweden.

Today, 16 per cent of the roughly 35,000 people living in Vesterbro are foreign citizens – especially from Turkey, Pakistan and the former Yugoslavia. Had it not been for Istedgade's greengrocers and barbers, the street would have been defunct years ago. The immigrants' shops kept it going in bad times.

In Reventlowsgade behind the Central Station there are three Asian food shops, in Colbjørnsensgade another one, in Reverdilsgade one more, plus a travel agency and a barber's shop with its prices in Danish and Chinese. On the corner there is a Cantonese restaurant, and round the corner in Halmtorvet there are two Thai markets. That is the nearest we come to Chinatown in Denmark.

Then there are the hotels, which account for a third of all the rooms in town. Next, there is the porn stretch on Istedgade, while half way down the street again becomes respectable with a mixture of shops: Freak organic bran stores alternate with hip shops, and then just a dress shop where small girls' princess dresses are in 200 per cent nylon. You find yourself drowning in grass roots, institutions, charity undertakings, religious coffee rooms and Vesterbro private initiatives – all in a special, relaxed style. No one will use them otherwise. In Vesterbro they say that Frederiksberg rolls up its pavements at 8 o'clock in the evening, that there is too much space at Østerbro and that simple sunbathing in Kongens Have in central Copenhagen requires the body of a model and a frisbee, whereas Enghave Plads accepts you unkempt with coffee, newspapers and general confusion. Just as you are. The author Martin Andersen Nexø was quite wild about Vesterbro's "luxuriant life", which he found very different from that in the other districts.

You don't believe it when you are standing in front of it – Vesterbro's colossal, mysterious curiosity, the wall of the Shooting Gallery. You have to look right up. "Within only three months it was virtually conjured up out of the ground, and now it is there with peaks and towers and golden weather vanes and waving flags and looking like the façade of an immense Gothic castle, the other wings of which can be imagined stretching out over wide open spaces," wrote Illustreret Tidende in 1877. "This same wall,

Vesterbro is a rare, intact district of a kind that has been pulled down in other major cities. Nørrebro just managed to be martyred by the installation of nice new houses and green lawns for the lower middle classes. Vesterbro escaped.

Copenhagen City Museum on Vesterbrogade is in what used to be the Shooting Gallery members'
clubhouse. Built 1786 and thus one of the few very old buildings in the district.

The garden behind Københavns Bymuseum (the city museum). Is this really the pauper district of
Vesterbro?

however, is a dummy – there is no castle behind it. There are only the houses of Istedgade, which the wall is to protect against the members' bullets on the great days of royal popinjay shooting."

Grotesque as the wall is, it is also wonderful. Although several of the churches and schools in Vesterbro also look like impregnable castles from the age of chivalry, this work is especially enormous, ungainly and alien. The royal upper class popinjay marksmen went right over the top with it, possibly because the king was a member and could not be expected to see a simple plank hoarding, and for that we must be grateful. This district is not exactly full of monuments. Just imagine they could be bothered making so much of it. They built the wall in 1887, left the place immediately after the Second World War and moved to Sølyst to the north of Copenhagen. Their old headquarters is the most elegant and one of the oldest in Vesterbro, and the garden is one of the few green spots in the entire district.

On the other side of the wall lie Istedgade and Skydebanegade, completely unrecognisable. Is this really the Vesterbro slum?

The whole of Skydebanegade has been revived in glorious yellow brick, terracotta friezes, towers and spires, balusters and zinc vases, lions' heads and Roman numerals, just as when it was built in one fell swoop in 1891. The old, black breeding ground for fungi is scarcely recognisable now, half a billion kroner later. Urban renewal has taken over and spared no expense. The towers had gone before this exercise. Most of the roofs were covered with roofing felt, the Roman numerals had disappeared, and most of the balusters had fallen down. The houses were so filthy that no one had any idea what they really looked like. The apartments were very poor. People living there had a single paraffin stove,

The Shooting Gallery Wall. Built in the style of a magnificent Gothic castle by the members so that people in Istedgade should not be hit by stray bullets. They used to shoot at popinjays, birds made of wood.

and during the winter they turned the gas stove in the kitchen on at full. Many of the windows couldn't be opened for fear they would collapse.

Here, anyone could come in from the street and obtain a cheap and nasty flat. Now there is a waiting list that has been closed because there is now a seven-year wait. Skydebanegade is technologically almost avant garde as the country's biggest private housing association with its own low-price telephone exchange, intranet and a home page on the Net. And a big, new, green courtyard. Families with children go on living there; the street is no longer a place from which you move on to something else. There are as many children here now as there were in the 1930s and 40s. At least, just as many sign up for Christmas and Shrovetide parties as did then, as can be seen in the papers from the old tenants' association. When Skydebanegade was built on part of the huge site belonging to the club members, it was a private street shut off by wooden barriers at each end and with its own guard to keep it all under control. He sent the children home and locked the entrance doors to 48 staircases at 10 o'clock in the evening. It was a nice, elegant street until the families began to move out in the 1960s. The same story can be told of many other neglected houses in Vesterbro.

The members of the popinjay club came to Vesterbro 250 years ago, before there was anything other than lots of space out there. Then Carlsberg, the brewery, came 150 years ago, and shortly after that the classic industrial workman, who came completely to dominate the bridge district, despite the fact that there was a middle-class element there all the time.

In contrast to Nørrebro, Vesterbro has more quality building and luxury flats along the main streets. Vesterbrogade was one of the most elite places that Copenhagen could boast of about 1900. All the elegant stores from the city area opened branches with large plate glass windows on the splendid new street. Magasin du Nord for instance. Even Viktoriagade was once elegant!

In Tove Ditlevsen's autobiographical novel *Barndommens gade,*

From the porn shop stretch of Istedgade. It is not particularly long, but is legendary. "Istedgade will never surrender" was the slogan during the 1944 popular strike, when the residents built barricades and bombarded the Germans with stones. Altogether 21 people died.

Vesterbro culminated with 85,000 residents around 1920. Now there are only 34,000.

The street of my childhood (1943), Ester is out with a friend collecting for Shrovetide. They go further and further away from their own, safe streets, Hedebygade and Istedgade, where ordinary people live, and end up feeling rather insecure in this affluent street:

"She goes into a fine entrance in Viktoriagade, and Lisa follows in amazement. 'You're surely not going to rattle your box here,' she whispers in disbelief. 'Why not?' Ester starts up the carpeted broad staircase. She sniffs the air like a hungry mongrel with all her senses alert. This is where the rich people live – it might just be possible to get something out of them. At the first place a maid dressed in a cap and a white apron emerges. The mask Ester is wearing grins at her, a little melted and soft after so

Girl in white dress and sunshine. It is a new feature that some people go on living in Vesterbro with their children. Previously, everyone who was able to moved out. Vesterbro is more affected by removals than any other part of Copenhagen.

many hours' hot breath. Lisa, who has taken courage again in the hour of danger, shouts 'Collecting for Shrovetide.' Bang! The door was slammed without a word. Sour puss!" The two girls stand open-mouthed at the glimpse they caught of soft carpets, shining mirrors and silk-lined furs hanging up in an entrance hall with subdued lighting. This brilliant street of affluent families was

transformed into one of the worst in the district within less than 50 years.

During the 1930s, Vesterbro was still the place to which all Copenhagen went in the evening. Vesterbro *was* Copenhagen's nightlife with cinemas and bars, theatres and restaurants with ballrooms,

Tattoo artist in Abel Cathrines Gade. Nørrebro was toil and moil and a petit bourgeois lifestyle, while parts of Vesterbro constituted a festive artistic district before the transformation starting in the 1960s.

varieties and cafés. "When twilight falls over Copenhagen in the evening, the old part of town around Kongens Nytorv becomes more and more depopulated, and people stream to Vesterbro. It is the Town Hall and Vesterbros Passage in hectic neon lighting that more than anywhere else convinces Copenhageners they live in a big city. You really have the impression of a city at the sight of the sparkling neon advertisements against the black evening sky and the tremulous light of red and blue that is emitted from house after house on to the thronging pavements and the broad, asphalted streets with their cars and buses and fewer cyclists than during the day," writes the journalist Carl Henrik Clemmensen in *Mit København, My Copenhagen* from 1939.

He is talking of the first stretch of Vesterbrogade, which in those days was called Vesterbros Passage and was the most brilliant piece of modernity that Copenhagen could boast of. But: "Vesterbro also has its poor area – not many paces from the dazzling neon lights there are drab side streets housing a great deal of human misery. This is something of which Copenhagen is reminded now and again when there is a murder or some dreadful sexual crime in these over-populated streets that are reminiscent of the squalid slums in London. The street corners are littered

with night birds on the look out; the Vesterbro demi-monde seizes its opportunity especially as the Valencia and other places of entertainment are closing." He describes the street walkers as less sophisticated than the Parisian variety, but "rather middle class and ordinary, almost pleasant in appearance", and an Englishman whispers to Clemmensen that "even the demi-monde in Copenhagen is idyllic!"

Vesterbro was not only abuse and back yards and grey desolation, but it was home both to provincial gossips and the features of a metropolis. A four-sided urban area delineated by Vesterbrogade, Enghavevej, Sønder Boulevard and the Central Station. Several observers of the time found this part of Copenhagen more reminiscent of Paris than any of the others.

"It is the only place in Copenhagen where there are piquant little hotels with a scent of levity and charm. There are real bars here with the genuine bar atmosphere. Everywhere there is the sound of music from the big restaurants and a swarm of people out to enjoy themselves. Why do you think that all the great foreign artists live and stay in Vesterbro when they are in Copenhagen? On account of the international atmosphere, of course," wrote the author Aage Brodersen just before the First World War.

When the workers gave up the small, cheap apartments in Vesterbro and moved out into the suburbs in the 1960s and 70s, things went seriously downhill, and everyone realised that the place was becoming bogged down in problems. But now things have changed, and Vesterbro is transforming its appearance and, to some extent, its residents. This is an object lesson in how radically a political decision can alter people's lives and surroundings. By 2010, Vesterbro will have been completely metamorphosed. This is to be no modest little improvement such as putting in new windows, doing up the façade a little and fitting a shower unit in the kitchen. The old houses are being turned inside out; all the insides are being taken apart and new kitchens, bathrooms and central heating are being installed. Small flats are being combined into one. Back yards are being cleared and filled with professional landscape architecture. Price in all: 4,400 million kroner. This is about 1.1 million for each renovated flat.

Buildings suffering from subsidence are being supported on new concrete piles. New skewed windows are being made by hand; sculptors are recreating the façade ornamentation; hand-moulded tiles are being ordered from Southern Jutland, and budgets are constantly being exceeded. The biggest urban renewal scheme in Scandinavia is going to be expensive and magnificent. What was elegant is going to be elegant again, and ordinary or directly awful houses are going to be made beautiful for the first time. Fascinating, luxuriant gardens are being established behind the chasmic streets. In the mouldy old back yards of Skydebanegade, everything has been cleared to make way for an undulating landscape with a meandering lovers' lane and a path up to the vantage point at the top, wild strawberries, woven willow hedges, an open air theatre, nice homes for the local cats, trees, bushes, benches and tables. It certainly didn't look like that in 1891.

In Vesterbro, no one has dared to pull down the old and build something new, although in many cases it would have been cheaper. They daren't risk new architecture. Since the redevelopment of Nørrebro, which changed that district into a battle zone, the authorities have become wiser – and more wary. Town planners and architects from all over Europe come to Denmark to have a look at the democratic urban renewal in which the City of Copenhagen, the Ministry of Housing and redevelopment undertakings have opened a centre with the sole object of hearing the wishes of the residents. After a crude redevelopment only about ten per cent of the residents come back when their homes are ready. In Vesterbro, almost all come back if they have come from a housing association, and under half if they lived in rented

property. Unofficially, the intention was also to attract new, self-sufficient people with money, children and energy to move in.

When the propagandist and art teacher Broby-Johansen reached Vesterbro on his perambulations, his acutely critical sense proclaimed a state of extreme emergency, and he complained bitterly at all the unnecessary decorations being foisted on the houses in Vesterbrogade and the forced appearance of culture being produced by the builders. "The whole roundabout of styles has been set going, a trial menu of everything the 1860s, 70s and 80s could offer in the way of spurious collations," he writes grumpily. And the street does indeed contain everything from Italian Renaissance, Parisian elegance through red brick mini-castles to one of the few perfect art nouveau buildings in town, the Savoy Hotel. Nor did Broby-Johansen approve of the "mountainous chasms teeming with people" being given the most glorious names from Danish history – Saxogade, Valdemarsgade and Dannebrogsgade. In the way the houses were being decorated he saw mendacity, speculation and an attempt to cover over something that was fun-

Shop in Viktoriagade.

Modernism near the Central Station. From the left: the Astoria Hotel from 1935 with the DSB winged wheel, then the ultra-modern Handelsbanken building from 1935, and on the right the verdigris Vesterport office building from 1932. A little bit of America in Copenhagen and something of the highest built and most way out the city could think of.

Matthæusgade School from 1897 in a solid bourgeois style with towers. A quarter of those living in Vesterbro send their children to private schools.

damentally shoddy. What on earth did they want with all those alien flourishes?

This mixture of styles is known as historicism and arose because people were sick and tired of the simple, subdued architecture of neo-classicism, and because the new class – the bourgeoisie – wanted something of its own. They searched through the enormous archives of history. Genuinely newly rich as they were, they had no tradition for anything at all. They invented their own symbols and false coats of arms, and quite a lot of it was overdone. They went from stark to exuberant buildings and from no decorations to intertwined flowers, cherubs, garlands, balustrades, grinning bearded figures, caryatids and strong men to bear balconies and cornices.

At Vesterbro and Nørrebro and outside the Copenhagen ramparts in general, you must not be taken in by churches which look medieval. None of them is medieval, they were simply built in a historical style. After the First World War the façades again become bare and decoration forbidden. The function of the house is beautiful in itself, the rest is simply superficial small talk. In his book *Pynt på gesimsen, Decoration on the cornice* (1983), the historian Kristian Hvidt calls these demands for stringency and functionality puritanical and alien to ordinary people. "These buildings were a perfectly serious effort to create something splendid and festive," he writes.

The façades were varied, and no one bothered if their neighbour was building in the Venetian style while they themselves were engaged on something Byzantine. The age was one of individualism and liberalism, so how could people's new houses be any different? They associated neo-classical houses with absolutism, rationalism and the bad old days. They wanted to build in the opposite way. Much of this can be admired in Vesterbro, where you can also see people from the provinces and other parts of Copenhagen going around the streets with guide books. It is a new town. People know the Marble Church and Christiansborg and the old town from end to end, but Vesterbro is exotic and new.

The most outrageous and cosmopolitan city architecture we possess is gathered together on a very small area at the start of Vesterbrogade. One after the other, we find epoch-making buildings from the great days of modernism in Denmark, 1920-45. In towards the old working class district, there is a generous array of them. For people who are fed up with the Golden Age, 1800-1850, and the everlasting celebration of *golden days* and the charming, neo-classical houses of the period, Vesterbro is ready with *modern days* and an entirely different view of life. Concrete, glass and steel are the acclaimed liberators, and brick a terribly ponderous thing from the past.

Leading architects have built here and have gone to ultra-modern extremes. They broke completely with the established manner of building in which you built in brick on a solid foundation. The façade and the walls held the building together, and spaces for the windows were built in brick. Above the windows, bricks were firmly interlocked to prevent the wall from collapsing, which meant there was a limit to how big the windows could be. Seen in that light, the buildings on Vesterbrogade are a revolution. A manifesto.

The enormous green, copper-clad office block called Vesterport dates from 1932 and is constructed over a steel skeleton like the American skyscrapers. So you could have just as many windows of whatever size you wanted. And the outer walls are only intended to provide shelter from the wind and the weather. They support nothing. The new building came to encompass the so far biggest overall office space in Copenhagen, 20,000 square metres; it had an in-built pneumatic post system and an underground garage. The dividing walls could perfectly easily be moved to accommodate the wishes of the lessees. Everything was madly new, and the building was covered with neon advertisements, which epitomise the city and are an accepted decoration in an architecture in which ornaments are banned.

The building rises like a ziggurat or a step pyramid. At the top there was a resplendent gigantic revolving yellow neon banana advertising Fyffes, and up there, too, there was a restaurant called the Ritz. The modernists swore by flat roofs because they went in for pure right-angled shapes, but also so as to make use of the roof as a sun terrace and place to sit out.

Functionalism had come not only to Vesterbro with this building, but to Copenhagen as a whole. Alongside it stands Nordea in number 10, made up of hardly anything but windows. A flawless building that is said to have had the great honour of surprising Gunnar Asplund, the chief architect of the 1930 Stockholm Exhibition, which is always named as the start of functionalism in Scandinavia.

"If you tell anyone that the bank is from 1937, they won't believe you. Asplund came to Copenhagen and was quite shocked that anyone could build in such a modern way," says the architect Ola Wedebrunn, the chairman of DOCOMOMO Danmark, an association dedicated to preserving modernist buildings. The minimum for listing buildings was recently reduced from 100 to 50 years, which turns the spotlight on all these buildings. The bank's façade hangs there as unsubstantial as a curtain, fixed to the floors – a *curtain wall* is the technical name. It supports nothing but itself, and so it has the freedom to look as it wants. It is not responsible for holding the building up. It was the concrete and steel that did that.

So it was also possible to build an hotel on a site no more than six metres wide. Without reinforced concrete there would be no Hotel Astoria – built with corbelled storeys like a narrow locomotive with the DSB symbol of a winged wheel on top. It looks like the winged goddess of victory Nike. The building is like a machine that is moving off somewhere. There is a white fence at the top where you stand as though on the deck of an ocean-going liner and watch the trains passing down in the railway cutting below.

This little bit of down town Copenhagen was not completed until 1960 with Arne Jacobsen's 19-storey Royal Hotel – a slender and elegant skyscraper with a low, broad block of shops as its base – the American dream. Jacobsen designed knives and forks and spoons for his hotel along with tables and chairs and everything else conceivable. The modernists simplified and reduced all the time, but they designed right down to the least detail. So fans today can stand and look lovingly at a gently shaped door handle in melamine in Radiohuset in Rosenørns Allé, the cult site over all cult sites. All the foreign modernism tourists in Denmark make their way there before going on to Vilhelm Lauritzen's other masterpiece, the old airport building from 1939. In 1999 this was gingerly placed on 744 wheels and driven to safety just under two kilometres away. The great architect later designed

House in the style of a castle in the unusual Valdemarsgade, where institutions and free residences provide an open, green aspect. Almost like Frederiksberg.

Transformed Viktoriagade with a heart. The houses have been subjected to radical alterations and are more beautiful than ever. The Rosenå, the Rose Stream, used to run here, and so the street still curves slightly to follow its course.

Back yard with car repair shop, soon also to be a rare sight. The yards are being cleared, filled with trees and plants and changed beyond recognition. Only 2,000 people lived in Vesterbro in 1850. By 1900, 65,000 were packed in.

Folkets Hus far out in Vesterbro, today known as Vega – a house of music – and so thoroughly restored that it seems just as ultra modern as it did when it was built in the 1950s, with an enormous underground bicycle shed and gable decorations showing working people.

Further down Vesterbrogade is the former Havemann store, now Føtex, in a state-of-the-art building with tower and blue neon spheres and stripes from 1938, "so that passers-by could be in no doubt that there was something special here," the owner of the building said.

This is like an enormous ship sailing along, and there was once a restaurant on the roof terrace at the top. The flat roof gave rise to beautiful dreams: "Tennis, badminton, football, swimming, racing car tracks, gardens big and small, restaurants can be established on the flat roofs. Entirely new concepts of beauty can be created by exploiting all this," wrote the architect Frits Schlegel in 1937.

Vilhelm Lauritzen's Folkets Hus on the corner of Enghavevej was once called "an impressive factory for collective intellectual life" by the communist Broby-Johansen. The factory was sold and has arisen again as Vega, the house of music – the absolutely trendiest place in Vesterbro. People from all Copenhagen and the suburbs go there.

The artist Dan Sterup-Hansen decorated the gable of Folkets Hus with hard-working people in the 1950s, inspired by a specific poem: "I am the people, the flock, the mass/ Do you know the floor of the world was built by me?/ I am the worker, the inventor/ who manufactures the food and clothes for the world / When I, the people, learn to remember / then shall I come, the people, the flock, the masses."

No one any longer talks of the *masses* in connection with Vesterbro or Nørrebro or anywhere else in the country. It requires hunger, poverty and unemployment to mobilise the masses in an old-fashioned sense, but the official opening of the Fisketorvet

Elegant Westend, a side street off Vesterbrogade, which has always been the finest in this district, offering large apartments in magnificent buildings. Together with Sønder Boulevard the home of the district's middle classes. The proletariat lived in smaller flats in the side streets.

Shopping Centre on Vesterbro was not far off when 60,000 almost panicked on the opening day.

The classical industrial worker lived in Vesterbro for a hundred years, from the birth of the district in the 1860s and 70s until the 1960s and 70s, when he drove his car out of town and bought a little house in the southern suburbs. His wife began to work, they had a double income, and their incomes rose rapidly. Inflation and tax allowances made it ridiculous not to buy a house. The Minister of Housing, Erling Olsen, said at the end of the 70s to the new houseowners: "Start by eating rissoles. The steak will come before long." And so it did. After a time it almost cost nothing to live in a house. But Copenhagen was once a working-class city with thousands of industrial workers.

There were 160,000 inhabitants in Copenhagen in 1860. By 1900, the number had doubled. The new inhabitant was simply an agricultural worker who moved to Copenhagen or America and became an industrial worker. There was a flood of people who were all going the same way. As for instance the novel character Pelle the Conquerer: "There was heavy traffic on the high road; they drove past people driving and walking, people with their trunks on the back of the truck, and others carrying their tackle in a bag over their shoulders as he was doing. Pelle knew some of them and nodded good-naturedly; he knew about them all. They were people who had to get to town – his town. Some were going straight on across the sea – to America or to serve the king ... But the real ones were those who had their trunks with them on a

No fun, please. The apartments were so small and the children so numerous that they neither could nor were allowed to spend the whole day in them. They played in the back yards and especially in the streets and knew exactly what was their territory and what was enemy territory. The boys in the various parts also had their own language. ▶

211

wheelbarrow or came along carrying it with one holding each handle. Their cheeks were red and their movements feverish; these were people who had said goodbye to life in the country and the accustomed way of life and chosen the town just as he had done," wrote Martin Andersen Nexø in *Pelle Erobreren, Pelle the Conqueror* (1906-10).

"A smallholder came along wheeling a little green chest, broad in the base and with delightfully home-painted flowers. Beside him walked his daughter; her cheeks were glowing, and her eyes were all over in the unfamiliar surroundings. Her father spoke, but she didn't seem to hear him: 'Well now you'll have to accept responsibility for yourself. Remember that and don't waste yourself. The town's good enough for anyone wanting to get on and able to stand up for themselves. But it doesn't bother too much if people are trodden underfoot. And don't trust anyone too much –they're experienced in the art of seduction in there. But you must be mild and gentle.' She made no answer; she was more preoccupied with not turning her feet over in her new shoes."

Pelle was a country bumpkin come to town. He had to discover everything from the start – his new job, a place to live, his finances, culture, and how to behave towards the others who had also just arrived. The historian Søren Mørch compares the refugees and immigrants of today to the people from the last century who moved into the slum districts in Vesterbro. They were in the same situation. They came from Jutland and Funen, from very alien circumstances. They could neither read nor write decently, and they had attended dreadful village schools. They were poor, peasant-born and stupid.

That was the time when the decision was taken to build the finest new schools near the bridges so that children from rural workers' homes could be have a better education. Copenhagen was a melting pot for those coming in from the provinces. Several thousand families moved in every year, so where were they to live? They had to build up a life starting from the bottom, and this they did in Vesterbro, a rapid, high and dense ghetto where so many people of the same type settled together for the first time. One member of the family would often go ahead and rent somewhere or live with relatives who acted as the gateway to the big city. It was quite common for six or seven people to live in flats of under 25 square metres.

Ida Swirski, born in Vesterbro in 1892, worked as a girl for a pawnbroker in Saxogade: "It was incredible what people brought in to pawn. They could come and get a loan for a shoemaker's last, porcelain, table linen, outdoor clothing, children's clothes, ladies' and gentlemen's underwear, tools, musical instruments, gold and silver... People could come and borrow bedding for a certain price per night. You can hardly imagine that people were really so poor that they needed to hire bedclothes, for that can be said to suggest utter poverty. But people came unconcernedly and pawned things without thinking what they gave in interest.

I remember there was a woman who came every morning when I arrived, waiting for me to open up. She could come several times during the day. In the morning she stood there with her husband's cylinder watch. She could borrow one krone on that, but her husband came home for lunch at 12 o'clock. He mustn't know she had pawned it so she would come with a sheet or something else she could borrow a krone on. Then she got the watch redeemed and paid five øre in interest, and just as soon as her husband had gone, she came back with the watch and redeemed the sheet and paid another five øre in interest, and in the evening she had to have the watch home again. And things were constantly exchanged and exchanged in this way." (*Københavnere fortæller, Copenhageners' tales* 1972).

The countryside sacrificed 80 per cent of all its children to the city. You could easily recognise them, their incredible numbers and their poverty. People living in the old town inside the ramparts became alarmed. If they got together, all these new people might start a revolution. They could get up to anything at all, and so they did. Copenhagen was the first city in the country to elect a Social Democrat mayor in 1903. In 1917 the party achieved an absolute majority in the city council and since then have decided the political life of Copenhagen. There was a lightning attack by the new class as they hurried to collect money so that by 1878, via a front man, they could buy a site and construct a communal building with a splendid assembly hall in middle-class Rømersgade.

In 1910 Lenin rented a room for a month from a seamstress in the middle building in 112 Vesterbrogade. From there he participated in the conference of the Second International in Copenhagen and studied in the Royal Library. In Denmark, the workers took power without a revolution. Suddenly, the country had ministers with everyday names ending in -sen: Hansen, Sørensen, Christensen and Madsen. A former cigar sorter, Stauning, became prime minister.

With the industrial workers came the divided city. Before this, rich and poor lived in the same districts, the rich on the ground floor and first floor in the front building out to the street. The less affluent were on the other floors, and the poor in the back building, side building, cellars and attics, but in the same district. Even the most distinguished streets broke down a couple of metres into the back yards and the alleyways.

Suddenly, huge number of people of the same class were living in one district; they walked about in the same streets, used the same shops, met in the streets and lived close together.

On New Year's Eve it was as though all Vesterbro poured into Saxogade to let off fireworks. At the turn of the century 1899/1900 fireworks were thrown down from all windows – firecrackers, jumping jacks, Chinese lanterns, Bengal lights. "When it was almost twelve o'clock, the young people brought out old sofas, straw mattresses and other household implements that were going to be thrown away in any case. Then they poured a bottle of paraffin costing six øre over the inflammable stuff, and it flared up to the accompaniment of shouts of delight," recalls Evald Andersen, born in Vesterbro in 1888, in *Københavnere fortæller, Copenhageners' tales*.

"But that was not all. Then, roughs and toughs, whom the newspapers the following day called the trouble makers, brought out the latrine barrels from the privies in the yard and threw them on the bonfire to the amused screams of those watching. On the same occasion, old handcarts were also sacrificed to the flames."

An intolerable stench lay over the district. You couldn't open a window for several days into the 20th century, which was later to be called the century of Social Democracy. People took their curtains down and washed them. Copenhagen exploded during these years and became a modern metropolis, a socially divided, scattered metropolis, while the old city within the ramparts, which a few years ago had housed everyone, became almost empty. Within a few decades, the new class created its own culture with breweries, housing associations, cremations and self-confidence. The idea was that the movement should take care of its members from cradle to grave and keep the basic things of life outside the control of capitalism.

Vesterbro deals in meat: meat from pigs and cows, and also the female kind. The butchers were the first profession of all in Vesterbro, because even by 1577 they were asked to leave Copenhagen itself with all their blood and stench. They settled down by the shore at Vesterport and later in Trommesalen ("The Drum Hall"), where business was done to the accompaniment of drum beats. Then they built the Brown Meat Market, and when that became too small and old fashioned, they built the White Meat Market alongside it in 1934. That is listed as a perfect example of functionalism's commercial building, where hygiene and health suddenly became very important.

With the butchers and their markets came the prostitutes, too, and as they were also moved out of Adelgade and Borgergade, and when Nyhavn became fashionable, they concentrated their efforts on Vesterbro, especially Halmtorvet just opposite the Meat Market. The last cow was slaughtered in the Meat Market in

1993; Danish cattle are slaughtered in Jutland now. The Jutlanders' colossal EU-approved refrigerated vans with the meat packed in plastic arrive in the mornings, and you can no longer see the farmers driving their herds of cattle down Valdemarsgade.

Now, Kødbyen, the Meat Market, deals in packed meats, stoned prunes and Béarnaise sauce, sausages, hams and paté de foie gras. But before it all became so neat and tidy, the butchers and their customers helped to keep Vesterbro going as Copenhagen's entertainment district. "When this market was held, there was a completely provincial atmosphere to Vesterbro. Cows lowing and horses whinnying easily drowned out the noise of traffic. Buyers and sellers from large parts of the country had turned up and a lively trade was done until the market shut at two o'clock. However, a good deal of business continued after this time in the nearby cattle market restaurant or in the spacious premises of the Landmandshotel," recalls John Ekvall, who was born in Vesterbro.

Today, the Landmandshotel has been transformed into exclusive apartments, and nothing is as it was before. Restaurants and pubs around the Meat Market were kept in business by the butchers and their customers, and now they are all closed. The abattoir workers went around carrying calves weighing 150 to 200 kilos on their shoulders. Fat, blood and their own sweat ran down their brown overalls. They drank. Today, a man is not allowed to carry over 30 kilos, and the 3,300 employees in the Meat Market aren't even enough to keep the pub and billiard hall going that was once in the arch under the Bull, the potent sculpture and trademark of the place. That's where the administration is now installed.

Before the age of the supermarket, Vesterbro was full of butchers' shops. In 1935 there were 107 of them in this part of Copenhagen. There was scarcely anything else in Værnedamsvej, and a large part of the Copenhagen population bought their meat there, while the locals preferred the improbable multitude of shops in Istedgade. It was possible for one shop in Vesterbro to exist on selling only bones, another on liver and offal, a third on horsemeat. As can be seen on the old butchers' signs, a distinction was made between meat and pork. Meat was beef and veal and beyond the reach of poor workers. They found their calories in rye bread and dripping, gruel, gravy, potatoes and fat pork if they were to have any kind of meat. In former times, pigs were much fatter than today, as was indeed the intention.

The prostitutes are disappearing from the Copenhagen night street scene. They are moving indoors into massage parlours or becoming escort girls, and that is where most of the market is to be found – invisible and in every district and town. Fewer women are walking the streets, and window prostitution has died out.

Concepts such as immorality and vice have died out. They are from the time when missionaries from Home Mission and the Midnight Mission patrolled the godless streets and tried to make the young men from the country think seriously by standing on the brothel steps and asking: "What do you think your mother would say to this?"

There was plenty for representatives of the Church to do in the bridge districts. The evangelical pastors met in the Home Mission Bethesda on Israels Plads. Their first meeting in 1886 was simply entitled: "Work for the Unbelieving Masses in Copenhagen". With a sense of symbolism, they established Fredens Kirke, Peace Church, in a former dance hall. They were trying to convert the natives from their mission station in Redskin territory.

But in Copenhagen prostitution was legal and controlled by the authorities between 1874 and 1906, the very years that saw the rapid expansion in the bridge districts. The Ministry of Justice, the police, doctors and politicians were keen to control the infectious diseases, including the deadly syphilis, which the clients took home and passed on to their wives. Immoral and notorious women like Bisse-Oda, Anna Nifinger and Tora Næsebras had to go to the police station to be examined by the police doctor once a week. A special register was stamped OK, but if a prostitute's body showed any sign of anything infectious, she would be ordered to lay off for a time. This was expensive for her, and so most prostitutes took no notice of such orders.

If a prostitute broke the police regulations and for instance trawled in cafés or failed to go to the medical examination, she would be forcibly registered in a brothel that was organised and run by the police themselves. They would appoint an elderly, worn-out prostitute to run it. These were actually compulsory brothels. The right to freedom was only 40 years old, and it applied especially to respectable people. The fallen women were seen as vain, lazy and lascivious. In Copenhagen, some of these lazy but beautiful and young women earned four times as much as civil service departmental heads, but the cheapest would service a man for 50 øre.

When she was compulsorily registered, a woman could no longer move around freely. She also had to wear a special white dress. In Copenhagen, she was not allowed to walk across Christiansborg Palace Square and under no circumstance to approach the royals at Amalienborg. She had to have the permission of the chief of police to move her lodgings and was not allowed to have children of more than four years of age living with her. The police had the right of access to her home at any time. She was to dress decently in the street, never spend time in restaurants and pubs and not walk down the main streets of the city. In 1900, 900 prostitutes were registered under this ruling. At least as many lived secretly without being registered.

The YMCA sent people out to work in the Copenhagen world of entertainment, and they were scandalised. There were hordes of prostitutes in dance halls and pubs, and the guests sang bawdy songs. Shops sold obscene pamphlets along with French articles – condoms, pornographic pictures, sex aids and sanitary towels.

The Midnight Mission, in association with Home Mission, was also on the spot, and their members kept watch and distributed admonitory pamphlets. They rented rooms in houses and held prayer meetings or continued them by talking to brothel clients they had picked up on the street. They had no contact with the prostitutes themselves. They were beyond redemption.

Ane Marie Petersen, born 1846, was registered and photographed by the Copenhagen vice police at the age of 21. The photograph forms part of a collection of portraits of "Public and other immoral women". The girl is standing smiling in her neat checked, long-sleeved dress. Her hair is well combed, she is supporting her arm on a pillar and looking the photographer straight in the face. It is almost too much to bear.

Evald Andersen lived with his parents on the corner of Istedgade and Eskildsgade at the beginning of 1900. Several of the houses opposite were legal brothels, so there was plenty going on at all times. "It was the girls and their pimps who dominated the district," he recalls.

After the introduction of parliamentary government in 1901, when the Liberal Party came to power, one of the first things the Minister of Justice did was to repeal the act concerning public brothels. And in 1906, the rules governing the police registration of prostitutes were cancelled. After 36 years, all the visible signs had gone – brothels, white dresses, visits to the doctor and police checks on the home. Of course it didn't all go away. The ladies continued with their profession in Vesterbro and elsewhere in town.

Tove Ditlevsen's little 1930s heroine, Ester in *Barndommens gade*, lives next door to a woman of easy virtue for a brief, delightful period until the occupants of the tenement discover what she is and have her thrown out. She represents a breath of life and luxury. Ester's mother, too, is enthusiastic and entirely without suspicion, but suddenly Miss Thomsen has vanished again with those generous hands of hers that were always ready to distribute chocolate and small change. "She had something to offer a child," thinks Ester in spite of the mysterious nastiness that is suddenly associated with her neighbour's name.

In the middle of the 1960s, Annie Feltmann and her husband moved to Vesterbro. Annie's mother was horrified: Decent people couldn't live there. In one of the roads there were often men standing looking up at a specific house. They were known as the "property agents". She wondered what they were looking up at and only understood the joke many years later.

Carlsberg

Vesterbro doesn't have many places of interest in an old-fashioned sense, but Carlsberg is a sensation. Behind the gate lies both a dramatic family history in which father and son take it in turns to love and fight each other, but also extravagant architecture extending from the old brewer's first gaunt and functional buildings to his son's wild affairs with every conceivable style from Venice to the Vikings.

Industrial plant and buildings are almost always pulled down and scrapped when go-ahead men want to move on quickly. It's only an old factory, you know. So they steamroller old machines, stores, boiler houses and main buildings and build something bigger and better. So a complete industrial plant complete with its equipment is a very rare sight, but all that stemming from J.C. Jacobsen's Gamle Carlsberg from the 1870s is there in good order and with open doors on Valby Bakke.

Fortunately, there was so much space that it was possible to leave the brewery standing and move on to the next. Miraculously, it survived as though in mothballs – long enough for the functionalists in the 1920s almost to swoon over its subdued architecture, its "honest expression" and the fine relationship between form and content. The buildings are gathered together as in a monastery yard in yellow and red brick with no fun and games.

In Carl Jacobsen's taste: the Elephant Gate from 1901. Some of the most amusing and bizarre architecture in Copenhagen. Further down, through the arch, mosaics can be seen of the brewer and his family, plus some employees. ▶

On the other hand, you had to go right up to the 1980s before anyone dared or wanted to praise the son, Carl's, main works – the Elephant Gate, the Brew-House, and the Double Gate. The author Ole Wivel called the style of that time "grotesque over-exertion and obvious confusion", but he encourages people to look at things humorously and with a certain sense of solidarity. Those people had just lost Southern Jutland in 1864. They had abandoned the firm, strong and sober style – neo-classicism – and launched out into excessive luxuriance purely and simply for the sake of surviving. There was a need for something new.

J.C. Jacobsen was the first industrial magnate to break out of the constricting city behind the ramparts and out of his father's little brewery in Brolæggerstræde, where they made a kind of alcoholic barley soup and called it beer. He applied for royal permission to go west and settle on Valby Bakke as a pioneer. That was in 1847, and it was a revolutionary step. Everyone else – 127,000 people, 3,000 horses, 1,500 cows and 1,000 pigs – lived claustrophobically close together in town.

He lacked space and had to get out, irrespective of how ridiculously far out in the country it was. The king gave him permission to build in stone out there, where this was otherwise not allowed because the enemy mustn't have anything to hide behind during a possible siege or attack on the capital.

J.C. was a brilliant businessman, but a martinet and a wretched father. This led to trouble later, when he and Carl became such bitter enemies that they constructed a wall between their two breweries. The old man put up internal shutters in his house to keep out the view of his son's house. He also took over his son's first brewery and refused to allow him to use a label that resembled his own. Despite being forbidden to do so, Carl's wife, Ottilia, one day sent her daughter across with a bunch of daffodils for the old man, who was so touched that father and son were finally reconciled just before J.C. died.

Valby Bakke is the kingdom of these two fighting cocks, and

Carl's imposing buildings, towers, apophthegms, signatures and decorations ensure that no one forgets it. Go in through the Elephant Gate, where four elephants support the building and the initials of the surviving children: Helge, Vagn, Paula and Theodora Jacobsen. The elephant can be interpreted in several ways. It is a royal symbol, and as neither J.C. Jacobsen nor his son was awarded the Order of the Elephant, but they were both keen on demonstrating, they took possession of the animal's fine associations and awarded the knighthood to themselves. At all events, a papier mâché gateway in the shape of an elephant was erected on the occasion of a royal visit to the brewery, a not particularly discreet hint. Perhaps the four bulky animals are only an architectonic whim, inspired by an elephant bearing an obelisk on the Minerva Square in Rome or a similar one bearing an organ in Vor Frelsers Kirke in Christianshavn.

There is a swastika atop the Elephant Gate tower. There was a discussion in the brewery after the Second World War as to whether all Carl's swastikas should be removed from the building, but most were allowed to remain as intended: as an ancient sun and fertility symbol.

Further down the hill stands the Brew-House from 1901 in the Italian style, looking for all the world like a Venetian palace. On top of it stands a statue of Thor rumbling with his goats through clouds of steam from the boilers. There is a giant lying beneath the chariot with one leg hanging out over the guttering.

The amusing thing about historicism is that it doesn't consider itself too good to borrow bits from everything and everyone and mix it all up into a glorious mess, and Carl Jacobsen is a master at this. His self-glorification and his urge to decorate know no limits. The critics said that his style was "unmanly", that is to say feminine, open and light, and there were also some who didn't approve of his going about with a red rose in his mouth later in life. He wore a Roman cloak in the winter and a broad-brimmed artist's hat in the summer.

Further down the hill: the double gateway with the gold

mosaic above. Here, we have come to Byzantium. The industrial prince Carl stands in the midst of the altarpiece beneath the clock. He has had himself represented holding a drawing in his hand, always busy with great plans, and turning towards us. His son, Alf, the object of his affection, is on his right hand side and has also been allowed to stand and look ahead, and so, curiously enough, has the brewery worker. The other figures stand with their sides to us, bowing respectfully to the brewer. At the extreme of each panel we see the two men responsible for the building, Bechmann the builder and Vilhelm Dahlerup the architect.

Ny Carlsberg's original main building is a laboratory now, but if you stand on tiptoe you can look through the main door and catch a glimpse of the incredible hall in which Carl went amok with effects. To begin with the magnificent elephant-shaped handles are so high up that everyone will feel like a humble dwarf on an unimportant errand. If you have once been allowed inside, the porter is seated so high up in his fine glass cage that a visitor must look up to come into contact.

The third lesson is the brewer's proclamation over the door: "Complete your errand, quickly go your way, remember time is money and time is short". He loved to scatter apophthegms around him. In the floor mosaic: Ora et labora. The hall is strewn with hop flowers, a little barley, cherubs, fabulous monsters and three small bearded owls with human features standing beside each other: the architect, Carl and an anonymous figure. Carl knew how to do things. His house is a cultic site for the family and it is full of amazing objects and decorations. Each little keyhole, each hinge, lamp, handle is a miniature work of art. All the woodwork is mahogany, finely carved. In the garden, there is an avenue of classical statues.

For some functionalists, socialists and classicists, he is too much. But Carl's father, who as the thriftier and more gifted is always the recipient of the praise of a later age, was not exclusively in favour of aesthetically pleasing functionalism. He, too, liked to impress. Part of his house is a garden room with built-in artificial moonlight – constructed after a similar device in the Royal Theatre. And then there is the Pompeii greenhouse in glass and steel, where he had dried fish and porridge made with water several times a day, surrounded by busts of the great men of Antiquity plus three Danish exemplars: The sculptor Thorvaldsen, the scientist H.C. Ørsted and the arch-conservative businessman and politician L.N. Hvidt.

After the death of Carl Jacobsen's widow Laura, the house became an honorary residence, and five Danish men lived in it in turn. The world-famous scientist Niels Bohr resided there for 31 years, beloved of the brewery because he had no objection to standing on the steps occasionally and receiving people. Bohr had the lake in the garden filled in because he had lost a child at sea and was now nervous for his grandchildren. The last real honorary guest was Søren Egerod, Professor of East Asiatic Languages, who lived in the house until his death in 1995. Now times have changed. Honorary guests live only on the first floor and only for a specific period, and now they are internationally recruited.

Fortunately, the brewery has kept its horses, and everyone can go in and see and touch the 12 enormous Jutlandic horses, the breed preceding the tractor. Some of them weigh a ton, and they use size 10 shoes, whereas ordinary horses use size 2. They are cold-blooded in the sense of being very, very calm. The brewery once had 238 horses in a two-storey stable. Now they are in Gamle Carlsberg, fed on freshly rolled oats and steaming and snorting and smelling strongly of the past.

The management is seated nearest to heaven on the top floor of the towering corn silo. The lower half is taken up by malt, so some things haven't changed. The Jacobsen family lies buried in the crypt of their splendid basilica with free-standing bell-tower at the Jesuskirke church in Valby, a couple of wonderful upper middle-class roads away from the brewery. The father and son brewers have given Vesterbro and Valby a sumptuous, eccentric feature, a temple dedicated to lager beer, which it is easy to laugh at but even easier simply to visit and become engrossed in.

Frederiksberg

On Vesterbrogade we are on the edge of a razor-sharp boundary dividing young and old, poor and wealthy, left and right. A step to the right into Frederiksberg Allé and the boundary is crossed. There is no no-man's land to smooth things out. You are immediately in Frederiksberg – royal, classic and conservative.

Would one ever talk of a lady from Vesterbro?

In some mysterious way ladies are only found in Frederiksberg and, at a pinch, Østerbro, but they are thickest on the ground in this splendid old district with the royal castle and its own coat of arms. Here they go about dressed in hats and light raincoats, carrying handbags and with a small dog on a lead. They are slim and well dressed, and their beloved main street, Gammel Kongevej, is brimming with elegant ladies' dress shops in which furs, gold buttons and navy blue play a constant role irrespective of fashion. An elegant dress lasts longer here. People don't rush breathlessly to keep up with passing fashions, but they keep to what is classical. The sewing is excellent, and Gammel Kongevej society is at the top of reliable conservative circles in the country. It was a

long time before cycle paths were installed in this street, which over two kilometres can boast of at least ten different shops selling kitchen equipment and offering total solutions to the most expensive, prestigious and emotive room in the house.

Frederiksberg also reveals an obvious predilection for *reproduction furniture*, which wants to look like antique furniture, but isn't. It can be bought all over the district, either in the form of large, heavy oak furniture or as light rococo furniture in glossy, polished wood. English country house style, Chesterfield sofas and smoking rooms like those so appreciated in Oxford. You won't go in there if you're a day under 50.

Vesterbro and Frederiksberg are two neighbourhoods as different as chalk and cheese. The first is historically closely associated with the industrial worker and Social Democracy, the other with the upper middle class and the Conservative People's Party. Frederiksberg has twice as large a proportion of incomes in the middle and top classes as Vesterbro has. In Frederiksberg, people have been educated for longer, they are wealthier and they have more children. They have two jobs, two cars and two of everything. To Frederiksberg, autonomy and independence from Copenhagen are sacred. All politicians who want to get anywhere here have to swear to that. Frederiksberg is a municipality and even a county on its own with its own hospital, its own educational and fire authority, its own power station and it own waterworks.

"Frederiksberg isn't a district, it's a town," emphasises Mads Lebech, the sixth Conservative mayor in the country's biggest non-socialist municipality. He doesn't change anything.

Frederiksberg tends towards neatness and good order, not to the Liberals, but to calm conservatism in which ideological lines are not so distinct as to really matter. On the other hand, there is no one else to blame if things go wrong. The party will soon have run Frederiksberg for 100 years – with one of the ten lowest local taxes in the country.

The constant nightmare of the different mayors has been that anyone should start altering boundaries and contesting the district's independence and its own police force – which has nowhere near as much to do as the others. Criminality is low, and the most frequently repeated word heard when a Frederiksberg citizen has to describe the neighbourhood is security. Others say peace and quiet. Your pulse rate drops the moment you cross the municipal borderline, they say. Frederiksberg has a tradition for three quite distinct groups settling there: kings, ministers and gays.

In 1711, Frederik IV, a man who liked ladies' company and knew how to enjoy life, built his castle on a hill, indeed almost a mountain – *berg* – from which the town derived its name. Later in the same century, Frederik VI grew up in the castle together with his young mother, the queen, her lover Struensee and his strict "natural" methods of upbringing, and with his mad father. You would think the boy would hate the place, but as a grown man he stayed there every summer and constantly had himself rowed around the canals in the garden, while people stood and watched. He brought prestige and brilliance to this part of the city, and Frederiksberg is still mad about him. His statue stands at the entrance to the park, Frederiksberg Have.

Then there are the politicians. Of all the 298 ministers Denmark has had since the introduction of democratic government in 1901, 80 have lived in Frederiksberg before, during or after their period in office. Aksel Larsen was the only communist among them. Eight heavyweights – prime ministers –were among them. Preben Hansen has worked this out in the book *I kongens råd – og på Frederiksberg, In the King's council – and at Frederiksberg* (2000).

The place appeals more to Conservative and Radical ministers than to Liberals and Social Democrats. Heaven knows what Aksel Larsen did in his terraced house on Fuglebakken (distinguished and just opposite prime minister Jens Otto Krag) in a municipality entirely in the power of reactionary forces. In the book, writer Lise Nørgard guesses that he wanted a level of service that Copenhagen was not able to offer its residents in the 1950s, when she herself moved to Frederiksberg and experienced an enormous difference. It was like going up from the bowels of an immigrant ship to the luxury cabins on the top deck.

"Everything was different, including the tone in the public offices. Never in my long life have I experienced so many ill-mannered and insensitive petty officials, so many endless queues, such enervating periods of waiting, such humiliating stays in hospitals and such poor chances of a decent house as in Copenhagen during those years. And then we came to Frederiksberg and met polite and helpful people in the public offices, respect and understanding in the hospital, and a different and better tone also in the case of the police."

And the gays? They themselves say that there is a remarkable concentration of them in this part of town – a larger proportion of the population than anywhere else in the country, but that is difficult to demonstrate. At all events, the ruling Conservative People's Party has had gays in the town hall for many years. It was an open secret that the theatre critic Svend Kragh-Jacobsen was gay. He made play with it himself and was on the town council for ten years, from 1974 to his death in 1984.

The radio host Michael Juul Sørensen is openly gay and has lived there since 1998. Apart from the classical meeting places such as Amigo Bar and Café Intime in Allégade, the other cafés, libraries and theatres attract them. "And then we spend a lot of money," says Michael Juul Sørensen as an extra explanation for why there are so many just there." There are plenty of places to spend money in Frederiksberg. You can get everything."

Only ten percent of Vesterbro residents are over 60. No less than a quarter of those in Frederiksberg are. So the most common prejudice – that Frederiksberg is the home for mincing steps, blue rinses and pearls – is not entirely wrong. The elderly and old residents promote a special, subdued atmosphere in the streets. Things don't move so quickly. There is a rate of breathing and a tempo that makes you relax your shoulders and breathe more calmly.

The critic Jens Kistrup lived in Frederiksberg Allé in an apartment block where nice people live who treat each other nicely, say good day nicely and don't see too much of each other. He called Frederiksberg a place of security. "It lies at the edge of Vesterbro, but the two are essentially different. The moment you leave Vesterbrogade and go down the avenue (Frederiksberg Allé) you are in a different world," he said. "Frederiksberg is peace."

A conservative politician on the town council says quite outright that Frederiksberg has enough in itself, a provincial town where everyone knows everyone else and where they tend to look down a little on people from Copenhagen. It's nice to have a city just round the corner, but it's best to live in a little, secure and manageable town where people would rather watch BBC World than Danish television. That's what they say, at least. But there is a question mark nevertheless. Even in this conservative realm some children are born with withdrawal symptoms, and even the

fine old royal park has problems with mainliners in the toilets. Classical Frederiksberg citizens call that *the other Frederiksberg*. Even though Frederiksberg seems to be open and green, there are 90,000 people living together in an area of nine square kilometres, and the social geography makes just as great an impression here as in Vesterbro, which also has its good and less good and awful addresses. Even if there were only two streets, it would still be like that.

There is a rustling of huge trees in Frederiksberg. Huge chestnut trees, lime trees, acacias and poplars grow in the quiet streets of large detached houses, and the green gardens close and become mysteriously dark from all that grows in them. There are no small measures here. Suburban houses have no soughing trees, for there people think in terms of unobstructed lawns open to the sun and harmless dwarf trees that only reach up to your nose.

The gardens in Frederiksberg are dense and old and have been written about by so many poets and authors that it would be nice to think of one who couldn't stand them. In certain places Frederiksberg simply *is* a garden, green and filled with rustling leaves. Kamma Rahbek, the hostess to the great personalities of the Golden Age, invented the potted plant out in Bakkehuset, and Frederiksberg invented the Danish villa. The first was built here. It was brand new in 1847 when the Villa Taarnborg was built unimaginably far out at the back of beyond for the von Bibow family. And how did they dare live there, scarcely half way up Gammel Kongevej? Those people were pioneers. They defied both the loneliness and the military, which could order houses to be demolished immediately if the enemy approached the capital.

Denmark's first villa looks charming and idyllic in drawings, with climbing plants, winding steps, combined garden and high wall to keep out thieves, a wooden veranda and a square tower on one side, taken straight from a building in the Borghese gardens in Rome, where Raphael is thought to have had his mistress living. So artists flocked around the tower house as a romantic place

Frederiksberg Allé is the closest Copenhagen gets to a grand axe.

Mysteriously, ladies are only found in Frederiksberg and, if we are hard pressed, in Østerbro.

to which to make an excursion, and the building acquired several Danish villa offspring.

People used to live either in an apartment in the towns or a house out in the country, not this curious freestanding thing in between. The last cholera epidemic in 1853 killed almost 5,000 Copenhageners with a little comma-like, rod-shaped bacterium. The exodus from the dangerous city increased in intensity. In the 1860s, villas were built on vast areas of Frederiksberg, for the king and the military had finally given up the line of cannon round the city. And so people rushed off to the green fields, where they quickly displaced the peasants and cattle. The wealthy constituted the first wave in this flight from the city. All housing policy is like that. The rich do something new, and then the idea percolates down into the general population. In the inter-war years, civil servants and smaller independent businessmen left the city for the villa, and in the 1960s the industrial workers moved out. By then the villa had turned into a small, detached house. Today three Danes out of five live in such houses. But Frederiksberg has its first generation villas – the historical monuments to a new way of life.

The elegant green streets around Gammel Kongevej are hardcore Frederiksberg, the quintessence of all that is old and solid. Uraniavej, started in 1867, is the best place to find the original Danish villa, for many of the original, simple villas are still there, for instance numbers 15 and 17. The same is true of Lindevej, where some of the first houses can still be found, for example two double villas down towards Gammel Kongevej. The tall trees on either side of the road meet in the middle and form a green tunnel.

Dogs are smaller and better behaved than elsewhere.

"The silent, enclosed world in Frederiksberg's peaceful villa streets, where blue clematis flower on white walls and there is a scent of fresh roses after the summer rain," sighs Carl Henrik Clemmensen in *Mit København, My Copenhagen* from 1939. And this is how this upper-class district is described in book after book, poem after poem.

But the real distinction has gone. Most of these spacious villas are now inhabited by several families or even communes, which the municipality fought against from the start in the 1970s and 80s. The people themselves can be seen in the gardens. There are bicycles leaning against the walls, and the hedges should have been cut long go. Gardeners, artisans and nursemaids have become expensive, so things are not what they used to be. And owners fight against institutions and offices in the old houses, for they spoil the "villa feel" with parking spaces where there ought to be a luxuriant green front garden.

A very small number of these huge houses are still inhabited by one family or one married couple, but when they move on, the huge building is easily converted into five or six owner-occupied flats.

Even when you stand and look at Frederiksberg from the other side of the lakes, from the city side, you can see that that place wants to be different. To begin with, the lakeside is left wild with grass, nettles and waving reeds. The lakes in all the other districts are bricked up and urbane. Secondly, the whole of the Frederiksberg side of Sankt Jørgens Sø is lined with mammoth villas. There are no villas on any of the others. Frederiksberg isn't massive, as Vesterbro so decidedly is. Frederiksberg is open.

"Frederiksberg is a provincial town, where everyone knows everyone else. I live 20 metres from Vesterbrogade, and I know *no one* from Vesterbrogade," says a man who has lived here for 16 years. "We have enough in ourselves." There he agrees with countless other people from this part of town, who bring out a picture of themselves that is exactly the opposite of Vesterbro. Vesterbro interprets itself as commonalty and noise. Frederiksberg is orderliness, quiet and distance – something that very often goes with money.

"In Frederiksberg, we live in villas or large apartments and like to keep to ourselves. We treat each other politely, but there is no misplaced sentimentality. This is not negative. People who move here want it like that. It is a respectful sense that 'that doesn't concern us'," says a man in his late 30s. "The quiet and the distance are at once the best and the worst of Frederiksberg. People are so keen to have peace and quiet that they prevent new cafés from opening, so it's a bit dreary out here. Gammel Kongevej is deserted after eight o'clock in the evening."

The fine villa-lined Amalievej, Kastanievej, Lindevej and Urania-vej are all typical of the early Danish streets lined with villas, and all were far out in the country when they were built.

Wealthy people don't like all living in houses that resemble each other. They didn't in those days either, and so they delved deep into the architectures of former ages and mixed them all up on a single road of fine houses – Swiss style, medieval, Italian country houses, pompous or modest, and all the owners were satisfied and felt they were individual. A white villa in the style of a country mansion stands brilliantly next to a profoundly serious set-up of red brick, almost a local town hall. Nevertheless, they all harmonise well with each other, for they were built at a time when people took the trouble to build a charming room opening on to the garden and lavished attention on elements from finely carved banisters to the chimney. And the new people look after them.

"The people living here are very interested in getting the houses back to what they were originally. None of them are keen to put up a conservatory or to install ridiculously big windows in these houses, as people were otherwise inclined to at one time. That is a thing of the past," says a relieved member of the local residents' association. A generational change is taking place at the moment, as older couples or people living on their own move out and sell their houses to television bosses, IT representatives and directors of various creative undertakings. Or perhaps the old people stay in one part of the house and make room for grown-up children and their children. Before the enormous price rises at the end of the 1990s, journalists, architects and musicians could also afford to buy houses here. "No one – or hardly anyone – lives alone in the villas any more. They are all houses of between six and seven hundred square metres and prices are sky high," says a man who has lived in Kastanievej for 25 years. When the villas were built, there had also to be rooms for maids, chauffeurs and other indispensable persons. They are no longer needed.

You have a feeling that trees are protected in Frederiksberg. And more are on the way. For the first time in living memory, trees have been planted in Gammel Kongevej. And in Pile Allé below Frederiksberg Castle a labyrinth of beech trees as tall as a man has sprung up. It is typical of Frederiksberg that large terra-cotta pots of flowers have been placed along Gammel Kongevej. Typical, too, that they should award prizes for nice, discreet shop windows, windows that make things look nice. This would never happen in Vesterbro. The historian Kristian Hvidt calls Frederiks-berg something completely and entirely on its own. Out in this "district of social aspiration", suitably close to the royal summer residence, the residents appreciated dignity. People built in a different way – better – than in the other new suburbs. In the 1890s, some of them established the "Committee for the Appropriate Development of Frederiksberg Municipality", and this district is still vain and preoccupied with looking good. Everything must be green, nice and clean.

Even the dogs behave better here than elsewhere. Frederiks-berg is a place with bags and receptacles for dog dirt, headed: "Do you have a good dog?" and a contrite little dog is sufficiently well trained to reply: "I'm sorry, but I needed to." There is a host of little dogs on the streets. But here in Pekinese Land they leave

Frederiksberg – royal, classical, conservative.

Also typical Frederiksberg: a tiny strip of garden in front of the house. Frederiksberg means Frederik's Mountain.

relatively few traces. They behave decently, like their law-abiding owners.

"If you don't want to move right out of town, but can't stand the tumult, Frederiksberg is the place to be," says the poet Lars Bukdahl, calling this area "a qualified, urban idyll", where the dominant feeling is one of convincing, old-fashioned sophistication that can scarcely be destroyed.

Where Frederiksberg has peace and quiet, parks and a swimming baths, Vesterbro has all-night shops and a constant stream of people. They appear not to cross each other's boundaries very often, but they have one area in common, the shopping street of Værnedamsvej. The name is a corruption of Werner Dams Vej. He was the owner of a hostelry and died in 1762. The street links the two districts and is divided between them. You turn the corner from the narrow and chaotic Værnedamsvej, where cars crawl along in both directions even if it looks like an impossible task,

and suddenly you are on the broad and empty Frederiksberg Allé.

There is something French about Frederiksberg Allé, and with a bit of good will it could be called Frederiksberg's *grand axe*. It goes from Mathildehøj in Frederiksberg Have past Fredriksberg Runddel to Sankt Thomas Plads and looks much like a French boulevard with four rows of lime trees pruned like candelabra. You rise several social classes and at the same time go back in time all at once. The road is magnificent and straight. It radiates gentle peace and is green as far as the eye can see. At the end stands Frederik VI, relaxed in bronze at the entrance to Frederiksberg Have, while the long axis continues behind him. The houses along the old royal road leading to the summer palace compete as to which can have the most towers, cupolas, bays and spires. One building aims to look like the Louvre in Paris, another Rosenborg Castle. Why be modest? That was not in the nature of the affluent new bourgeoisie. Lille Rosenborg from 1857 is the first block of flats in town in the new historical style – Dutch Renaissance like the real castle in Kongens Have. Later came all the incredible houses in styles from all over the world, but then that was the thing to do.

Henrik Jørgensen grew up in one of the endless apartments in Sankt Thomas Plads, where there are two fountains. "The house is redolent of middle-class affluence and enterprise from the turn of the century. The homes were clearly planned with an eye to the way of life of the more affluent middle classes: there are small apartments and large apartments, but even in the small ones there is room for the maid. The big ones are clearly arranged as suitable settings for middle-class social occasions: living room, cabinet, library overlooking the street, dining room with a single dreary corner window out to the yard (dinners for guests always take place after dark, so natural light can be dispensed with; and so you always have to grope around for your breakfast or light a candle!), a long corridor on to which the bedrooms open. At the end of this a kitchen, and behind that the maid's room, obviously smaller than any other room in the apartment.

In the long corridor, some small folding tables have been set up on which to place the dinner service when you move from the roast to the ice. The remains of the soup and the fish are already taking up the space in the kitchen. Yes, you can live there, you can even live well there; but you can't get away from a sense of a middle-class theatre – and, I must admit, that is just a little intoxicating." (*Barndomsbyer, Cities of childhood*, 1998).

When Frederiksberg Allé was established in 1701, Frederik IV erected an iron gateway out towards Vesterbrogade. It was closed to anyone but himself. As more Copenhageners built their elegant country mansions along the avenue, they were given keys. And later, quite ordinary people walked along it when they were on their way to Frederiksberg Have on a Sunday. The gate was taken down in 1862 and moved to the corner of Roskildevej and Pile Allé, where it still stands at the entrance to Søndermarken, the park. But the area is still royal, classical and conservative.

Nevertheless, neither Social Democrats nor socialists have anything against living there, and they reluctantly admit that despite its unbroken Conservative rule, Frederiksberg is not in the Stone Age as seen from a liberal point of view.

Frederiksberg has always had the reputation of being rural, so it is quite obvious that the Royal Veterinary and Agricultural University should occupy part of this area and make it still more airy and leafy with its park and its beds and plenty of room between the buildings. The Rolighed farm with a main building and three stable wings, rough cobbles and a meadow full of flowers is almost too much of a good thing only five minutes from Rådhuspladsen. A sign warns: "Live animals. Drive slowly" and husbands and wives walk into the University's garden to admire the begonias and variegated boriecole and to talk quietly together. On special days you can also see men in plus fours. It is strictly forbidden to walk on the grass in this fine and well-tended garden from 1858. Flowerbeds from a vanished age still have a chance, and some of them look like absurd sofa cushions from the Victorian age in aubergine and ox-blood with a palm tree in the middle and winding patterns of succulents.

The lawns are cut sharp at the edge by their paths, and the trees from foreign lands reveal themselves as the rare sights they are. The laurels in the park stand in square, bottle green containers on legs so they can be taken inside during the winter. Carps swim in the pond. The park embraces it all: the magnolia lawn, the collection of medicinal plants, the biggest collection of summer-flowering plants in the country and one of the few remaining formal rose gardens with 50 historical roses with fascinating names. Rosa Mundi – how beautiful can you get? There is also a dark patch, as there must be in all real gardens. A good, old-fashioned sepulchral atmosphere reigns down at the bottom in the little wood of thuja, pine, giant sequoia and ivy.

The first main building in yellow brick with large iron windows was designed by Gottlieb Bindesbøll, the man behind the brilliant Thorvaldsens Museum. Later, another architect built a block on to it, so you have to go on to the back of it to see Bindesbøll's contribution and right into the internal courtyard to see his façade.

Enormous plane trees shade the large yard behind the main building. Their blotchy, smooth stems are enclosed in ivy. This is a large, simple space with lawns and gravel paths like in front of a country mansion. Incredible here in the middle of town.

Frederiksberg Have

There is no longer a guard at the entrance to Frederiksberg Have with the aim of preventing cripples, down-at-heels and drunks from entering, but you might well think there was, so quiet and orderly it is in there. Everyone walks about decorously. The park is closed at night like Kongens Have, because, like all museums, it is irreplaceable and full of cultural history. The grand opera events have been moved over to Søndermarken, as they did too much damage to Frederiksberg Have. A man with an ear protector is hoovering leaves up, fat geese are waddling around, and the herons that have escaped from the zoo are circling high above. Almost every day you can see the heron man here with his strange, waving arm movements combined with a whistle and a cackle to tempt the nervous birds down in a circle around him. He thinks it's too easy to feed geese and ducks like the other bird lovers, for instance the man known as Hansen the Moorhen.

Frederiksberg likes to present itself as a place of peace and tolerance, and it has succeeded even in the park, which isn't even Frederiksberg's own, but belongs to the State. According to the 1849 constitution, the royal palaces and gardens became State property. It is as though the old people of this area have taken massive possession of Frederiksberg Have; at least they dominate the literature. And the Palaces and Properties Agency has constant problems with them in spring because they tiptoe around and dig up bulbs and smuggle them out in plastic bags as though it were their own garden. When the guard confronts them, they swear that they didn't know it wasn't allowed and then they hide behind a tree until he has gone again. "I understand that this park attracts old and lonely people. The rumble of the city stops at its gate; it opens up as a place for quiet thoughts and silent sorrow. It is like a cemetery for hidden memories and broken hopes," wrote Peter Nansen in 1891.

Johannes Jørgensen wrote five novels about young men coming from the provinces to Copenhagen to study at the university. They all come to grief in their encounter with the metropolis. But Jørgensen always consoled himself with Frederiksberg, which was something different. It was rural and peaceful: "The autumn makes its refreshing way through Frederiksberg. The days cool down beneath the shades created by the foliage – and there are fewer nursemaids. The evenings are cold and wet from the heavy dews of autumn – and the lovers withdraw. All that are left in the old park are the old men – the tall, thin, tightly wrapped up old men that the happy life of summer frightened away, but who can now settle down with pleasure on the old benches."

Sophus Bauditz describes the park as a kind of wondrous forecourt to death in 1912:

"Frederiksberg Have must be seen in the autumn, and Frederiksberg Have must be seen towards evening, when old or at least elderly people slowly walk about on the tortuous paths on which no one, or scarcely anyone, is at home. It best suits people whose task in life is finished, and for whom it is quite a miniature experience to stand on the hill by the Swiss house and watch the sun set over the 'country' and cast a last glow on the little island's birch trunks behind, or to sit on one of the benches and hear the bells ringing from a church, the location of which one doesn't know."

Frederik IV placed his castle on the top of the Valby Bakke. In fact a mountain – in German: Berg – hence the name of Frederiksberg.

The citizens of Frederiksberg are older than in other districts of Copenhagen. They are almost always mentioned as a kind of natural fixture in literature depicting the old park.

Frederiksberg Have, the pride of the district and a place to which Copenhageners have made excursions for hundreds of years.

Drachmann used the expression "bourgeois-philistine" of the park. Philistine implies petit bourgeois and fatuous, but Drachmann was always there, and he knew it from end to end. The park has maintained a certain lofty and majestic quality because every summer's day, Frederik VI (1786-1839) doggedly sailed around the canals in the park while half the town's population stood with bared heads along the muddy waters.

"And the entrance to Frederiksberg Have! With yellow walls and yellow gardeners' houses and wrought iron gates in the style of the eighteenth century! You felt that you were in a little European kingdom as you entered this park. You felt it was lovely with this monarchist illusion hovering in the yellow light." Tom Kristensen, *Hærværk, Wilful damage* (1930).

Every time an elm tree dies or a gale has a go at Frederiksberg Have it is good for something. Then the experts take out the castle gardener Petersen's old plan of the park. It is thought to be from the 1790s, and it acts as the Palaces and Properties Agency's master plan. That is how the park ought to look again in time. This man Petersen was so kind as to draw in all the trees very carefully, and his plan is supplemented with lists of plants in which you can see what they bought in those days. And the plan contains surprises: There was an incredible number of coniferous trees in those days, so in future the visitors to the park will see many more evergreens. That won't suit everybody today, when deciduous trees are so much loved and spruce are heartily disliked for being sombre and unvaried. But that's what it looked like in here when the romantic park was finished in 1804. A very deliberate play was made on the dark and the light and the difference in the colours in the deciduous trees – pale green alongside copper beech.

Cypresses, thujas and other evergreens were placed strategically so that you couldn't see right through the garden in winter when you walked in it. If that happened, the surprises would disappear, and they were the whole idea. You couldn't see from one experience to the next.

This historical garden can be compared to a national museum, in which garden art and aesthetics are to be preserved. It is considered to be one of the country's finest romantic parks because so many of the original treasures have survived – the summerhouse, the temple, the dolmen, the grotto, the Swiss cottage – all those *objects* they suddenly had to have in their gardens.

If fashion so dictates, a woman can easily buy herself a pair of flared trousers and throw them away the following year. In the same way an absolutist king could without more ado turn his enormous park inside out according to fashion. He could transform his stiff and formal baroque garden into a free, winding romantic garden if garden fashion required it. And that it did at the end of the 18th century. It was no use owning a run-down, old-fashioned park even if it had once been the most beautiful. And garden fashion is merciless. All parks in Denmark were generally speaking redesigned in the romantic style in the 19th century, and Frederiksberg Have was completely transformed by 1804. It has previously existed as a baroque garden for a hundred years: a *parterre* garden is quite low and clings to the ground. Small box hedges twenty centimetres high form intertwining patterns and monograms. Seen from above they look like a complicated piece of embroidery, and it is just from above that it has to be seen, from the castle. Typically, the most expensive and splendid things in the park are closest to the castle.

The baroque requires everything to be under control, and so you establish customs and excise, tax authorities and all kinds of other authorities – and of course, nature must also be controlled. The gardeners cut everything into shape, and the landscape architects use rulers and design long axes through the castle and out into the landscape and infinity. Frederik IV strolls around with his court on planned walks at specific times, so it is important to have men with spades well hidden. And the ordinary populace is also herded into the bushes when the king is approaching. Baroque culminated in Versailles, and then came the French Revolution in 1789 and put an end to absolutism in France. In the parks, natural forces were allowed their freedom, and rulers were discarded. Now feelings were to have their freedom in a free park. Denmark was a poor little kingdom fifty years out of date. Even rich Danes were further advanced than the king.

Frederik VI no longer wanted the stiff old French set-up, but a mysterious, wild park in the English style where an exciting surprise waits around every single corner. But he kept the two grand views from the baroque garden – from the castle looking towards Andebakken and from the entrance at the circus looking towards the prehistoric mound. People with knowledge of garden art were delighted at this and emphasised that the remains of the old garden were the best thing about the new one. The king retained the terraces in front of the castle and the avenue trees on either side, but the manically pruned trees were allowed to grow wild. Before this they had to be exactly eight metres tall with five metres of top and three metres of trunk.

In a romantic park, the intention is that a visitor should feel transported. It is furnished with all kinds of curios – a Swiss cottage, so you can feel transported to the clear air of the Alps, a Chinese summerhouse where you can take tea and dream of the vast empire, a Stone Age mound that makes you think of your own roots, a little Greek temple to represent the sublime, and a mysterious grotto that has been added as the result of Italian garden fashion. Everything one loves is represented here – antiquity, the Nordic universe, and the Chinese universe. Later, the neighbouring Zoological Gardens built yet another curiosity – Denmark's answer to the Eiffel Tower.

Søndermarken has a Norwegian section with something of the character of a mountain, a mountain hut and spruces so that no one will forget the twin kingdom of Denmark-Norway. Educated people could interpret these things in the park and knew what they ought to feel when facing one or other of these pieces of stage scenery. A ruin means decline, death and melancholy. A Greek temple is a glorious peak of civilisation. All is emotion, melancholy, reflection, sentimentality – feelings above all. People started travelling at the end of the 18th century simply in order to see something and collect views. Prior to this they had a real errand in foreign countries. Now they simply enthused about them.

The king set Holstein dike diggers, who had dug the Ejder Canal right across Jutland, to dismantle the park's splendid fountains and link them to several kilometres of the winding canals, in which the water stands motionless. The soil was piled up into small mounds and islands. He sailed around on the muddy canals in a gondola, went ashore on the Chinese island to the people's applause and drank tea from Chinese porcelain together with his daughters. The park was open to the people of Copenhagen, but he kept Søndermarken to himself, fenced in.

You have to look for a long time before finding anyone who doesn't like Frederiksberg Have, for everyone loves it. But the art historian Hakon Lund is critical. It is one thing for the terrain to be flat and so naturally unsuited to a landscape garden. Something quite different – and worse – is the diversity of ideas: "There are too many and too diverse curiosities to achieve splendid views," he writes in the authoritative *Danmarks havekunst, Denmark's ornamental gardens* (2000). And he is not alone: "Under Frederik VI the grandiose baroque garden, which today would have been a site comparable to Versailles, was transformed into what from a professional garden architect's point of view is an amateur English park. And it is best not to show it to foreigners because its charm is to a considerable extent undoubtedly based on unfortunate garden features such as the muddy canals and the candelabra limes that are deformed thanks to a shaping that was given up half way," was the opinion of Broby-Johansen, who also disliked the king so much loved by the population.

Elegant Allégade. About 20 descendants of Christian II's Amager peasants settled here to cultivate the land in 1651. The village was called Ny Hollænderby and was the first urban development in Frederiksberg.

Sankt Jørgens Sø is different from the others: wilder, with reeds and a lakeside. Called after a leper hospital dedicated to a saint, which lay here in the Middle Ages.

Copenhagen Zoo

Of all the showpieces in Frederiksberg, Copenhagen Zoo, Zoologisk Have, from 1859 is the strangest. In the midst of the metropolis the task is to make the public feel closely related to the wild animals. And they make use of all the classical theatrical methods at their disposal. Much more than one would imagine.

In the old days, people went to the zoo to stand face to face with the beast. You could prick the tiger with your walking stick, watch it rush at the bars and feel the rush of fear. The installations were virtually deep wells, for the animals had to be kept down and the public had to feel safe. What the animals have to tell us today is a completely different story: Now the innocent animals must be protected from the greed of human beings. Now we have to feel solidarity with them. The public isn't neutral when it comes to this show. Most attribute human qualities and feelings, mainly longing, to the animals. Biologists say that longing is exclusively a human feeling. No animal longs to be anywhere else in the world. But the management of the zoo knows that its public thinks along these lines. So if an animal is sitting looking miserable, that can't be allowed. The management stand on their heads to avoid it and to engineer settings so that the animals don't look miserable. An orang-utan sitting on a branch relaxing looks upset. It is its nature. It looks apathetic when it has had a meal.

"We want to speak to people's emotions; it's as banal as that," says the director about his theatre, in which the animals are actors in settings with carefully controlled lighting and sound tracks. In the tropical house, the birds are encouraged by a tape recording of jungle sounds – frogs, cicadas and a bird's whistle – then they find it easier to join in. The animals are in very precisely staged surroundings. The jungle isn't a jungle but a feeling of the rainforest, of its warmth, sounds and luxuriance. It is an idea and a cultural phenomenon, and there is neither an ecological balance nor anything else at all natural about it. This jungle is in a city. On the other hand: the most admired and fantastic zoological gardens in the world are in the Bronx, New York.

The Zoo contains a workshop that works exclusively on decoration, light, sound and swindle. For instance it makes a city setting of rats scuttling around in a horrible, underground network of sewers scattered with used condoms and syringes. In another place, the American possum pretends it's at home in a back yard with an overturned American dustbin and artificial American rubbish. And the fruit bats flutter around in a vampire-inspired setting bathed in moonlight. Here, too, the sound is supplemented with owls and frogs. These not particularly spectacular nocturnal animals have been given a real boost with the setting. Cuddly tiger cubs do better.

The masterpiece is the tropical house, where the public goes around among tropical birds and enormous butterflies. Sloths and chameleons cross the paths on their lianas above visitors' heads. The waterfall has been fixed and moved several times because it didn't splash in quite the right way. This can be done because the mighty rocks are made of dyed fibrous concrete and can simply be lifted.

The cliffs are made of the same seven perfect cliff shapes cunningly fitted together, but clearly distinguishable individually if you look carefully. The mangroves are made of conduits, epoxy and gauze, and among the real trees and bushes there are many artificial ones made up of good branches and adorned with artificial leaves.

The designer has also made a number of dioramas (miniature reproductions of reality), in which the "sun" is low in the "foliage", and where artificial stretches of rock have inlaid heating elements. Then the animals can lie and warm themselves in front of the public just as they would in greenery where they can't be seen. The major, trend-setting zoological gardens in the West are all moving in the same direction – into nature, into the idea of nature. The public must become one with the place – without being eaten or kicked. A mental eternity has elapsed since Niels Kjærbølling opened his embarrassing little zoological garden in 1859, when the animals that his friends and contacts had sent him had to be shown in a pretty awful way: birds of prey in small cages, waders in vats, a tame seal in a bath, a tortoise in a bucket and so on. Kjærbølling laboured on, and people's good will grew and grew.

Copenhagen Zoo has abandoned the conservative old method according to which 20 birds were kept in 20 cages so that you could determine the breeding, open the nesting boxes and keep a proper eye on the birds. Now they fly around in artificial rainforests. In the old birdhouses, the keepers cleaned droppings from the branches, raked the gravel and put small boxes of food in to them. Today, they have to use a telescope to see the birds in the tropical house, where they no longer clean up in the same way as when there were tiles and walls. Sterility has come to an end.

When the author Viggo Stuckenberg (1863-1905) went into the old gardens "where such a great world is enclosed" a few months before his death in 1905, he caught a glimpse of paradise. No less.

"Every morning is beautiful in itself; over the morning of every day there is a breath of rebirth and renewal. But in here, where so much and such varied life is assembled, the morning possesses one charm more. Every sound from all these animals' throats, even the most familiar, seems to be new and young in the pure, untouched air, and the sunlight falls as though for the first time on the hoof marks in the enclosures and over the squirrel's bed of cracked nut shells. Everything is as though just having been brought into existence from some remarkably fresh eternity." Stuckenberg was completely in love with the gardens when the mornings were light. "But then go on a winter's evening after sunset in Frederiksberg Have and to hear the wolves howling up there in the frost and drifting snow, while the cold makes the naked trees creak. Then you need little imagination to understand that the gate of Paradise was shut long, long ago, and that terrible things have taken place in the world since then."

Nørrebro

When they are having coffee at a communal table among relatives and friends somewhere in the provinces and say where they live, people from Nørrebro can be sure someone will always exclaim: "How do you dare to live there?" It's always been like that. This old, left-wing, violent Copenhagen bridge district always causes a nervous sense of awe and turbulent associations merely at the sound of its name. You can't just say "Nørrebro" and think that others will remain neutral. "Nørrebro has such a reputation in the press and among the population that you wouldn't believe it. As though there's a civil war going on here. It's not like that at all. The surface cracks once a year, that's all," says a man who has had a shop on Nørrebrogade for 16 years. When he moved in, he was also on edge because of the old working-class district and its thuggish reputation. But he quickly changed his views. The *dangerous* folk were not dangerous, just exciting. Now he enjoys being in the part of Denmark where the largest numbers of people and nationalities are gathered together in a very small area. There are not many places like this in the country.

A woman born in 1919 says that she has never been worried by anyone or ever felt threatened in Nørrebro – though she admits that there are elderly ladies who still dare not walk through the once wild and overgrown cemetery, Assistens Kirkegård. This woman doesn't even have a sense of living in a rowdy district, but admits that it was "not really so nice" in the 1970s, when sleeping drug addicts lay in all the entrances to blocks of flats in the mornings. That's all gone. One day, the pack took off and went elsewhere, mainly to Vesterbro.

People moving into the area are almost all surprised at what it is really like in Nørrebro. They expect something different and rougher than what they find there. The peace and quiet of Nørrebro in the evening is striking, for people go to bed and sleep. Most of them have to get up and go to work or school. 70 per cent are under 40 years of age. Nørrebro is a demonstratively political area in relation to, for instance, Vesterbro and the other districts. It is left wing and angry and won't put up with anything, certainly not the police. That's what they say at least. The truth is that Nørrebro is becoming more and more middle class. There are lots of Conservatives and Liberals living there. The Liberals are as important there as the very left-wing Unity List, and every single election result shows Nørrebro moving towards the right. A large, silent majority is fed up with social agitators and they would rather have peace and quiet and the right to eat as many burgers as they want in the multinational McDonald's that the agitators have tried to drive out of Nørrebro.

Although there is still a lack of doctors, lawyers, office heads and others from the respectable middle classes, Nørrebro is moving away from its historical left-wing traditions. The agitators can't just hang up a banner across Nørrebrogade with the inscription Union-free area. It is getting close to being unacceptable. With every referendum that has had anything to do with the EU, the old bridge district has become more and more in favour of the idea. "The spirit of the 1970s nevertheless still survives in some way or other out here. But it's funny that you can no longer be sure that your neighbour will say no to the EU," says a man from Blågårdsgade.

On the other hand, Nørrebro is also the place where the local council made the black, American murderer Mumia abu-Jamal an honorary citizen, and where the Socialist People's Party and the Unity List had an absolute majority. Later, the Ministry of the Interior forced them to take back the title from the condemned Abu-Jamal because it was not within the council's competence to distribute honorary citizenship.

It is also a place where a publicly supported music venue such as 30 Stengade insists on having written into its statutes that it organises anti-fascist activities. Music is not enough.

In Griffenfeldsgade you can still buy Marx and Engels' Communist Manifesto and the communist youth movement Rød Ungdom's *Den ultimative sangbog, The ultimate song book* in the workers' bookshop. So some things haven't changed. The dark and dirty Elmegade, on the other hand, has developed into an very fashionable alternative to the old town's most sophisticated side streets. After urban renewal, the buildings are resplendent in classical

colours, and the shops think they are in Strøget, with exclusive makes in architect-designed interiors. Behind these buildings there are green courtyards, where the daylight pours into the flats. When the sandwich shops, the Chinese takeaways and the dark brown pubs with their one-armed bandits and terylene curtains disappear, and second-hand Arne Jacobsen, hand-built bicycles and bagels with chorizos suddenly make their appearance in the district, then it will have happened.

In Sankt Hans Torv, you can find people eating pâté de foie gras, something totally incorrect and alien to Nørrebro. You can find croutons with rouille, acacia honey yoghurt and organic blue cheese. Now they flash debit cards in the old working class district. At the beginning of the 1990s there was nothing of that kind: dark and with too many cars, it was the sort of place where you could buy a second hand gas cooker. All this came in the wake of the Barcelona restaurant in Fælledvej, founded in 1989 as the first chic restaurant in Nørrebro. Then came Rust and the new Sankt Hans Torv, renovated and transformed at the beginning of the 90s with Jørgen Haugen Sørensen's sculpture The House That Rains. Before that, the square was really only a traffic roundabout. Copenhagen paid for an elegant cobbled surface that had still not been properly laid when Nørrebro exploded in more than five hours of violence on 18 May 1993 because the Danes voted in favour of the EU opt-out clauses. And the Union. That didn't suit the agitators. The cobblestones were used as ammunition in the worst street fighting in recent times. An eyewitness reported to the newspaper Berlingske Tidende:

"About 2-300 thugs have gathered on Sankt Hans Torv. They are throwing cobblestones at the police on Fælledvej. The front line of police can't hold. A member of the riot squad goes out behind them and shouts down to the units in Nørrebrogade: 'Let's have a group down here. Then we'll put an end to them. Be quick, they mustn't run us down.'

There was a pause in the battle for a time, but then it started up again. The police withdrew. No one in the front line was in

The autonoms and their sympathisers have made their somewhat tiring mark on Nørrebro. The locals are generally speaking fed up with them.

Typical Nørrebro.

The avant-garde has moved from the centre of town to the bridge districts.

any doubt. This was really dangerous. And it was for real.

Finally the group from Nørrebrogade reacted. Accompanied by shouts of hatred from balconies and windows, where youths were shouting "nazi swine" and "hippos" after them, they ran up towards Sankt Hans Torv, where the bonfires were burning. They ran, stopped, ran, stopped. Nervously, hesitantly. And then it started. Veritable cascades of cobblestones flew through the air. Dull thuds could be heard when the stones hit shields and shin guards. Officer after officer was knocked over. "3-0" came the shout from a balcony as the third one went down. Despite the police cordons there were many civilians here. Their hatred only went in one direction.

Several policemen were carried away by colleagues. Seven officers were lying on the road in the middle of Fælledvej. A Swedish journalist from Expressen in Stockholm watched speechless: 'This is war'. Then the final boundary was passed. And there was only violence, blood and chaos left. In between the sound of cobblestones raining down like a thunderstorm on the police shields, there was a sound of pistol shots. Warning shots. Not one or two, but almost a constant salvo rang out. No one could fail to hear them. Finally it stopped. But the cobblestones continued their inhuman curve, and the youths were forcing their way forward.

Then there was a second salvo. And these were no longer warning shots. The police were shooting to save their lives. Shooting to hit."

113 shots were fired. 14 people were hit, none fatally. These disturbances started in 1993, just as the district was being transformed. Shortly afterwards, the four tons of small cobblestones were knocked into the ground, the houses around the square painted and row after row of café chairs put out on the pavement. Ironically, the Museum of Police History is in this square as one of the infinitely small number of museums in Nørrebro.

The price of owner-occupied flats rose many times more quickly around Sankt Hans Torv than Nørrebro prices in general, for now the square had suddenly acquired a Parisian atmosphere. Squares are popular and are worth a lot of money, as can be seen in a game of Monopoly. Sankt Hans Torv also pays off well. During the summer, students come drifting down from their flats at about 10 or 11 o'clock to have brunch and read the newspaper. In the evening, the revivified square hums with voices, and people come from all over town, for this is an unusual place. Six streets lead to the square, and visitors have a view of the first church in Nørrebro, Sankt Johanneskirken, consecrated in 1861 when the new town outside the ramparts was growing rapidly.

The numbers of classical smørrebrød shops and Chinese grill bars are reducing.

Healthy and lean in Blågårdsgade.

The habit of going out has become decentralised. The flow of people is no longer only towards the centre, but it also moves unpredictably around the bridge districts as they are upgraded with new and interesting places to go to. Leading DJs work in Nørrebro and Vesterbro, not in central Copenhagen, because students no longer live there. They have taken the music out with them.

The workers left in the 1960s and 70s in order to find a bit of land and a small house or to move to the social housing schemes in Ishøj. At the same time, industry and workshops also moved out. Time ran out for the small flats and squalid back yards.

From 1970 and far into the 1980s, Nørrebro looked like a devastated city with large empty spaces and deserted buildings. A large number of famous battles took place between residents and sympathisers on the one hand and the police on the other.

The squatters in the 1980s were met with a certain sympathy, but since the autonoms took over in the 1990s it has been difficult to find a single Nørrebro resident who doesn't think the diffuse trouble on the streets isn't a nuisance. There is no popular support.

But Nørrebro recovered slowly, and from 1990 new people be-

gan to move in. To some people, the picture of Nørrebro changed from being a squalid place to something artistic, hip and suitably radical, where *one* could live after all. Spirited and slum at the same time. Perhaps they are the same people who wander around wearing a navel-length t-shirt bearing the inscription 2200 Nørrebronx. At all events, they move in whenever a smoky old pub becomes vacant, for instance Det Gyldne Krus on Kapelvej, which has taken on a new lease of life in a young, light version with the gradually inevitable concept of brunch and drinks, DJs at the weekend and unromantic ceiling lights.

Self-assured shopkeepers in Elmegade think the central area of Copenhagen seems provincial because everyone goes around in the same fashionable clothes, and everything is so nice and safe. "If Nørrebro hadn't happened, Copenhagen would have been provincial," said one of the leading figures, whose elegant clothes shop has been in Wallpaper, Vogue and Elle – just before he moved his shop to the centre of town. He compares the area around Elmegade and the square with Chelsea in London and East Village in New York. The people passing in the street are not 1980s style yuppies in sharp suits and gold watches, but a softer, creative and more "casual" version of the same type. An equally

Dronning Louises Bro (Queen Louise's bridge), Peblinge Sø and Nørrebro. Pebling means a
pupil of a choir school, but nobody knows why the lake was named after a person like that.

Sjællandsgade. One of the new, green courtyards that make Nørrebro nicer to live in.

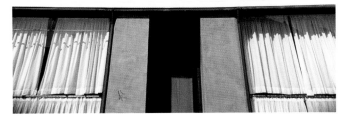

Folmer Bendtsens Plads near Nørrebro Station. Bendtsen (1907-93) was first a sailor, then a street vendor and then a painter. He took his motifs from the Copenhagen working-class districts.

Nørrebro became modern in the 1990s, and not a second before. But this is only true of the dense old built up area, the real part of it, not the new, low-built suburban housing. The prevailing myth about Nørrebro is that it is rebellious, political and knows better.

rigid set of rules applies, but they mustn't be too obvious. And the smart job is no longer a stockbroker, but something or other in the media or design.

But there are still some native-born citizens, old people and eccentrics, to be seen in the streets, and the smart ones always accept them provided they behave properly. Any dangerous traits must be kept under control and softened up with smoothies and tapas under pink neon lights. Here you can buy designer clothes that are only sold in New York, London and then Elmegade. And here you can see the other Nørrebro, a Nørrebro that might think of saying yes to Europe. A Nørrebro that is completely indifferent to politics and slogans. And a Nørrebro that has expensive cars parked in the streets. The new residents are students, side by side with well-heeled types from '68 and youngish people who move into the large apartments – advertising agents, photographers, graphic artists, artists, actors, IT folk, lawyers. However, it is possible to buy a black scarf inscribed *No nazis* or a cap inscribed with *No racism* on the square. The laundrette and a pub with chequered tablecloths and potted busy Lizzies has survived so far.

The area around the square has gradually acquired charm and some style because it has something that large areas of Nørrebro lack: old, high and dense housing. Its urban quality.

When the monotonous slum clearance of the 1970s and 80s turned much of Nørrebro into an open, green and low-rise suburb, Sankt Hans Torv, Elmegade, Ahornsgade and the other streets named after trees escaped. When their turn came, the authorities had learned to preserve instead of pull down. And so the estate agents have grouped together here. The traditional district is experiencing a renaissance.

The dividing line between the old and the new is roughly speaking Nørrebrogade. On the right as you come from town there is the old part. On the left you have the Green Square, where entire streets were demolished and replaced by prefabricated elements with a red "wall carpet" and concrete bands as a contrast. "These are in a way the suburbs' anti-modern revenge

on the bridge districts, the real town," says Frederik Stjernfelt of what he calls "this sentimental hatred of the city", where you puncture the intensity by reducing the urban density, breaking down the structure of street networks and squares and establishing melancholy patches of shrubbery and empty lawns between the houses. These newly built areas are constructed entirely without provision for shops, and so the streets are deserted. Occasionally a little ordinary life in diverse forms emerges in the more or less well-preserved streets, Blågårdsgade and Griffenfeldsgade. The new houses turn their backs on the street and open inwards with rustic balconies and enormous janitor-friendly areas with lawns, benches, paths and playgrounds. With the slum clearance, half the residents disappeared, and it was also the intention that the most densely populated area in the country should be thinned out a little. But as soon as it had been done, the regrets came in droves.

People suddenly began to look more positively at houses from the 1870s, when Nørrebro sprang up. Perhaps it wasn't so ugly after all. They discovered that the new buildings were anonymous, uninteresting and alien in a town where closeness and intensity are natural, and where nature in the shape of large lawns is out of place. There is much to suggest that these buildings will end up as a time capsule: This is how we did things in the 1970s. We shall never do it again. In Vesterbro we see the official endorsement of older houses, where apartments are being renovated to the tune of a million kroner each. There they simply daren't build anything new for fear of destroying the old districts and for fear of the fury of the people living there. Confidence in the new architecture is minute, so rather preserve even if it costs a fortune. But the Nørrebro experience had to come first.

"Nørrebro is a martyrdom. One suffers and bears witness so that it will never happen again," says the anthropologist Anne Knudsen.

Anne Knudsen moved there in 1987, and her friends viewed Nørrebro as a place exclusively inhabited by social security cases.

All that changed completely around 1990. Suddenly, other people's reaction was "Oh, how exciting" when she gave her address as Blågårdsgade. It has become enormously smart to live in Nørrebro, precisely because it doesn't signal middle class. But even so, you can quite happily have your coffee with others like you on Blågårds Plads, dance in the clubs around Sankt Hans Torv and buy your designer clothes in Elmegade.

A paint dealer says August is the best month in the whole year for him. His shop fills up with families talking with a Jutland accent. They take litre upon litre of paint away, and finally dad puts his debit card through the machine. It is all the new students whose parents have bought small flats for them in Nørrebro. Now they are over to help them to settle in. The children live there for three, four, five years, and then they move to something bigger or right out of town. Then the new students come, and it all starts over again.

The poet Søren Ulrik Thomsen misses something: "I feel a great loss of reality in connection with the disappearance of the old Nørrebro. I come from the provinces, of course, and moved to Copenhagen when I was 16, and I had a very strong, intense experience of *reality* in the vast old slum districts. Now there are only a few places left, for instance in Nørrebrogade between Assistens Kirkegård and the lakes between four and five o'clock when people are on their way home.

It reminds me of the time when reality existed, and I feel the need for a flat where I can stick my head out of the window and see all the bikes and cars and shops. For that is *life* – in all its tumult, decay and abundance," he says to Peter Øvig Knudsen in *Børn skal ikke lege under fuldmånen, Children are not to play under a full moon* from 1996. Thomsen would like to have the world rebuilt as it was on 12 August 1972, when he came to Copenhagen.

In the 1830s, 40s and 50s, the young Nørrebro was a lovely, rural place inhabited by respectable, sensible people – officials, pensioners, widows, artisans, gardeners and cemetery workers. The

cemetery Assistens Kirkegård was one of the few old features in the area, established in 1760 on account of a desperate lack of space in Copenhagen behind the tall earthen ramparts and the moats. Cows grazed out there, the military exercised occasionally on Nørre Fælled, the birds sang, and the odd wanderer could be seen making his way across the wet meadows. Although the city was beginning to suffocate because far too many people were grouped together in far too little space, there was no chance of living in the inviting, green country district of Nørrebro, which they visited on excursions.

The military had the supreme authority and decided that no one should be allowed to build or to live in the area around Copenhagen, for the enemy was not to have anywhere to hide during a siege of the capital. Out in Nørrebro, the fortunate few who had been given special permission were able to live in single-storey houses. In 1830, there were three side roads in Nørrebro – Blågårdsvej, Fælledvej and Jødevej, now called Møllegade – and 1,500 residents who wanted to live close to each other.

In 1852, the military gave up the idea of defending Copenhagen in the old way, for it was no use in any case. Copenhagen was no longer to be a fortress city, so building was now to be permitted: a few streets appeared straight away, including Tømrergade and Murergade, but otherwise little happened for the first twenty years. The first generation of houses was three storeys high at the most and was surrounded by villas, gardens and uninhabited green areas. Nørrebro attracted nice people. Dentists, merchants, directors and office heads once lived in the large luxurious apartments in the elegant streets – Dosseringen, Nørrebrogade and Blågårdsgade, where forty per cent of the new apartments were of more than three rooms. Some were up to six or eight.

These respectable people slowly began to drift away when cheap housing started in earnest in the 1870s, and hordes of country labourers poured into the new bridge districts. All the greenery was swallowed up, fresh air was at a premium, and the superior residents gradually moved from their large apartments

to respectable new suburbs like Østerbro and Frederiksberg, leaving Nørrebro to an increasingly homogeneous population, as a result of which it finally became a purely working-class district. In 1884, Nørrebro elected the first Social Democrats to the Folketing, the Danish parliament, a tailor by the name of Holm and a shoemaker called Hørdum.

The Danish architect and town planner Steen Eiler Rasmussen was outraged a hundred years later. What were people thinking of finally to let Copenhageners out of their prison behind the ramparts and then house them in dense, high-rise, cramped conditions when there was plenty of room? People living in Copenhagen were first oppressed by their rulers for hundreds of years, and now these servile masses had to bow to land speculators. "In London, slums *emerged* little by little when stately houses were allowed to decay and were taken over by lower classes than they were intended for. But in Copenhagen, slum districts were systematically *built*. I will not describe in more detail how unfortunate it is when the underprivileged are gathered together in special districts of this kind," he wrote in his classic *København, Copenhagen* in 1969.

Even when the later parts of Nørrebro were being built between 1870 and 1890, there were those who believed that this was a new slum. And historians and architects have held that view ever since. But according to recent research, this is a myth. When Copenhagen City Museum appointed Luise Skak-Nielsen to undertake a major cultural-historical study of inner Nørrebro and she described it in *Alle kender Blågårdsgade, Everybody knows Blågårdsgade* (1989), the doctrine was overturned: "A later age has called this development bleak, and in time it has become a dogma that it was built as a slum. Seen in relation to the general standard of housing at the time, this is too harsh a judgement. The workers' homes in the bridge districts – cramped and lacking in amenities as they were – were better than what was on offer to workers in central Copenhagen." A study from 1870 shows that the workers in Vesterbro lived in bigger and better apartments than those in

Christianshavn. And the houses in the old part of Copenhagen were more crowded than in the bridge districts. In addition, the housing act distinguished between the two localities in 1856 and demanded larger open areas in the new district. And finally: Most of those coming to Copenhagen were escaping from miserable conditions out in the country. Nørrebro was not wonderful, but many other places were worse.

The author Martin Andersen Nexø called Vesterbro a place teeming with life and Nørrebro petit bourgeois: "It is a case of food and rent and food again, as regularly as in no other part of the city. Traffic moves more slowly here than elsewhere, there is a special steely trustworthiness imprinted on this area, where every step comes with the entire weight of work. Ordinary times pass in a steady, old-fashioned manner with birthdays and little excursions on Sundays; the bad times cling on to their coat tails. Here, they make do with their own belongings and use them again: the rags are left from the overcoat they bought themselves. Life is honestly one's own down to the last stitch," he wrote in 1910.

Slaget på Fælleden, The Battle of the Common, on 5 May 1872 was the first of a long succession of political battles in which the people of Nørrebro were implicated, and perhaps the nearest Denmark has ever come to a revolution, at least one of the violent kind. The police had the previous day arrested the socialists Louis Pio, Harald Brix and Paul Geleff and prohibited a popular meeting on Fælleden in support of striking Copenhagen bricklayers.

For foreigners in Denmark: Go straight to Griffenfeldsgade. More immigrants live in Nørrebro than anywhere else, mainly on account of the housing. Danes live in the old, renovated apartments and the immigrants in the council housing, of which there is a great deal in Nørrebro. Twice as much, for instance, as in Vesterbro.

When a great crowd of people nevertheless turned up, the police, soldiers and hussars set about them. No one was killed, but many were injured, and the battle came to symbolise the adversity facing the workers' movement. But the next century was to be theirs.

At the heart of Nørrebro a square has been constructed specifically for political meetings and confrontations, and it is still regularly used. When Heegaard moved his foundry out of Blågårdsgade in 1898, the municipality bought the site and established Blågårdsplads. It was to be decorated in 1919. The intention was originally that the new square should be adorned with a good-humoured sculpture portraying "men and women whirling and dancing" and two brewers carrying a barrel from which a fountain sprang. That was too much for a district where the men dropped dead blind drunk after beating their wives and children and drinking up their wages if there were any.

The temperance societies believed the sculpture glorified drinking, and the artist withdrew his proposal. Then the idea took a serious turn. The sculptor Kai Nielsen took over and excavated a rectangular sunken space, clad it with stone and placed a heavy, huddled sculpture of the working people in the low surrounding wall. "I have tried to create a space for popular meetings for the many people living in Nørrebro," he said. "While the speaker is standing on the great stone rostrum, the tiled sunken space is full of listeners, and the women and children sit all around on benches under the trees."

And that is how it turned out. The square became a popular centre. The children played there, and the women sat and talked. Photographs from the 1920s, 30s and up to the 60s, when families moved out, show a host of children, young people, mothers, scavengers and meths drinkers. Of course, the socialists' May Day always started there. Other parties tried to use the square as a forum, but they were driven away. The Young Conservatives marched to it in the 1930s, at which every window was opened and people shouted "Blågårds Plads is red, Blågårds Plads is red.

The Fifth Ward is red." The streets were the setting for many skirmishes. Between 70 and 80 per cent voted for left-wing candidate.

"The rule forbidding you to appear better than the others applied. For instance, our uncle kept quiet for many years about having bought a weekend cottage. My parents' car ended by being acceptable because they had to use it to buy goods for the shop. But it was dreadful at first: fancy being an owner-driver as they said in those days. And I was called the greengrocer's stuck-up daughter because I wouldn't go to dances in the Danish Bicycle Club," says a woman about the 30s and 40s in *Alle kender Blågårdsgade, Everybody knows Blågårdsgade*.

Blågårdsgade has come to life again after the long decline. There are restaurants and cafés there now, bakers, flowers, books, meat, bicycles, greengroceries, boots, shoes, clothing, furniture and takeaways from various continents. It was once one of the finest streets in Nørrebro, a commercial street with stucco and double doors giving access to the large apartments, and now there is again life and variety here such as you rarely see elsewhere. On a good day on a good bench on Blågårds Plads you can get an impression of the most important groupings in the district.

"The impression constitutes a kind of archaeological section through the more recent history of Nørrebro," writes the anthropologist Anne Knudsen in *Nørrebro – træk af en bydels historie, Nørrebro – features from the history of an area* 1997. First there are the well-brought-up young people in the café drinking soda water and freshly pressed carrot juice. They are the most recent segment of the population in the district. Then there is a pub for the usually pensioned-off remnants of the Nørrebro population from 1960. Another pub provides the setting where the last and next-to-last Danish communists congregate and call the police capitalist lackeys, while outside it sit the all-day beer drinkers with beers bought from the kiosk. The young immigrants on the square don't drink. And among them there is an unproblematic sense of living together that distinguishes Nørrebro as a "real town" in contrast to the suburbs and the provinces, where people live in ghettos with others exactly like themselves. All this is according to Anne Knudsen.

The square is still impressive despite its historical reputation for trouble, a reputation that still clings to it, and despite the fact that on two sides it is framed by, new, red low buildings. The church and the pompous super-middle-class houses on the other two sides raise the level. In the 1980s, beery men with big dogs used to cause trouble on the square. Now it's mainly immigrant lads who make trouble, but they will probably be replaced by other types one day, for nothing is certain here. Not even the regular spots.

The first shanty town in the country was in Nørrebro, locally known as a rhubarb district after the exciting new Chinese vegetable they had started cultivating in the fields outside the ramparts, not least in a large market garden just behind Peblingesøen.

So Rantzausgade and its side streets were never known as anything but the poetical "Rhubarb Land". The first time the red vegetable is mentioned as being found in Denmark is in Dansk Have-Tidende, Danish Gardening Journal, in 1835, but it really became common only in the 1860s. There was an upsurge of building in Nørrebro and on the land belonging to the market garden in the 1870s, and since then everyone has known what a rhubarb district is – small, poor, bad buildings inhabited by roughs with an over-sized ego.

> We tough guys from this Rhubarb Land
> we chew tobacco and drink our schnapps.
> we beat up all the others
> when they invade our patch.
> In Rhubarb Land
> in Rhubarb Land
> it's good to live
> in Nørrebro.

Newly arrived from the Danish island Lolland, the five-year-old Christian Christensen listens excitedly to the Rhubarb Land national anthem, sung by a hundred boy's voices and accompanied by the slapping of naked feet and the tramp of clogs on the pavement. His mother says it's a nasty song and he mustn't learn it, but he does. He also hears other women call her "a holy shit from the country". The family is only a tiny drop in the ocean of people coming to town from the country districts. It is 1887, and many years later he writes his unique memoirs, *En rabarberdreng vokser up, A 'rhubarb boy' growing up* (1961). It is so far from what we know today that it could just as well be set in China. At first, his father always comes home sober, but the schnapps is cheap and you are considered a wimp if you don't drink. Then the family history develops in the classic way with an incredibly strong mother, her violent, drunken and useless husband, and a host of children whose love for their mother knows no end.

At the age of five, the boy makes his début in the world of work. He and his mother make firelighters at night when the others have gone to sleep: "Afterwards, mother told me that I often fell asleep while working in this way at night. I myself only remember a single night. I awoke to hear mother pleading me to go on, as we would have nothing to eat the following day otherwise. I remember I made a colossal effort to pull myself together, and started tying, but for how long? I could hear mother's voice far away. I had passed out. Mother shook me, and finally I heard her promising me a piece of Danish pastry costing two øre if I would only go on tying. And I tied and tied in a battle with hunger and sleep. And finally, when morning came and the colour of the windows changed from black to pale grey, we had won – the 500 firelighters were finished. I was awakened by my mother carrying me across to the bed and kissing me good night. I appreciated that kiss. I don't remember whether I got my Danish pastry, but I do remember the kiss."

The rhubarb land is so poor and so rough that mother and child are terrified of the others. Gradually, it dawns on them that

Details from Nørrebro.

they are really in safe hands, and that there is an enormous sense of cohesion in the district despite the poverty. The police only dare come in large numbers, for they are quite simply beaten up by the men in the tenements when they turn up to take a prostitute ("one of our girls") or arrest another of the residents. People help each other to move house, with food, with births, with clothing, with work and with funerals. The principled ones try to protect the women from their drunken husbands, and the children from their drunken fathers.

A quarter of the men in Copenhagen died from drink as against only three per cent of the women. Around 1900, almost half of the tenants in Nørrebro were single female breadwinners. They survived on their own and their children's work and by taking in lodgers in their small flats.

When the author Jeppe Aakjær (1866-1930) came to Copenha-gen to attend teacher training college, he rented a room from a brave woman in Nørrebro: "Her husband was a drunk who, when he wasn't at work sat around at home with a couple of mates and slavered over his beer ... Petersen was an able worker, but every-thing was drowned in the beer." Mrs Petersen, on the other hand, was "a very competent and unusually good-looking woman ... It was a shame for Mrs Petersen; she worked and toiled to keep the home together and to make up for her husband's sins. She was a peasant girl from Sjælland and still had the countryside's rosy cheeks. She was in her mid-20s and deserved a better husband."

The children bathed in the Workhouse Stream and played in the enormous churchyard Assistens Kirkegård. When they were out, they fought like mad with boys from other streets and espe-cially boys from other schools. "There was a feeling that people living nearby were of the same kind. You knew it by the smell

and the signs; these were the ones fate had put you together
with, and they were the ones you felt safer with than if you went
over to the other corner – only six paces and you were in Bagge-
sensgade, and that was enemy territory. And Wesselsgade, you'd
better not go there either. Todesgade, that was too nasty, it was
bloody nasty, it was the end … there were territories marked
out, strictly marked out," says one man of the 1950s in the Black
Square. There was no room for the children in the flats and hardly in the courtyards. The houses were five storeys high, and in the
old days the only things built as high as that behind the ramparts
were towers. At the bottom there were long, narrow alleyways,
and there also had to be room for sheds and privies. Water closets
were not installed until the 1930s.

Rhubarb Land has gone now. The Workhouse Stream flows
in pipes beneath Åboulevarden. There is no sign of water there.

Apart from the stone in front of Åhusene, which was placed
there as a memorial to four people who drove into the stream
one November night in 1812 and drowned. Rantzausgade, where
Christian Christensen lived and was so proud of his tenement
flat, is unrecognisable. Almost the whole of one side of the street
has been removed and replaced with new houses. Jægergade is
completely new. In Skyttegade there are just four houses left from
Christian Christensen's time.

Christian was a "bit of holy shit from the country" when he
came in 1887 to become a Copenhagener and a worker. So were
all the others. Agricultural workers who wanted to do their best
for their families packed up and came here. This was the future.
Everyone could recognise them in the streets because they looked
different: They were poor, badly dressed, uneducated, clumsy
and ill at ease. As soon as they found work, they sent for their

families and they grouped themselves together in ghettos. They were simply immigrants, but only from the provinces. And their children became second-generation immigrants and their grandchildren third generation. In time, they became Copenhageners.

A hundred years later, Yugoslavs, Turks and Pakistanis moved into the district in the same way. They have settled with their own associations, schools, parties and businesses. Admittedly, there are now cafés, money and designer clothes in Sankt Hans Torv and the surrounding area, but nothing has changed Nørrebro so much as the immigrants. A fifth of Nørrebro's 70,000 residents are foreign nationals, immigrants or their descendants. They are the new proletariat. Fifty years ago, no one would have guessed that Islam would become the second biggest religion in Denmark, and that mosques, prayer rooms, Koran schools and Arab cultural centres would move into the back buildings. In Copenhagen, not a single church has been closed although 300,000 people have left the city since the 1950s. There is a host of churches in Nørrebro – 11 Lutheran churches and five catering for other Christian denominations, but there is not a single proper mosque. When the churches were built in these numbers between 1861 and the 1930s, there were crowds of people milling around in Nørrebro, and there were simply not enough churches to cater for them, resulting in multiple weddings and multiple baptisms.

In those days a church fund was established to speed up building. The objective was a church for every 10,000 residents. Now there is more than one for every 5,000 in a district where particularly large numbers are not members of the Danish State Church and very few attend church services. "It has been known for the pastor to turn round, look out into the church and say: Let us both pray," says one church representative. "And it has also happened that he has turned round and found there was no one at all." Churches in the rest of the country fear the advent of Copenhagen conditions. Perhaps this irreligious neighbourhood is a sign of what they can expect. In Jutland, 90 per cent are members of the Danish State Church. In the City of Copenhagen it is 69 per cent and in Nørrebro only 30 per cent of the 0-17-year-olds who are members. Nørrebro is the "weakest" area in the whole country. Half of Nørrebro's enormous population disappeared with the slum clearance and as a result of the general desire to own a small house, and a large proportion of those left are Muslims. So there is over-provision of churches and under-provision of mosques. There probably won't be any in the near future, but Muslims have difficulty in fitting into their prayer centres.

The shops selling jewellery on Nørrebrogade attract immigrants from all over the country. Nowhere else is there such a selection as in this row of jewellers. For her wedding, every Arab woman has to wear a splendid necklace in meticulous and intricate filigree and earrings to match. The finest sets are handmade in Pakistan and sold in the market in Dubai, from where they come to Denmark. You pay according to weight. Immigrant women and their husbands don't want pale, shiny "Danish gold". That is only eight, ten or 14 carat, while the Pakistan kind is 22 or 24 carat. It is wonderfully dark in colour and more matt than ours.

Griffenfeldsgade is international, typically with shops stuffed from floor to ceiling with tinned good, beans, lentils, rice, spices, hulled grain, nuts, tea, glass and all the other things that make them indispensable. In a building formerly called Sabbatshvile (Sabbath Rest), Christian Association for Young Men and Women, built in 1889, we now find Daban, a salmon-coloured barber's shop with coloured lamps possibly bought further up the street from the lamp dealer, whose staggering selection of crystal chandeliers in plastic is as far from the popular, but expensive PH lamps as is humanly possible. And he also has electrical wall installations with shimmering waterfalls, plastic flowers, small mosque alarm clocks, singing jewel cases and Oriental carpets for 148 kroner. This street can supply gold and silver shoes and clothing, including the famous princess dresses with their many layers, which Danish children with cotton fanatics for mothers have long ago discovered when Shrovetide approaches. In the restaurants you can eat food from all over the world, and from small travel agencies with large photostats of Mecca all these people can buy tickets to all their various native countries.

A school class of 18 in Nørrebro can easily include more than eight different nationalities – for instance Morocco, Pakistan, Iraq, Turkey, Russia, Bosnia, Albania and Denmark. For the same reason, in Copenhagen one child in three attends a private school. Nørrebro is the home of more immigrants and their offspring than any other district in Copenhagen. This is related to the fact that they live in social housing schemes, which came after the slum clearance, and there is plenty of it. Rents are so high that you can only live there with social support. When you are working with sums such as these, it pays better for families with work and with the right finances to buy a flat or house. The "old" Danes live in the old houses in the district.

In Nørrebro it is difficult to find anything at all to buy, for less than ten per cent of all dwellings are owner-occupied. This is the lowest percentage of owner-occupiers in Copenhagen, and at the same time it helps to keep people with a little more money out of a district that really needs them. Just under ten per cent of all the dwellings in Nørrebro are council flats or houses as opposed to only five per cent of those in Vesterbro. Nørrebro also has more residents on social benefits, a higher unemployment rate and more residents not in the employment market than Vesterbro.

Outer Nørrebro is a reaction to inner Nørrebro. A self-assured counter-reaction from people who would no longer put up with property speculation or housing shortages and had now acquired power. Outer Nørrebro is better built and more aesthetically planned, and so people have stayed there. Many of the residents were quite young when they moved in in the 1920s and 30s.

After the First World War, Copenhagen was for the first time forced to undertake its own house building on account of the terrible housing shortage: 11,000 Copenhageners were homeless in 1922. It was tempting to embark on a programme of jerry building, but this was not done. The architects simply invented an entirely new type of dwelling for the purpose – the enormous, bare and simple apartment blocks in heavy, red brick comprising several hundred flats around a large, open courtyard with gardens. No privies down there, no back buildings, no industry, but simply an unfamiliar luxury in relation to the tightly packed houses in inner Nørrebro behind Jagtvej.

The first four blocks admittedly were not in outer Nørrebro, but in Struenseegade and Hans Tavsensgade in inner Nørrebro and were designed for the City of Copenhagen by Povl Baumann in 1920. They are entirely flush, enormous and massive. Larded with windows and more windows, one after the other in mathematical order. It was a style that could go on for kilometres. The smart thing was that the young architects were so keen to build simply. They were tired of the historical style with its extravagant mixture of Renaissance and Gothic and its abundance of decorations. And the City of Copenhagen wanted to build cheaply. The two wishes were a perfect match. And so: no ornamentation, no expensive bay windows, projections and angles, no flourishes or stucco. It came as a shock. People thought it was terribly uninteresting and monotonous (and they still think so today). The windows represented the sole relief. That was what you could play with as an architect. Experts enthuse about Hornbækhus from 1923 by Kay Fisker. You can see the building even from a fast-moving car on Ågade, for the façade is 200 metres long.

After this, large blocks appeared all over the outskirts of town and in outer Nørrebro, and so it was both finer and better to live there – at least for a time. Now, the dense mass of dwellings in inner Nørrebro is in demand, especially as the courtyards have been cleared of back buildings and asphalt and planted with trees and grass. Now they stand there as the large blocks did from the beginning.

Copenhagen had a Social Democrat majority from 1917 and built enthusiastically despite protests from the non-socialist par-

Nordbanegade. In the outer part of Nørrebro, the large blocks of apartments from the beginning of the 1920s were provided with something quite new: a large park at the centre – without privies, sheds or back buildings.

ties at this interference in the free play of forces. The Worker's Co-operative Housing Association was also building homes. Both improved the quality,so that private landlords were forced to raise the standard of their buildings in order to compete. Rungstedhus on Rungsted Plads is just such a block, built in the 1920s with over 200 apartments grouped around a large, well-tended courtyard. Families lived there on a single wage, for the women out here did not go out to work. "At either end of the courtyard there was a large, semi-circular wooden bench, and then there were low box hedges, trees and flowers, a gravel path and fine lawns that we were not allowed to walk on," says Inge Pedersen, born in 1925 just round the corner in Alexandravej. She comes from the kind of working class family that was *also* found in Nørrebro. Her father was not a member of a political party, but of the Danish Ramblers Association. The family went walking in the forests or in Utterslev Mose every Sunday, and the daughter went to dances in Concordia in Fasanvej with a colossal ribbon in her hair. Boys out here joined the Scouts. In her class at school, all the fathers had a job. Everyone knew that the poor people lived in around Blågårds Plads.

"My father was an unskilled worker, employed by Tuborg throughout his life. He came to town from the country, where he had worked on various farms. My mother was a Copenhagen girl. Her mother washed bottles in a chemist's shop. My mother didn't go out to work, but we didn't lack anything. My mother sewed and knitted, so I was always neatly dressed. We had decent food, went to the cinema and visited Vordingborg, where my father came from, once a year. But a school trip to Stockholm costing 30 kroner was more than I could manage."

She met her husband at a dancing class during the war. He had also been born in Nørrebro, at Rungstedhus, where the young couple found a flat and remained all their lives. His parents lived there, and later hers as well, plus his grandparents and her brother. If you knew someone in the block, you had a chance. Otherwise you could forget it. Later – in 1951 – they bought a weekend cottage down the Køgevej. Many others from this block also had cottages there, and they all went out there on the red DSB bus that did nothing but transport Copenhageners out to the country in the summer. Her husband was also a factory worker, and he, too, remained in the same place, Atlas, all his life. You stayed in a good apartment. And you stayed in a good job. That's what things were like. Inge Pedersen still lives there: "I have been to dances with lots of the men in the block when they were boys. Now we've reached the stage when those of us who moved in when we were young are beginning to disappear. In five or ten years, this will be a completely different block. The flats are being combined; people move out again so quickly, and the young people play loud music in the evenings. We didn't do that."

Inge Pedersen and her husband quickly discovered that Nørrebro is not a neutral word, but a notorious name. They have had visitors who spontaneously exclaimed: "Is it possible to live like this in Nørrebro as well?" when they came into the big, bright apartment on the third floor overlooking a garden instead of a back yard and with the tall trees in Rungsted Plads on the other side. "We got used to saying that we lived by the telephone exchange on Borups Allé when we met other Danes while travelling or attending a folk high school. Otherwise we had to sit and explain all kinds of things every time," she says, willingly admitting to having her prejudices – about Vesterbro.

The café hiring out boats on Peblinge Sø. Behind it lay the Black Square – one of the poorest, most overcrowded and most squalid districts in Copenhagen.

Sankt Hans Torv, the centre of modern, affluent, hip Nørrebro. People from town have started taking a trip out to Nørrebro, something that would never have happened in older times.

The other side of the square, the small cobblestones of which were used during the dangerous battle between police and demonstrators on 18 May 1993.

Assistens Kirkegård

Remarkable as it may sound: the greatest attraction in Nørrebro is its dead. A large proportion of the country's intellectual elite lie buried in two fantastic cemeteries a couple of hundred yards apart, Assistens Kirkegård and the Jewish Burial Ground in Møllegade. They were both here long before the densely packed high-rise housing sprang up around them. The Christian cemetery still keeps up with the times and shows what Copenhageners have now thought up. All kinds of new burial customs and rituals can be seen here long before they appear elsewhere. The Jewish burial ground came to a standstill in 1967 for good reasons. 5,500 Jews are buried here, and there is no room for more, for the graves cannot be levelled and used again after a number of years as the Christian ones can. So the burial ground and its 14,000 square metres must lie here for all time, while the old gravestones sink into the ground or deteriorate and the houses around the green space are pulled down or replaced. These houses have only been there for 150 years, the burial ground for 300, and the City of Copenhagen has guaranteed eternity to the Hebrew Community. That is something quite special in a world that is pressing on. Beit Olam, as the burial ground is called in Hebrew, means the House of Eternity.

Assistens Kirkgård creates a fashion and allows things that are not tolerated in the provinces. At Christmas, a young man's grave is decorated with red ribbons, gold-sprayed pine branches and Christmas pixies. The bench is wrapped in red ribbons, and from the tree hang mistletoe and an inflatable plastic heart. Everybody is a star, is the inscription on it. The tree trunk is adorned with a string of Christmas decorations, and in front of the gravestone there is a pig with a ribbon round its neck – along with a lot of other trinkets. The young man lived from 1974 to 1999, and, to-gether with all the other new individualists, those he left behind are changing Danish burial culture. Gone are the modest wishes not to be a nuisance and to be laid to rest in the big, anonymous common grave. Gone are the small inscriptions – "Peace", "Rest in Peace", "Mother". The new graves are overflowing with personal references, declarations of love, photographs, poems and pebbles placed on the gravestone.

Copenhagen leads the way, and Assistens Kirkegård is right out in front and the nearest you will come in Denmark to the Père Lachaise Cemetery in Paris, where people flock to visit the graves of famous figures. Behind the long, yellow wall facing Nørrebrogade, there are now candles flickering everywhere. Prisms or mobiles hang in the branches of the trees. Families celebrate the dead relative's birthday at the grave and decorate it with flags, and a Christiania resident has had a heathen rune stone inscribed. A hash pipe is occasionally placed on the author Dan Turéll's grave, or someone might put a beer there. Children's graves most resemble small nurseries adorned with favourite toys and teddy bears, cars and sweets, bead plates and penguins, angels, Winnie the Pooh and Piglet. They won't have that kind of thing in the provinces, but it's more difficult to refuse them in Copenhagen. And the authorities know that when things start in Copenhagen they spread out across the country a few years later. "Provincial rules can't be enforced here. People from the city will not accept being refused," says a deputy head of office from the Copenhagen Cemetery Authority.

This avant-garde cemetery has always been something special. It was the first Christian cemetery outside the city, consecrated in tobacco fields in 1760 and a hundred years later surrounded by the rapid developments in this part of town, whose cheerful resi-dents took it over, bringing to it life and pleasure, packed lunches and tablecloths spread across bed-sized flat gravestones. Of course

The author Martin A. Hansen was a teacher in the school in Kapelvejen, close to the cemetery, in the 1930s and 40s. He knew "dense, busy, violet Nørrebro" and wrote: "Petit bourgeois Nørrebro is host to many great people. If Nørrebro, which possesses no cultural institution, were to reckon its dead, it would nevertheless be the intellectual centre of the country".

Assistens Kirkegård, consecrated on tobacco fields in 1760 far out of town and so only for the poor. Later, Nørrebro was developed, and the residents used and still use the beautiful cemetery as a park.

there were some who disapproved of so much life in the garden of the dead. There still are. Assistens is run politically and financially by the City of Copenhagen, not by a parish council, and so the prices are Social Democratic. They are nowhere near those in Frederiksberg for instance. "Is there anything you need in the cemetery: Tables, benches, bicycle racks and that sort of thing?" ask the City authorities accommodatingly in a brochure advertising the cemetery as a place where "you can take a walk with your two- or four-legged friend, take your daily exercise, enjoy the special silence and atmosphere or study for your examination." And it is used far more than might be expected. Nørrebro is not a green part of the city, but on the contrary it is under-provided with trees and open sky. Of course, 49 acres of obviously beautiful land can't just be left without being used.

In former times, you could buy brandy and ditties at the entrance or you could hire musicians. People sat in the cemetery and relaxed, even then to the great annoyance of those who owned the graves. The local authority tries to strike a balance with the population, some of whom now and then go too far and sunbathe naked in the grass between the graves. Assistens is still the liveliest cemetery in the country, and a third of it is slowly being turned into a park as the graves are levelled, and there are no new burials in the part furthest from Nørrebrogade. People walk their dogs. A woman sits on the back of a park bench eating her packed lunch. Another leans against the wrought iron railings smoking a cigarette. Outside the walls you can hear the ambulance sirens in Nørrebro and children playing in a school playground. The newspaper B.T. is photographing fashion here "in one of the hippest places in Copenhagen."
The name Assistens Kirkegård could perhaps best be translated as The Relief Cemetery because it relieved another cemetery. Copenhagen simply didn't have room for more burials within the ramparts after the plague of 1710-12, which had killed 22,000 Copenhagen citizens, infected by fleas from rats suffering from the plague. "The corpses were so numerous and so tightly packed

beneath the floor of the church that the stench rose up through the flags, and the sermon simply *had* to last at least an hour," said Jørgen Schrøder, the cemetery's most dramatic guide. But people wanted to be buried in the expensive sites close to the altar to have closer contact with God. The poor were pushed outside the church and the churchyard altogether and out on to the grassy patches round about. The city was forced to establish a cemetery outside the ramparts and preferably beyond the lakes, for that is where the drinking water came from.

In 1760, walls were built around a piece of land of a few acres so far out that no one wanted to go there. Only paupers were buried here for the first 25 years. Finally, a wealthy public servant, Johan Samuel Augustin, decided he would be buried in Assistens. He did not want to be a burden on his city by polluting the air in there. He had an enormously grand funeral and an expensive monument made by the leading sculptor, Wiedewelt. He started a fashion. People began at the same time to wax enthusiastic about nature, and the churchyard without a church was right in the midst of it. 1805 saw a regulation prohibiting the burial of Copenhageners in the city churches, and from 1851 neither were they allowed to be buried in the churchyards in the overcrowded and stuffy town behind the ramparts.

The garden paradise of Assistens is filled with a 250 year-old mixture of modesty and pretension, anonymity and adulation. Since the site was consecrated, 250,000 people have been buried there – including Hans Christian Andersen, the physicis and Nobel Prize winner Niels Bohr, the author Martin Andersen Nexø and the philosopher Søren Kierkegaard, who had personally prepared himself by frequent visits to the cemetery and the family grave. "Strange," he writes in his diary. "There, outside the city, lies the garden of the dead – hardly as big as a smallholding, and yet here there is room for all the contents of life. It is a compendious representation of reality, a brief epitome, a pocket version."

The cemetery reflects modern life. So it has quite quietly also been given a jazz section, in which Ben Webster was the first to be buried in 1973. After him came Kenny Drew, Jazz Kay (Sørensen) and Ole Nezer. The journalist Nils Ufer is there, too. Assistens has become *the* place, just as a nightclub can. It tells more stories than any other Danish cemetery. It tells for instance that the Danes have begun burying their stillborn children and their aborted foetuses and erecting a gravestone for them with a name on. People wouldn't do that 20 years go. The hospital saw to what was required. But just as people have begun to draw back from anonymous graves in the midst of big lawns, so parents are unwilling to let their stillborn children disappear into anonymity. They must be somewhere, and they want to know where.

The House of Eternity – The Jewish Burial Ground

Møllegade was once simply called Jødevej, Jew Road. It is a side street off Nørrebrogade and turns off a couple of hundred metres before Assistens Kirkegård. This is the site of the old Jewish burial ground, tightly hemmed in by high houses on all four sides and cut off from Nørrebro by a red wall. Only in one place can you peep in through a grating. Otherwise you have to go up into the apartments and look down. Behind the walls, the world has come to a standstill. One single woman still comes and visits her mother's grave. It is closed to everyone else. The custodian in the little red house in the wall in Møllegade looks after this rare and listed place. The residents in the houses all the way round can enjoy the greenery and the bird life, and occasionally a group of interested people is allowed in and shown round by the Hebrew Community. The old gravestones stand row upon row in the grass, and in the middle there is an avenue of tall lime trees. Some of the stones have fallen, and others stand at a dangerous angle. Some have sunk down into the sandy ground, so that only the very top sticks up. A beautiful sense of decay has taken over the place and given all the stones the same grey patina, mixed with green moss. There is a mysterious fairytale atmosphere.

In 1693, the widow of a jeweller by the name of David Israel struggled out here with her husband's body. Until then, the Jews had buried their dead as far away as Altona near Hamburg, for there was a Jewish burial ground there. This woman couldn't manage that for some reason or other, and the Copenhagen Jews were given permission to buy a plot of land far outside the ramparts, where the husband could be buried. He was the son of the first Jew that had been allowed to settle in Copenhagen. The following year, the Jewish community was given the right to the land and was thus ensured of a cemetery that would be undisturbed to all time. The incredible thing is that the man's gravestone is still there with a Hebrew inscription. He was the first of the 5,500 burials within these walls, which were extended eight times and finally enclosed in the new district of Nørrebro.

Half of the gravestones have decayed and disappeared. The rest tell us a good deal about the history of the Danish Jews. The inscriptions on the oldest gravestones are in Hebrew. In the first half of the 19th century they are both in Hebrew and Danish, and in the second half of the century usually in Danish. The Jews were integrated, some even so thoroughly that they wanted to be cremated, which is not according to the rules. You must be buried whole.

The beautiful Harriet Camilla Brandes was engaged to the politician and writer Edvard Brandes at the age of 15, and they had two children together. When she was 23 years old, it was discovered that she was having an affair with her music teacher, and Edvard threatened to divorce her and take the children from her. She drank a bottle of Prussic acid and was buried here. He married twice more and after his death in 1931 was cremated in Bispebjerg Crematorium, as he wished. On the other hand, his

The four unmarried Bendix sisters lived in Copenhagen in the 19th century. They were buried beneath four identical angels, although strictly speaking angels do not belong to a Jewish burial ground. This attractive sight is – as is also the case in Assistens Kirkegård – by the wall.

wish to be buried alongside Harriet was not fulfilled because the Jewish burial society would not accept cremation. So the space beside her is empty. His ashes are buried in an unmarked spot in Bispebjerg Cemetery. Those of his brother, the famous critic Georg Brandes, were at his request scattered near the Slesvig Stone in Dyrehaven in 1927.

Today, 10 per cent of Jews want to be cremated as against 80 per cent of Christians, so by far most follow tradition. Since 1886 they have been buried in Mosaisk Vestre Begravelsesplads near Vestre Kirkegård at Kongens Enghave, where there is also a guarantee of undisturbed graves for ever.

According to tradition, the gravestones face east, except those that are placed along the wall by Guldbergsgade and Birkegade. As in Assistens Kirkegård, the most distinguished graves are along the wall, so there tradition yields to a good spot. Here lie the four unmarried Bendix sisters, each beneath an identical relief by Thorvaldsen – the famous Night with her children, Sleep and Death. Strictly speaking an image of an angel ought not to hang here, for Jews are not allowed to portray one. But the Chief Rabbi allowed it in those days, and so now the presence of Thorvaldsen in the burial ground is interpreted as a proof of tolerance, integration and pragmatism.

At first, all the gravestones were identical because no one was to be any better than the others in death. They were of sandstone and of the same height, but later on they were infected by Christian individualism, and affluent Jews made more of it than the rest. At one time there was a conflict between the German Ashkenazi Jews and the Sephardi Jews, whose forefathers had been driven out of Spain and Portugal at the end of the 15th century by Queen Isabella and King Ferdinand. They had a tradition of horizontal gravestones. The others wanted them vertical. So the first Sephardi Jews bought a piece of land, put a hoarding round it and laid their stones down flat. Later, in 1748, the two groups reached an agreement and amalgamated the two burial grounds. But even so, all gravestones after this date stand upright.

Here, too, are eight Christian soldiers who died during the British bombardment of Copenhagen in 1807, buried here by their fellow countrymen who took little notice of the religious significance of the place. The Jewish burial society protested in vain, resigned to the situation and placed a wrought iron fence around the foreigners' graves. It has been removed now, and the soldiers have been guaranteed a grave undisturbed to all eternity. This promise of sepulchral peace also encompasses a genizah, which is a burial place for discarded papers and letters with the name of God on them. They must not be destroyed. Today, the chief rabbi buries such papers for all time, including photocopies, in a new genizah in Mosaisk Vestre Begravelsesplads. The whitest gravestone in the ground is a memorial to the merchant Sophus Berendsen (1820-84) and has just been restored by his firm, which still exists. Berendsen produced iron girders for the entire construction of Østerbro, Vesterbro and the Nørrebro in which he now lies buried.

The burial ground is called the House of Eternity – in Hebrew Beit olam – because the graves may never be levelled. They must remain undisturbed for all time.

Østerbro

Østerbro can be approached by ship, as almost 200,000 tourists, mostly American, do in the summer when cruising in the Baltic. They come in through the channel between Amager and Saltholm in towering cruise liners and tie up in rows at Langelinie. They are awaited on the quayside by shops selling amber and porcelain and hand-painted wooden clogs, and the assistants are kept on their toes. One of the biggest cruise liners, "Splendour of the Seas", carrying 1,800 tourists, is actually known by the expectant name of "Big Spender of the Seas".

The quay at Langelinie is today one of the most visited cruise destinations in the world. Tourist buses wait to take the passengers straight to Tivoli. They have bought their tickets beforehand. Everything is planned. Every fourth passenger stays on board and only sees Copenhagen from the deck. Danish organisers have long understood that passengers prefer to stand in a winding queue like at home rather than in a long line, that 400 Americans eat 1,500 pieces of Danish pastry with their coffee, and that Copenhagen is sold on safety and security. Copenhagen is *safe*, and this attracts them just as much as the Little Mermaid. The organisers

hire nice young Danes to chat with the passengers while they are waiting in a queue. They mustn't be bored. The poll firm Gallup's head psychologist has called the ships floating rest homes, whose passengers are confirmed in idyllic, peaceful Denmark in their belief that the world is a good, kind place after all. The Little Mermaid, the waterfront, the neat, tidy Fairytale City with those polite people are perfect elements in the passengers' eyes. These passengers average more than 60 years old and are in search of safe, peaceful experiences, so Østerbro is the perfect arrival point. This district has a long tradition of peace and quiet and lots of money – three things that often go together.

"It happens occasionally that tourists from the big ships take the wrong turning from Langelinie. Instead of going through Kastellet, the Citadel, to the centre, they go over the bridge to Østerbro. That is where they spend their sole day in Copenhagen, which they leave with a feeling that the Danish capital is a kind of miniature Paris, with good-looking, well-dressed people sitting in expensive cafés by a slow-moving river. All the shops are expensive, too, even the Turkish greengrocer, and everyone is quiet and polite. Tall buildings alternate with picturesque town houses and elegant districts of large villas. The streets are quiet and elegant. You can sleep late here every day. What a lovely town, think the tourists; how beautiful and clean, and how everyone looks like a model, and how well they play their music, and how beautifully they live," writes the architect Merete Ahnfeldt-Mollerup in an essay.

"Østerbro is the place you move to if you want to move into town but don't really dare," says one woman. A kind of city light. This is also the place where the most nervous wealthy parents from North Sjælland find flats for their children, because it's like where they come from. Frederiksberg is all right, too.

If you are at all able to choose, you move to the part of town where the dominant set of rules corresponds to your expectations, where the rules of etiquette suit you. In this way, the people living in a place become more or less homogeneous of their own accord. Those moving to Vesterbro know what to expect. And so do new people in Østerbro.

Estate agents also play on people's expectations and the mythology of the districts: Life and dynamism in Vesterbro and Nørrebro. Peace, respectability and brisk trade in good shops, also known as a "Parisian atmosphere", in Frederiksberg and Østerbro. All four districts still reflect their origins and histories. And no one needs to go right up into the apartments to discover where on the social scale the particular area is placed. It can be seen in the street: Is it a place where people stroll along with bare stomachs and a bottle of beer in their hand? Where dogs are big and people eat cakes straight out of the baker's bag? Do they smoke in the street? The truth about a district is quite concrete.

The various Copenhagen neighbourhoods divide the tasks among themselves, and Østerbro has always made sure to be finer. Always. "My grandmother lived in Østerbro all her life, and even though she cleaned for people and had a privy in the court-yard, there was never any doubt that she was finer because she lived in the distinguished part of the city," says a woman from Nørrebro, the district with the opposite reputation. You can't be called a lady from Nørrebro, but a lady from Østerbro sounds all right.

Foreigners living here are primarily embassy staff, whose children go to private schools: 70 per cent of all the foreign citizens living in this area are from Scandinavia, the EU countries and the USA compared to 31 per cent in Copenhagen as a whole. This is because they can find suitable accommodation in Østerbro and because it is nice and safe and respectable. There are apartments of as much as 5-600 square metres in Østerbro.

In the 1890s and 1900, some of the wealthiest families in the country built themselves splendid mansions in Kristianiagade, Dag Hammarskjölds Allé and Kastelsvej and created one of the most magnificent districts in Copenhagen. The first generation included the margarine manufacturer Otto Mønsted, one of the founders of Magasin du Nord, Theodor Wessel, the painter P.S. Krøyer, Hofjægermester Sehested-Juul, whose pompous title, now awarded to several people, means Master of the Royal Hunt, and so on. The timber merchant Harald Simonsen's mansion with 11 bays, built in Dag Hammarskjölds Allé in 1918, is appropriately called "little Amalienborg". This was previously the site of a new phenomenon produced by affluence – a dog's cemetery for the bourgeoisie's deceased pets. No one had thought of anything like that before. Later, when merchants and manufacturers could no longer afford to live in them, the houses were perfectly suitable for embassies, lawyers' offices and management consultants. The Russian, Spanish, British, American, Chilean, Colombian, Egyptian and Peruvian embassies are grouped together in this affluent district, once the home of the newly rich, while a further 20 embassies and consulates are to be found elsewhere in this district, the postal address of which is 2100 Copenhagen Ø.

The low terraced houses, the Kartoffelrækkerne ("the potato rows") can be vaguely seen at the other side of Sortedams Sø.

Langelinie with cruise liners. Copenhagen is sold for confidence and safety.

Hjalmar Brantings Plads near Stockholmsgade and Østre Anlæg. Østerbro was born with a silver spoon in its mouth. The place for bay windows, wide three-part windows, balconies and a great deal of money.

As is the case in central Copenhagen and Christianshavn, immigrants from Third World countries account for less than six per cent of the population of Østerbro. They virtually do not live at all in these three neighbourhoods, but they have shops there. One woman tells how, when out shopping on Saturday mornings in Østerbro, her Israeli husband is forever being stopped by customers who think he is the greengrocer. "People do it quite automatically because most brown-eyed and dark-haired people here are either greengrocers or kiosk owners."

"Østerbro was born with a silver spoon in its mouth," concludes Hans Helge Madsen in so many words in *Østerbro, før og nu – og aldrig, Østerbro then and now – and never* (1993). The district is historically aware of itself as an almost mythical idyll. Rural, beautiful and quiet, even though the signs of this have been removed.

This was where people spent their summers before the city expanded. Beaux-esprits, intellectuals and quite ordinary rich people left their winter residences within the ramparts and spent their time in the country, that is to say in Østerbro, in the summer. Even when Rosenvænget, Denmark's first neighbourhood consisting exclusively of villas, was established in the 1860s and 70s, some of the residents still had winter addresses in town. While memoirs dealing with Vesterbro and Nørrebro are largely literature about misery, those from Østerbro tell of its glories. Julie Sødring lived at the end of the lakes and could scarcely sleep at night because "the nightingale sang so powerfully for us". As a child in the 1830s, she lived amidst "a glorious array of flowers, large areas of fruit trees, small lakes, spreading lawns, meadows with cows and lambs, long avenues one of which led right down to the shore and ended at a mound, and woodland from which there came a ravishing sound of bird song in the early summer". All these were things of the past by the time Julie Sødring died in 1894. Østerbro had been transformed into an area of concentrated apartment blocks, though built to a higher standard than those in the other bridge districts.

The apartments are bigger here, the streets wider, the windows taller, the bays enormous and the entrances further apart – a sure sign of wealth. Østerbro is younger than the other three bridge districts. Only 13,000 people lived there in 1880 as opposed to 46,000 in Nørrebro. Østerbro was so far away; it fought against the trend to the end and refused to do as the others and sell its paradisiacal quality, its summer residences, its magnificent gardens, lakes and ponds and its view of the sea. Because development was slower here, it saw a better housing act passed in 1889 ensuring that the height of houses and the width of the streets were suited to each other, and that apartments along long corridors were prohibited. Wretched back buildings hardly existed in this younger part of town.

In purely architectonic terms, the Act also established a dividing line that makes it easier to distinguish between houses from before and after 1889, as it allowed bay windows and other "bulges". Prior to this you were only allowed to build straight up and down with the exception of open balconies. Østerbro is a district full of decorations and balconies, while the houses in central Copenhagen are bare and totally "flat" by comparison. Another thing that became modern in the 1890s was broad windows. So there are lots of them in Østerbro, too.

Østerbro is roughly speaking from the 1890s and was developed so late that the area was better built than Nørrebro and Vesterbro. It was also built to a larger scale, for people had acquired more money by this time. Builders looked to a more affluent public from the start, and the local authorities had learned a bit about space, light and greenery in the meantime. No fewer than 35 per cent of the apartments have four or more rooms as against the Copenhagen average of 22 per cent.

Of course, there are also many small flats in Østerbro – in Ryesgade and in some of the more distant side streets off Østerbrogade, but the general picture is that this part of town is privileged from end to end.

On a Saturday morning you can see the affluence in Østerbrogade and Nordre Frihavnsgade. Well-dressed young people are strolling along with an unusually large number of black prams with thick *off road* tyres in the crush, where Christen Købke's cows walked scarcely 170 years ago. This is not a place where you drink beer out of the bottle, but a part of town for brunch and mocha, where you can buy hand-sewn feminine clothing and hats that are out of this world, chocolate body paint and ten different kinds of Italian coffee machines and paraphernalia. And people buy Italian wines, good bread, cheeses, vegetables and meat in specialist shops. There is also a real bookshop, which most unusually sells only books. The citizens of Østerbro are less likely to be unemployed, living on early retirement pensions or on social security, and they are more affluent than in most other places in town. Where the average citizen has an income of 100 kroner, one from Østerbro has 115, one in the centre of Copenhagen might achieve a maximum of 126, and one in outer Nørrebro is at the bottom of the scale with 84. As though that isn't enough, the Østerbro woman breaks all records with the average length of life and lives longer than any others – even women from country districts. She can look forward to no less than 79.1 years. People look after themselves and keep well out here.

"You have to dress up to go to the playground – both the mother and especially the child," says one woman in her 30s. "I have never seen to many expensive *Ticket to Heaven* snowsuits as here. The wardrobes of some of the three-year-olds are more valuable than mine."

This can also be seen in shops and restaurants. Østerbro is self-sufficient in luxury; you don't need to go to town for anything at all, not even arty clothes. The frequency of shops selling expensive children's clothing is very high in Østerbrogade, and the same is true of shoes. There are small, exclusive and individual boutiques with an abundance of clothes, gifts and equipment for the home – Kenzo cushions, thick towels, perfumed candles, silk flowers, Catholic church candlesticks and decorative, worn, white rustic furniture from Provence. A third of the residents in Østerbro have had a long or fairly long education as against 18 per cent in Copenhagen as a whole. Every third child goes to a private school. More people vote for the non-socialist parties than in Nørrebro and Vesterbro, but fewer than in Frederiksberg.

The core of Østerbro is at the end of the lakes. In the 17th century, the king had a dam built here so that the water from the lakes didn't just run out into the sea. The lakes were turned into reservoirs. And 200 years later, the Østerbrogade Riviera, as was the romantic name given to the short stretch along the lake, was constructed with slender spires on the corner buildings in Willemoesgade. Østerbrogade was fine, Nordre Frihavnsgade the second finest and Ryesgade not fine at all when the journalist Henrik V. Ringsted (1907-83) grew up in a villa in Rosenvænget in Østerbro as the privileged son of a doctor. Henrik had a taste for literature of such poor quality that it couldn't be found in any one of the safe and respectable streets. So he had to take a risk and go out into the working-class part of Østerbro. There, they immediately spotted this boy who didn't belong:

"As my unremitting urge to know everything about 'Texas Jack' and 'Nat Pinkerton' drove me further and further down Ryesgade, the dangers associated with acquiring these books increased. In those days there was not only a class struggle, and although I myself was also dissatisfied with my dress, it was nevertheless clean and nice and whole and un-darned and must immediately have given me away like a breath of air from the fine part of Østerbro. At the same time there was another kind of war between children ... This war was waged mercilessly against anyone dressed differently from the gang of boys dominating any one district at any one time," recalls Henrik V. Ringsted in *Lille dreng med trillebånd, Little boy with hoop* (1958). Snobbery ruled in his home, where it was not thought that Nordre Frihavnsgade was "quite in our class". Henrik's aunt, on the other hand, was brave enough to go far down that street – towards the harbour, ugh! – to do her shopping. Ryesgade and the harbour represented

Sortedam, Østerbrogade and the towers at the entrance to Willemoesgade. This short stretch was once romantically called the Østerbrogade Riviera. Still distinguished.

all those things a nice boy should fear. "There was a strange scent of fried onions in the air, undoubtedly from the civic restaurant that was there at the time, and you could meet men with open and half empty beer bottles in their hands."

All those wild and dangerous things were to be found in that direction. One day, Aunt Fafnersbane took Henrik's mother to one side and said, "You are silly. You can get it all for half the price if you shop where I do, and you don't need to tell Hans anything about it." Hans was the pater familias. The distinction between fine and less fine districts still exists, of course, although the class struggle and the gangs of boys have disappeared.

Even today, the most expensive address in Østerbro is still the quiet and distinguished Stockholmsgade with its pollarded trees, the view across Østre Anlæg and the national, upper-class Krebs School just round the corner. This is where the princes went to school, and the register includes many children of the aristocracy. The further you go along this classical street towards Østerbro, the bigger the apartments become, and the greater the numbers that have been taken over by lawyers, accountants and management firms.

When the street was built in the 1880s and 90s, high-ranking public servants and businessmen moved in and enjoyed the view across the park of the levelled ramparts and bastions. The middle classes could ride in the royal riding master Lørup's splendid new riding school on the corner of Stockholmsgade and Upsalagade with room for 80 horses. There was a bandstand and there were four enormous candelabra in the ceiling, and the aristocracy was wildly enthusiastic about it. But in 1931 there were no longer enough clients, and the riding school was pulled down. But then there were always the two art museums left in the park, Statens

Østerbro, and the centre of town and Christianshavn, have less than six per cent immigrants. They virtually do not live in those three parts of town.

Museum for Kunst from 1896 and Den Hirschsprungske Samling from 1911.

Despite all its obvious glories, Østerbro is often accused of being boring. It has always been easy to get at this district on that account. Historically speaking, it is also correct in the sense that in comparison with other parts of town there was right from the start a dearth of pubs, cinemas and entertainment. The authorities were miserly with licences because of the nice residents and relegated all the fun – and the trouble – to other parts of town.

In the book *København før og nu – og aldrig* (1990) there is a description of "the elegant, but stuffy and dreary Stockholmsgade". And in *Østerbro før og nu – og aldrig* (1993), the architect and author Poul Henningsen (1894-1967) is quoted as saying: "What is the point of living longer in Østerbro when you die of boredom?" To that, it has to be said that he personally lived in the upper-class suburb of Charlottenlund. However, countless residents in Nørrebro and Vesterbro point to Østerbro as the antithesis of their own dense, lively and mixed district. "It's very windy in Østerbro. It's too open, and people are all the same," says a Spanish woman who lives in Vesterbro's Saxogade. It irritates her that her fellow countrymen who work in the embassy or in multinational companies always automatically settle in Østerbro and think that *that* is the real Copenhagen. Another woman who over the years has lived all over Copenhagen and now has a nine-room apartment of 345 square metres in the famous prestige development Gefion og Gylfe in Østbanegade, says, "There's something very stuck up about Østerbro, and there are the elderly ladies who go into the shops and virtually hit out with their walking sticks so you hold back for them in the queue. It's all a bit stiff and starched out here, and people are very concerned with how things look. On the other hand, when I lived in Vesterbro I could feel a little insecure occasionally. Here, I can quite happily go out with the pram at 11 in the evening, and I would never have done that in Istedgade."

A third Østerbro resident, who moved to town from a house in

North Sjælland at the age of 50 says, "We moved here and not, for instance, to Christianshavn, because we have grown too old to put up with someone throwing up on the steps during the night. It's quiet out here, and I go across to Kastellet and look out over the sea every single day. The proximity of the water gives Østerbro a freshness you don't find elsewhere."

After Stockholmsgade, the Rosenvænget area is the most prestigious, say the Østerbro estate agents, although they do not generally speaking get anywhere near selling one of the historical mansions. No one moves. In *Bag hækken. Det danske parcelhus i lyst og nød, Behind the hedge. The Danish detached house in good and bad times* the architect Olaf Lind says that, along with Frederiksberg, Rosenvænget was the first district of villas in Denmark.

Rosenvænget is a legendary, leafy breathing space in the middle of all the apartment blocks, and one of the first areas to be built in rural Østerbro. Where Rosenvænget is today, there used to be a beautiful large private park belonging to the mansion of Rosendal. It extended from Østerbrogade right down to the Sound, which in those days lapped the shore along Strandboulevarden. The park contained small lakes, extensive lawns, meadows with cows and lambs and long avenues. In 1857, the royal wine merchant Waagepetersen bought the land and parcelled it out as something completely new in those days – plots on which to build private houses. The privileged were to live here in beautiful, green surroundings with no high apartment blocks, and so it was. Well-known painters, politicians, Mr. Krak of the guides and the much-feted actress Johanne Luise Heiberg moved in in the 1860s and 70s and were given the keys to the gates in the fence surrounding Rosenvænget. The local doctor had a key; Hans Christian Andersen was deeply flattered also to be given one; and people without an errand there had to stay away. At the end of Rosenvængets Hovedvej there was a little ditch with a bridge across. On the other side, a green meadow stretched down to the water's edge.

The court wine merchant imposed certain easements on Rosenvænget, which for fifty years has been able to keep through roads, tall buildings and apartment blocks out even though countless people have tried to make inroads into the area. In 1899, Dr Niels Finsen virtually sneaked into a villa and turned it into a clinic where patients suffering from lupus (skin tuberculosis) came for his revolutionary ultraviolet light treatment. The other residents protested at being forced to see disgusting patients in their quiet street and complained of the doctor running a business in what was supposed to be a purely residential area. They tried to buy him out by offering him a villa in another district, but in vain. Residents in Copenhagen's classical villa districts, for instance Frederiksberg, fight against exactly the same thing: businesses and institutions for addicts or the handicapped in the old houses, for it spoils the "villa character". The attitude has now been given a name: N.I.M.B.Y – not in my back yard. Niels Finsen was awarded the Nobel Prize for Medicine in 1903 and gradually bought up a third of Rosenvænget for his institute. In 1981, the Finsen Institute moved to Rigshospitalet, and Kræftens Bekæmpelse, the Danish Cancer Society, bought the buildings and the land. Johanne Luise Heiberg's villa is still there, now divided into six owner-occupied flats.

Kartoffelrækkerne – "The Potato Rows"

Østerbro has a number of idiosyncratic and alluring areas in which people would give their right arms or three, four, five million kroner to live: Stockholmsgade, Rosenvænget, Kristianiagade and – Kartoffelrækkerne, the "Potato Rows", a cultural relic full of live people, a much loved ghetto.

The 480 houses at four million kroner each are a living Who's Who in Denmark. Here live architects, artists, computer specialists, two former ministers, academics, film people, actors and a few old people from before the place became chic. The people who buy houses here don't boast of their money. The code word in this old development is understatement. Here, you hide your

*Villas and peaceful gardens in Rosenvænget, which, for obvious reasons,
people rarely leave.*

millions of kroner in a little terraced house with a strip of garden in front and a strip of dark courtyard behind. "Prices have gone mad, and I think the fact that well-known people live here is forcing them higher still," says an Østerbro estate agent.

The house must not be either run down or embarrassingly neat and tidy, but it has to maintain a delicate balance. Worn in the charming Italian way. Patina, not decay. Well tended, not newly rich. Precise in details – windows, doors, cobblestones, flowers, doormats, colours. Kartoffelrækkerne see themselves as a place for intellect, aesthetics, abundance and enjoyment. All are seen in a more intense form in the annual street parties, at which residents listen to live music – piano and violin – eat well-prepared, modern food and stage an amusing Hamlet afterwards. The residents are capable of that kind of thing.

"Although they are expensive, you can't call your house in Kartoffelrækkerne a *residence*," says one diplomat who, in defiance of diplomatic tradition, has rented a place there. His colleagues settle in Klampenborg or in the large, high-ceilinged apartments in Østerbro – not in these narrow terraced houses where people run in and out of each other's doors, and where children have unchallenged power in the street. You can't move in and expect to be left in peace. You are expected to take part in street meetings, street parties, putting up Christmas decorations and in every way to support the famous common spirit in this enclave. Also financially.

The potential for conflict which after all exists in this little paradise in the midst of the city is centred on the children, whose play houses, sand, footballs and noise in the street bother some residents who would really also like to park their cars in the play

Kartoffelrækkerne ("the potato rows"). "Prices have run amok, and I think it is also pushing them upwards that celebrities live here", says an estate agent in Østerbro.

street. And the street contribution, "a compulsory entertainment tax" that goes to tilting at a barrel at Shrovetide and street festivals, irritates them as well. The little residents' paper publishes anonymous complaints about both, for there is an unwritten law that says that children and solidarity in the enclave are of the essence, and people don't like openly to suggest breaking it. The "Potato Rows" have become a symbol of fun-and-enjoyment-seeking middle classes who feel on a par with the best in society, but have nevertheless ended in a ghetto for people just of their own kind. And these people don't want to live in a ghetto, they have simply chanced to because it's so lovely; there is a feeling of community, and the children play in the street and attend one of the few "white" state schools in Øster Farimagsgade. The headmaster himself calls it that because the number of pupils whose native language is not Danish is so low that Danish families don't move their children into a private school.

"Kartoffelrækkerne have turned into a small, strictly controlled community of academics," says the editor of *Arkitekten, The Architect* as one of the worst insults he can think of. The journalist Martin Kongstad shudders at the thought of his childhood in these houses, the archetype of blueberry tart and left-wing luxury living in the 1970s. There were posters on the doors: "No to the EEC" and "Support the striking lab technicians". And two thirds of them read the left-wing intellectuals' newspaper Information and voted for the left. "I can remember the slight sense of self-satisfaction hovering over the ranks in those days, and perhaps founded on the fact that the fortunate householder could both afford rump steak and a weekend cottage, a car and calvados, the Bernadotte School and sensible shoes for their children. And they had no problems with their consciences because they adopted a cast-iron and theoretically tested social attitude," he writes in Berlingske Tidende. He also remembers a street party in which the only remaining worker in the street finally took part one year and became so over-excited that he hung his loudspeaker in the window and put on a record with German popular dance music called 'party music'. That put an end to the tolerance. The new residents asked him to take it off.

From the outside it looks like a coup d'état in which the academics from the middle of the 1960s and onwards slowly pushed out the original working-class families from the old tenants' association, but that is partly a myth. "The original workers didn't protest, for they had never lived there," write Olav Harsløf and Anne Røssel in *Kartoffelrækkerne* (1986). On the other hand, some 30-40 new owners poured in every year. Suddenly there were women on the management committee, and the chairman, a caretaker, was replaced by an assistant head teacher. Then the central bit of each street was turned into a play area, and finally it has to be admitted that these are at any rate not the same type of people as before.

Even when they were built by Frederik Bøttger between 1873 and 1889, these houses were elegant and tried to look like the middle-class villas in Frederiksberg and Østerbro with their stepped gables, Romanesque windows and a pseudo-Byzantine style. And neither was it only "real" workers who moved in, but also artisans and low-ranking officials, and even doctors' widows. The general opinion of the old Victorian terraced houses was that they formed a breeding ground for petit bourgeois respectability. There is nothing like one's own house and front garden to pacify a worker. Not even if every house was built for two families. Now there is just one to each.

The list or residents in 1886 includes the following: office worker, policeman, ship's captain, merchant, postman, engineer, colour sergeant, married lady, shoemaker, butcher, unmarried lady, unskilled labourer, bricklayer.

Gravesen, the editor in Herman Bang's novel *Stuk, Stucco* (1887) lives here, and here, in this constricted space, he has his famous ball: "The guests started arriving, and it was impossible to move either forwards or backwards in the narrow corridor where the gentlemen were taking their coats off and blocking the way for the ladies, whose dresses caught on Vilhelmine's flower arrangement as they went upstairs. In the sitting rooms there was a general air of solemnity to the chinking of teacups (Mrs Canth's maid went round offering sugar and cream with such a stern face as though every flick of the sugar tongs meant an attack on her dignity). The six Misses Gravesen stopped all movement by all rushing across to the same new arrival to overwhelm him with hollow delight – as loud as magpies so as to elevate the mood. The gentlemen had already been obliged to leave the sitting rooms and move out into the corridor to make room for the ladies, who refused to sit down before the dancing, but stood up round the furniture, slightly embarrassed by the modern silk dresses that had been sewn at home to designs captured in the shop windows, and which, like all home-made things, pulled uncomfortably and hurt both here and there. And still there came more guests, while the daughters pulled at Mrs Gravesen to be introduced.

'Yes, we're a bit short of space here,' she said apologetically, 'so very short of space.'"

Kartoffelrækkerne have assumed a greater significance than they have in themselves. The old development *signifies* something all the time – in literature, in magazines and in newspapers. It is explained and interpreted – precisely because it is a ghetto for a special kind of people – and either irritates enormously or attracts tremendously.

In 1865, the workers at B&W founded Arbejdernes Byggeforening, the Workers' Building Association, on the initiative of the doctors F.F. Ulrik and Emil Hornemann. They wanted to ensure that things were decently built – and so they were, clean, plenty of air, more room. But they didn't get rid of the privy in the back

Shrouded in mist, the America Quay in the Free Port, where ships bound for America docked. The statue represents a Danish Mormon girl who emigrated to Utah in the second half of the 19th century when it took 52 days to cross the Atlantic. During the voyage, there were seven weddings, two births and 12 deaths.

Kalkbrænderihavnen. Denmark's new legal quarter with more than a thousand employees.

yard. The same was true of Brumleby near Østerbrogade, built by other sensible doctors as a healthy reaction to the cholera epidemic in 1853. Brumleby represents intellectual and physical origin of the Potato Rows and is the mother of all housing associations. It was and is closed to through traffic – a lovely open, little green area that has been copied by far too few. "A unique monument in the history of house building," thought Steen Eiler Rasmussen. Brumleby and Kartoffelrækkerne are famous far and wide precisely because they are the exceptions. High-rise, dense buildings were made all around them – by speculators. Today, the two small enclaves are nothing like each other when it comes to price, for Brumleby is a co-operative venture with strict waiting lists, whereas the private houses in Kartoffelrækkerne go to the highest bidder.

At the end of all 11 roads in the Potato Rows lies the Sortedam lake, where people still had their own private bathing jetties with flagpoles and a little hut with a lock during the First World War. In warm summer evenings you could hear music from the rowing boats out on the lake. For 30 years, fast passenger-carrying steamers plied between Østerbrogade and Gyldenløvesgade. Several hundred thousands bought tickets during the summer months. In the 1920s it all came to an end, and today sailing is impossible between Frederiksberg and Østerbro, for Fredens Bro is not a bridge, but an embankment with no gap through which to sail.

The Free Port

Things are happening along the Østerbro coast. The wealthiest private individuals and firms in Denmark are getting together in the old Free Port – a new and affluent enclave by the sea.

For some people security is being surrounded by other people, life and businesses. For others it is to see the wrought iron gates open, drive their car into the car park, hear it close behind them and take the lift straight up to their apartment without coming across anyone at all.

It is this last type who are moving into the most expensive apartments in Copenhagen, in the old free port behind Kastellet. A quite special new town is being built by the sea. A town whose inhabitants apparently have to live on ice creams and gourmet food from the restaurant on the America Quay. There is also an exclusive furniture shop, a kiosk and a baker who closes at weekends. A development for a group of extremely wealthy citizens who the Mayor of Copenhagen, the non-socialist parties and the estate agents say can't find homes in the centre of Copenhagen because over half the flats there are only of one or two rooms.

There is space enough for them here. Here they can live in peace. "It's like living in a huge park where there is nothing above you and above nature but the enormous vault of heaven and some swans that occasionally turn in the harbour basin," says a man from one of the houses.

"While Hamburg works, Copenhagen sleeps," said the country's financiers and businessmen towards the end of the 19th century, shifting uncomfortably in their chairs. In 1894 they inaugurated the Free Port, a splendid and carefully designed harbour complete with deep berths, warehouses as big and beautiful as cathedrals and a customs fence all the way round. The hot shot of the day, the architect Jens Vilhelm Dahlerup, who designed the Ny Carlsberg Glyptotek, Statens Museum for Kunst, the Pantomime Theatre and many others, achieved a technical coup with his beautiful and functional warehouses, all placed by the water in a filled-in area off the coast at Østerbro. Copenhageners were given the Langelinie Quayside – a cul-de-sac promenade laid out on top of a long, low warehouse. They were also given the little marina as compensation because they could no longer walk along a green path along the coast. The Free Port people simply laid a road and some railway tracks straight through Kastellet to gain access. That was where Østerbro sustained its worst and deepest wound. The district lost its access to the coast and was completely cut off from the sea by a customs barrier and, a little later, by a railway embankment.

Midtermolen in the Frihavnen with the headquarters built by ØK. On the right the Kalkbrænderihavnen.
Any trace of industry has disappeared completely.

The area between Østerbro and the Sound is like a piece of desolate enemy territory.

Scarcely a hundred years later, the Free Port, the hope and pride of the country, was decaying and finished. No ships, no trade, no money. The customs barriers were pulled down and the shipping company Ø.K just managed to build a colossal new prestige block on the central mole before the old company celebrated exactly a hundred years by moving its 12-member management to Singapore in 1997.

Now the Free Port is again attracting big money. Only one of Dahlerup's warehouses is left on Langelinie. A host of surveyors and craftsmen are busy going through the wind-swept area and transforming it into "the most attractive address in Denmark". The Free Port is such a place where one inevitably comes to talk of money and prices. You wouldn't spontaneously refer to such things in Holmen, for instance, the other new town under construction.

From the Free Port you can look over at the old naval dockyard with its canals, tall, old trees and historical buildings. Holmen typically attracts young people or "middle-aged people with artistic inclinations", as one estate agent put it. In short, this also means that people buying an apartment in Holmen must be able to put up with passing Christiania on the way. "I don't know anyone for whom Christiania is a plus," says the estate agent Poul Erik Bech of EDC.

The Free Port is dominated by offices and attracts a clientele consisting of businesspeople, many of whom use the apartments as their second home, or firms buy them for their directors when they are home from abroad for a time. The postal code means something. A luxury flat is not the same in Islands Brygge as in Frihavnen, 2100 Copenhagen Ø. Not least for people coming from places north of Copenhagen. This place *is* money. The two biggest

firms of solicitors are moving to the Port in newly built offices. They don't want just anybody as their neighbours. There isn't a seesaw or a child to be seen anywhere. Buildings are shooting up in the area. The biggest and most expensive flats are sold even before they are finished: seven-nine million kroner for a penthouse flat with terrace. The water and the view are the attraction, but the "smartest address in Denmark" is more like a collection of offices than a place to live. The 6-700 residents are not sufficient to provide any life in the place – yet. But the town hall has ambitious plans for building artificial islands with lots of dwellings in the harbour like in Venice or Amsterdam or in Christianshavn.

All that is left for grandiose projects is the harbour, and now the money is available. When Copenhagen Harbour was abandoned because the Free Port moved north to where there was more space, the whole country was broke, and nothing happened. But after decades of crisis and decay in the 1970s and 80s, it is now worth a fortune as something quite different from a port. The same process is taking place in all major cities: industry and the active harbours close down or move and leave the bare surroundings behind to be used for something else. The whole of the Copenhagen North Docks is one huge building site.

Around Kalkbrænderihavnen and Svanemølleværket, glass skyscrapers have been built for all the huge, amalgamated undertakings that can no longer find adjacent buildings in town. Three of Denmark's four largest law firms have placed themselves in this new law neighbourhood with more than a thousand employees. Before, they were behind discreet brass plates at the posh addresses in town. Now they display themselves in copper towers and large, open glass houses

There will be no residences out here. They are collected in the Free Port in something that might perhaps one day come to life and turn into a real neighbourhood. The social profile is one-sided, for only a small part of the population have enough money to settle here. The new town is populated by purchasers of a "certain calibre", as the estate agents say.

High-rise building in copper in the new lawyers' quarter of the city.

Most of the IT industry, where much of today's money, so-called *new money*, is to be found, is in the Copenhagen area. So are biotechnology, clothing and the advertising industry – and associated busy young couples without children, each with a good income. When the Americans put in at Langelinie in the summer, they stand on the deck and look into apartments that are not quite typical of Denmark.

Kastellet

It is no longer a secret that the Danish intelligence services have their headquarters in Kastellet, the Citadel, in Østerbro. The defence forces have always kept a little in the background, but one day when the former commanding officer of Kastellet was walking down past the long red buildings, he heard a teacher out with his class say, "That's where the intelligence services are." The address is in the telephone book. So is K.G.B. That abbreviation refers to Det Kongelige Garnisonsbibliotek – the Royal Military Library – open to the public.

Today, only ten families rent properties in Kastellet, in addition to whom there is the head of the defence forces, the chief army chaplain and the commanding officer, all in official residences. Everything closes down at ten o'clock in the evening. The sentry goes his round high up on the five-pointed star. Just as the real port is leaving the Free Port, so the real military is leaving Kastellet, which has not had any military significance for over a hundred years. War is no longer waged in the old way, and the soldiers have gone. Offices for 11 authorities with staffs of 450 in all have moved in. In 1894, just when the Free Port was being built, the last remnant of Kastellet's value as a fortress officially disappeared because it had to hand over a great deal of ground to the new Østerport Station and the new port. They even built a road and railway lines through Kastellet.

Today, the small number of inhabitants know that they live in one of the finest and best preserved fortresses in Northern Europe, a listed relic of the past – a tourist attraction – which is under constant supervision by Copenhageners. So there is scarcely any sign of life outside the dwellings. Nobody can stand the sight of old clogs planted with summer flowers, doormats, bicycles or plastic garden chairs. Everything must be beautiful, neat and clean. The public must not feel they are intruding on other people's private and personal territory. So the residents make themselves invisible. The tasks of the defence forces in the old military compound, which encompassed 1,800 men and women at one time, are scarcely what they were. Nowadays, they serve tea and buns to thousands of Copenhageners on one holiday evening a year and arrange ballets and concerts. Gentlemen in their 50s, 60s and 70s stroll around inquisitively. They were quartered here when Kastellet was a quite ordinary garrison, and they are back now to revisit their youth.

In 1999, the fortress was returned to its former state and surrounded by water on all sides, so that it came to look like Frederik III's original structure: When the Swedes besieged and stormed Copenhagen in 1658-59, everyone could see that things were about to go wrong. The king sent for the Dutchman Henrik Rüse to erect a fortress at the entrance to the city. It was constructed in the new Dutch manner – with earth and moats instead of the massive walls of stone that were otherwise used.

The king also wanted a final place of refuge from internal enemies if powerful opponents of his new form of government – absolutism – should appear. Rüse only took three years over it, although his important, covered road out to the shore – "lange linie" – kept on falling into the sea during gales. He compelled 6,400 reluctant and hungry men to carry out the work. The baroque pentagon with dual moats was ready to be taken over in 1664, six months before the contract required. Kastellet and Holmen on the opposite side of the entrance could together close the harbour and prevent enemy ships from reaching Copenhagen.

Kastellet was also Denmark's first barracks. Before this, soldiers were billeted on families in various parts of Copenhagen,

The Pentagon of the baroque period, Kastellet. The old military town held 1800
people at its peak.

The ten-metre-high ramparts around Kastellet. The tradition of going for a walk on the ramparts on the evening before the religious holiday "Store Bededag" is thought to go right back to the 1740s. There was a long pause when the ramparts were dismantled, but the custom has now been resumed.

Citadellet Frederikshavn was the name given to Kastellet when it was inaugurated in 1665. Restored 1998-99 according to the original drawings.

The English church and the ramparts around Kastellet, the Citadel.

which was a nuisance to both parties. Apart from Nyboder there were altogether 2,861 families in the capital in December 1659. And all, with the exception of the poor, were obliged to have soldiers living with them. Registers provide a record of who were rich and who were poor in the houses in the town. The number of soldiers billeted preceded the names of the residents. For instance, in the even numbers in Snaregade there lived, among others, "Jens Nielsen, tailor, poor" and "18 persons, His Honour Mayor Hans Nansen" and "1/2 person. Lene S. Diderich Baschers". The explanation of the half soldier is probably that it was possible either to share one with a neighbour or make a payment to reduce the full-time billeting.

There have been Danish soldiers here since the inauguration of the fortress in 1664, interrupted only by the 43-day-long British occupation in 1807 after the first and last battle for Kastellet. And by the Germans from 1940 to 1945. The Nazis stormed Kastellet on 9 April 1940, blew up the Norway Gate and took it without a fight. There were only nine sentries because, as said above, the soldiers had long been moved out and the place emptied of any military significance. The Germans set up their headquarters in the Hôtel d'Angleterre and turned Store Kongensgade and Bredgade into one-way streets to they could more easily drive backwards and forwards. After the war, the German chief administrator, Werner Best, was imprisoned in Kastellet. A court in Copenhagen condemned him to death in 1948. This verdict was later changed to 12 years imprisonment by the Supreme Court, and in 1951 Best was deported. The gifted Count Griffenfeld was imprisoned here awaiting the execution that at the very last minute was stopped by a royal pardon and changed to lifelong imprisonment. Johann Friedrich Struensee's cell can be seen in the old lock-up behind the church. He was taken out to Fælleden and beheaded in front of half Copenhagen in 1772. The citadel prison at that time was behind the church, where on one side you can still see the holes through which the prisoners could listen to services but not be seen by churchgoers attending them.

This state prison was the most secure in existence. It was isolated, strongly guarded and so the place where important prisoners were confined. Even so, the English pirate John Norcross managed to escape, so when he was caught again they built a strong oak cage inside the cell, where the adventurer spent 16 years chained to an iron bar. By that time he was weak and harmless and was kept for a further 16 years outside the cage, but still in the cell. Norcross became incredibly clever at taming mice. They lived in his enormous beard until he died in 1758.

Two other wretches arrived in the citadel prison in 1846: a tribal chief by the name of Adum from the kingdom of Aqvapin (now Ghana) and one of his ministers, Sabah-Akim. They were condemned to be deported for life because during a battle with a neighbouring tribe they had abducted and killed the chief's two small sons. After the murders, they smeared the boys' blood all over the tribal drums because then it would hurt them every time the drums were beaten. One drum is in the National Museum. However, the two men were only in prison for four years as the colony was sold to Britain in 1849. The following year the two were sailed back to Africa.

Fælledparken

Fælledparken was the first people's park in Denmark and opened in 1911. It was to be used rather than being seen as a place in which to take a stroll, as were the others. Ørstedsparken was designed as a sophisticated French park in which to take a walk and surrounded by a hedge, a place where you wore your best clothes, opened your parasol and strolled on a Sunday. Polite greetings, quiet conversation, closed at night, no walking on the grass and a park keeper to turn out the down-and-outs. This kind of thing was not the intention in Fælledparken, although that, too, was provided with some magnificent meandering paths in the old style. People ignored them, walked as they pleased and wore straight lines in all directions.

Football match in Parken. Originally, in the 1870s, the game was a Copenhagen phenomenon. Kjøbenhavns Boldklub (KB) from 1876 was the driving force behind the introduction of the game. The first registered members belonged to the upper classes.

Kongens Have and Frederiksberg Have were designed for kings, but were gradually opened to the public when revolutions spread across Europe. It happened everywhere, for the kings were nervous and keen to please their populations and calm them down. The "wave of democratic parks", where people made their own parks, followed in the wake of the constitution and the growth of the Copenhagen population. Fælledparken is the biggest in Copenhagen and was designed as an English landscape park – a dream of an idyllic pasture where shepherds and their flocks crossed great expanses, and where forested massifs block out the distant view. You would think that nature itself had created it. It is a typical grassy park, built up of vast stretches of grass and edged by forest so as to shut it off from Copenhagen and invite the public to believe they are suddenly in a different world. As a rare experience in a major city, there are spreading views in there – of the sky and unaccustomed distances. The beach forest at the edge is also unusual; other parks do not have one, for the use of quite ordinary Danish trees in a park was a new feature. They had not been thought fine enough before this. The forest is now of an age when the trees are beginning to die. The problem is that they can't sow and propagate themselves because the new little trees are tramped down and peed on.

A further splendid feature was that the new district of Østerbro swallowed Fælledparken, while Nørrebro's part of the old common had houses built on it. The main entrance to Copenhagen's biggest park was placed at Østerbro, and the Rigshospital was placed at the farthest end – towards Nørrebro. But Fælledparken is the Copenhagen park that most obviously belongs to the people and is the most visited of them all. The workers' movement made its mark on it once and for all: Mayor Jensen from the Social Democratic Party planted the first tree, and the park was used for the new workers' sport of football. Ever since the opening, the socialists have celebrated Mayday here, but the event has developed into the country's biggest party for high school students, and the 100,000 participants are not quite so left wing any longer. They are drunk, and the sun shines on them. Even the Liberals are present, for they argue that "The Liberal Party is Denmark's biggest workers' party".

During the summer, Copenhageners divide into groups: a large group of Africans meet and prepare food in one place, young skaters gather over by their rink, the children play in Sansehaven, the 'Garden for the senses', or by the paddling pool. And when the sun sets, the grass is dotted with small burned patches where people's disposable barbecues have stood. The biggest problem in this huge, grassy park is – the grass. It doesn't manage to grow before it is worn down. In fact, it is completely worn away in many places. The head gardener is forever at loggerheads with footballers concerning the grass. They want to start the season as early as possible in the spring, preferably in April. He takes the opposite line and wants a later start, preferably in May. However, the municipal gardener is the first to say that he neither can nor will protect the grass by establishing enclosures in the park. That is impossible. So is a prohibition against spontaneous football. So the grass gets worn down.

Fælledparken was so late getting off the ground that the authorities had had all kinds of ideas about health and sport since the conception of Ørstedparken and the other new parks on the former military terrain in the 1870s. And the Social Democrats had discovered what their voters needed now they had more free time. But then the prospect brightened. Young people went in for sport, bathed in the sea and in the sun. People talked of "the outdoor life", "sport hygiene", "general fitness" and "toughening up". And so Fælledparken was designed to cater for festivities and meetings, play and games. And alongside it there was a splendid enclosed sports ground, tennis courts and later a swimming baths with the most daring thing so far, mixed bathing, in 1930. This was the first major sports ground in Copenhagen. .

Mayday in Fælledparken. Even the right-of-centre Liberal Party is present.

Amager

There's a curious thing about Amager. All the messy and less than successful features about the island are becoming attractive. An exclusive little pocket of resistance has gradually emerged, as Nørrebro and Vesterbro have become neat and tidy. The resistance is made up of stylistically conscious, ultra-modern types who are tired of urban regeneration, miss the shipyard B&W and love everything that is trashy, gritty and genuine. By their mere presence they can transform a grim district into an attractive place that is gradually being taken over by an affluent public. And then they themselves will slip off somewhere else.

Their great fear is that the district is becoming too nice, that there are too many flowers and white fences in the newly renovated back yards, that things are too regulated or pompous. "I prefer the rather more rubbish-bin appearance," says one of them. And a woman wants "a more chilled, relaxed and smart Copenhagen – a bit more like East Berlin".

It is people like the poet Søren Ulrik Thomsen who want a Copenhagen just as dirty and lively as the day in 1972 when he moved into town with his parents. And there are people like the film director Nicolas Winding Refn, who made *Pusher 2* on Amager because Vesterbro had lost its rough character in the meantime, and because Amager reminds him of East Village in New York.

"Amager is probably the last real bohemian district in Copenhagen. After the urban regeneration and whatever, there is generally speaking no difference to be seen between Nørrebro and Østerbro. It has all acquired such a corporate feeling, and that helps to erase the original urban environments. But Amager is still something special. There is room for the little shop and for contrasts," he said after filming on Amager.

And there are people like the journalist Mads Brügger, who will defend his "liberatingly failed" Amager against the storm troops of niceness to the very end. When people like him say that a district has retained its authenticity, they mean that it hasn't changed, that time stands still.

Here, Amager comes into the picture as the last or second last bastion of the old Copenhagen. Amager is potatoes and gravy,

steak and onions and a beer. Amager is one of the few remaining places where the butcher's best buy might still be sweetbreads. People go to ballroom dancing or American square dancing wearing Stetsons and boots and get into all the intricacies of country and western. And you will go a long way before you see women eating salads behind large windows in cafés. This is the artisan's island with delivery vans parked in streets and in suburban residential roads in the evenings. This is where the little skilled worker lives, and pensioners, the unemployed, office people and a lot of immigrants in the big blocks. Amager is the sort of place where you can get a sewing machine repaired or have a new seat woven for a chair.

What makes Amager modern at the moment is precisely the fact that there are so many things left that are anything but modern. A woman living in Smålandsgade calls the whole island "retro" and a good place for people to go when they have had too much of hanging round in Sticks'n Sushi and walking about wearing Gucci sunglasses. "Everyone does that now," she says. "And so the brightest front runners try to go in the opposite direction by moving to Amager."

A man who has lived in the front of the island for 12 years says: "People go almost demonstratively carelessly dressed and are in general incredibly different from Copenhageners. The island is provincial and slow. I don't actually long for the old values, the "genuine workers", drunks and rockers, but for Amager to change – and that is happening now."

The island is prey to creeping regeneration because there isn't room for more money and more progress in town, and so people are spreading across the reserve area of Amager with Ørestad, Havnestad, Metro and Riviera. Young people who are choosy about where they live, and whom estate agents always keep an

eye on, have moved into Islands Brygge – the closest you can get to town on Amager – along with a number of radical galleries for modern art. Third-year students of design hunt around in Sundbyøster and Sundbyvester looking for trendy kitsch and fake Turkish gold watches, and families with children who can't afford to live in Kartoffelrækkerne or the northern suburbs buy houses in the good, lush residential streets, from which they sing the praises of this newly discovered territory. They are fantastic at *telling* how wonderful these places are and thus attracting others of like mind.

"People used to live in exile on Amager because they couldn't find anything better, and all they wanted was a rapid return to Sjælland. Now they stay there, buy a detached house and make a virtue of necessity. In time more of the same kind come and join them. That's how any transformation of a district starts," says Lene Strandbjerg Wolf. One man says that millionaires are moving on to Amager now, and that is true. But only to special, carefully delineated areas.

"I've always been proud of my island, so I feel irritated when people say that it's ugly and a place for losers. The residential roads are really wonderful, and people are always surprised when they come out here," says Malene Botof from Ingolfs Allé near Sundbyøster Plads. She was born and bred on the island and sees new groups of people moving into the other houses in the road – "some lovely go-ahead families with children". Malene Botoft is able to fill the atrium in her Ingolfs Coffee Bar with 130 guests, all buying tickets – for opera performances. Amager is constantly just on the move.

"When I was at the university in the 70s, Amager was the island for failures. Only Christianshavn was any good," says a 50-year-old woman from Tovværkgade. "Now everything is being thoroughly upgraded." Amagerbrogade is acquiring shops selling bagels and flower shops with charming galvanised tubs where there used only to be drooping tulips in a bucket. Ten years ago, this long street was in a state of crisis with rows of empty shops,

The entire island is retro *and a good place to go for people who have had an overdose of sushi and Gucci.*

but when something new turns up, it's a bit better and a bit fancier each time than what was there before. But there are still no striking fashionable cafés or interior designers. "There isn't any feng shui about Amager," as Mads Brügger says. On the other hand there are eccentrics and colourful people.

"Amager will never become so smart that the original residents are pushed out," says one woman. "I know people who were born on Amager, live on Amager and swear they'll die on Amager. And they are only 30 years old." The locals stay put. There is every chance that a woman from Amager will find a husband from Amager. There is a sense of loyalty on the island that reminds one of that in the provinces. You don't find that in the new Vesterbro. Vesterbro is the result of fashion. People here have roots.

The place where it all comes together is Amager Centret, where there is a smell of smoke and food, and where people meet and know each other. One woman remarks that nowhere else in Copenhagen has she noticed so many teenage mothers with prams as here. Take the Metro to Frederiksberg Centre and see just the opposite.

"I don't want to move from here, for I love the village atmosphere. You go to the Centre in jogging clothes or gardening clothes. People don't make too much of themselves," says one woman.

More than any other district, Amager is felt to be somewhere outside town. Copenhagen is simply another town and for many another world as well. People on the island might well say that Copenhagen is all right, but they don't go there often. They make a virtue of being idiosyncratic, and most of them will say at some time that Amager is like a big village. You don't need to leave it. Many also draw parallels with Jutland, for instance the author Vagn Remme:

"There is something rural about it. Of course, it is also an old peasant community that has developed into a working-class district. People here are a little slower and more deliberate than in the rest of Copenhagen. They can't really be bothered. They also speak more slowly than people from the centre of town. They are upset if you say so, but there is probably a bit of the Jutlander about Amager. Perhaps because a lot of Jutlanders live there. The Copenhageners I know don't want to live on Amager, so this is where Jutlanders can find a flat when they come to town," he says to the newspaper Jyllands-Posten.

In a report entitled *Københavnerlivsformer* (Copenhagen Life Forms) (2003), commissioned by the Town Hall, the sociologist Henrik Dahl draws a picture of the typical island resident. She is called a "home maker" and works primarily in order to earn money so she can take time off. The home is her castle, and she wants to have her family, friends and acquaintances nearby. She wants orderly conditions around her – quiet, room, greenery. She loves all local things and finds it difficult to leave. The homemakers especially make their mark all the way around the outer limits of Copenhagen, Brønshøj, Husum, Vanløse, Valby, but they are under pressure as house prices gradually increase and are driven further and further away from the expensive centre, and one day they will fall off the edge.

These are ordinary people with roots. They are neither particularly progressive nor the opposite, neither rich nor poor. They are not directors, project managers, scientists or anything else that is smart, but classical wage earners. They earn under 250,000 kroner gross a year, constitute 40-50 per cent of the city population and are undergoing a small but inevitable fall in numbers. Their places of work are closing, and other groups are putting pressure on them, for instance *life planners* in career jobs. They don't work so as to have leisure time, but in order to achieve responsibility and power, and they prefer to live in special enclaves with good addresses: Østerbro, Frederiksberg, Central Copenhagen and now Vesterbro and Islands Brygge. But because they can't always afford to live there, they also end up in Brønshøj, Valby and, increasingly, Amager, which they are transforming to conform to their own image.

The home makers have created special districts in town

Only 30 years ago, both Christianshavn and Amager were for the lower classes. To Islands Brygge, now so sought after, one just did not move at all. Nor to the low, slummy terraced houses in Sverrigsgade and Norgesgade. Now those are sold at a fortune.

The tone is tough. It is not as in the bourgeois culture where everything is wrapped.

◀ *On Amager, people have allotment gardens and move out to them in the summer.*

◀◀ *The Helgoland Swimming establishment where thousands of shivering children from the island learnt to swim.*

– Amager, Valby and Kongens Enghave – with something of the village about them and residences that pass on from generation to generation. "I love Amager and won't leave it. It's a bit more ordinary and it suits my Jutlandic roots. It's the only place where people talk properly to each other and say good day when they meet," says a woman in *Københavnerlivsformer*.

A young woman is fond of Amager because it is a relief not to have to live up to all kinds of things: Do you live in the right place, wear the right clothes, and you don't come to grief in "hot or not". Amager isn't the place for design. "Smartness is under pressure here. There are a few too many low-price shops such as Føtex and Tøj & Sko everywhere." It's as though people from Amager are agreed on saying that kind of thing when they are asked. Even when the distinguished author Klaus Rifbjerg was a boy on Amager in the 1930s it was like that: "There *were* rich people on Amager. But there was never anything stuck up about them. They didn't feel like aristocrats in comparison to people who were – not in strained circumstances – but not quite so well off as they were," he says in *Sundbyfolk, Sundby people* (1999).

A well-dressed woman in Amagerbrogade shouts at her big dog: "What's that you're doing, man? Are you daft?" People don't beat about the bush. For that reason there are new arrivals who give up the island after encountering the directness of the natives.

"I once moved out and lived in an affluent district up north in Birkerød near Furesøen with a bathing jetty and everything, but I couldn't stand it and moved back. The difference is that people here are modest and unambitious, but up there they are not. They have to earn a lot of money to be able to live there and maintain the family, house and status. Here, you are sheltered from all that.

If you want to live here, you have to give up all thought of status," says Jørgen Øllgaard, who moved into Haveforeningen Sundbyvester, Sundbyvester allotment garden association eleven years ago as the second academic to do so.

"The tone is down to earth. It's not like in the middle-class culture where you wrap things up. I know people who have moved here and left again because they missed the gentler, more rounded form of address they were used to. If you're from the middle classes and want others to be like you, Amager isn't the right place," he says.

Mentally speaking, Amager is a long way from lovely old Christianshavn, the bohemians and *radical chic*, but there are not more than a few hundred metres between the two parts of town. They are only separated by a moat, but there's a world of difference, and you see this at your first glance. The first small shops in Amagerbrogade show striking signs of advancing age: the pram shop Danmark with a telephone number that is far too short, 574430. The barber's shop behind dark brown mouldings offering pensioners' haircuts at 75 kroner and styling at 105. The wine lodge with potted plants on the window ledge and yellow lamps. And then there are manicurists and solariums, pizzerias, kiosks, second hand clothing, billiard halls and a pub called Bodega Klør 9 – the first in a long line of otherwise moribund establishments. Classical pubs? Come to Amager and see the last of them. Bakers, kebabs, aquarium fish and shops with ready-made egg smørrebrød on white paper in the windows – they are all here.

Amagerbrogade brings the island together and is its backbone. "My splendid Heart River" as Klaus Rifbjerg writes in *Amagerdigte,*

View of the Prøvestenen – an artificial island attached to the larger island.

Amagerbrogade. "If we had a brewery we could cut off the bridges", says a man who grew up on the island.

Amager poems (1965), where he loves the monstrous confusion and the sensational lack of taste. If you look down the side streets, most of them flatten out in a mixture of squat buildings and then open out with trees. Copenhagen's fourth bridge district is not nearly as high-rise, dense and concentrated as the others, but it varies enormously in height and breadth. Stately urban colossi alternate with squat, humble buildings, houses and workshops, even up on the main road where there is still room for needle-work shops, upholsterers and dealers in sports cups.

At the top of the hierarchy there is the contrast to the modern but dreary geometry of the Urban Plan – Eberts Villaby, further out along Amagerbrogade and then on the right. A small selection of detached houses from the turn of the century 1800/1900 in lovely curving streets around a kitsch white fountain with

Amager peasants, happy schoolchildren and a couple of fat babies on top. There are pollarded trees in the avenues and gravel to crunch beneath your shoes. The spacious houses are adorned with spires and balconies, portals and bay windows, garden rooms and names typical of the time at which they were built such as Sans Souci, Louisehaab and Ingers Minde. There is a feel of a vanished age, new families with children, and owners with a high degree of self-esteem. They become angry if estate agents try to sell a house outside Eberts Villaby and yet use its good name. This little neighbourhood, built by the Amager-born magnate Hermann Ebert, still attracts the highest prices on Amager, but as one estate agent says: "We don't have anything really expensive on Amager, and these are the closest we get to luxury houses."

Amager is indelicately known to a lot of people as shit island.

It has always existed in a closed circuit, in which the same people moved from place to place on the island and estate agents couldn't be bothered advertising in the national newspapers. 65 per cent of their purchasers were local, and those coming from elsewhere were typically Jutlanders. Even today, when estate agents always maintain that Amager is modern, they encounter more Jutlanders than Copenhageners. But the main core of residents is determined to stay. "If you get a girl friend who runs you, you move away with her. But if you divorce, you come home to Amager again," says an experienced estate agent.

A couple living in Italiensvej have many of their relatives living nearby on Amager – the parents, sister and brother of one of them and their grown children. "You simply stay here," she explains. "It's like a little town. For me, Copenhagen is something completely different I travel to. I *don't exist* in town. We buy clothes out here, go to the cinema here, bathe here, fly from here." And her husband adds: "We could close down the bridges if we had a brewery." She works in Amager Hospital, "a place for local appointees", and she knows all the patients. He grew up on the island and has never lived anywhere else. They have regular places on the beach at the end of the road and have no intention of moving.

Estate agents find it easy to sell good, high-ceilinged apartments in red brick buildings on Amagerbro – the very first stretch of Amagerbrogade and side streets such as Under Elmene, Ved Svinget, Hollænderdybet and Sønderport. Prices have risen inexorably since 2000. It is also easy to get rid of houses on Amager Strandvej and its side streets. The difficulty is selling the uninteresting functionalist apartment blocks from the 1930s further out, where the ceilings are low and there is no stucco. And then there is long, run-down, noisy Holmbladsgade with its long, dilapidated side streets. There are no sales there. Until a very late stage there were only bare fields here, farms and a few small houses. The first tall, urban housing only appeared in the 1870s, but it spread rapidly. Today, the local authority defines Holmbladsgade as a

problem requiring urgent improvement. It is a classical industrial and working-class district with blocks of flats, a dreary appearance and a population consisting of large numbers of immigrants, unskilled workers, single and old people. Holmbladsgade is off Amagerbrogade and goes down towards the sea. It ends in offices and industrial buildings, the Kung Fu School and Copenhagen Roofing. And then you can't get any further even though you can feel the sea is quite close by. You can follow the abandoned Amager railway line and walk along past car repairers, bus garages and Nordisk Gummi & Guttapercha Co.

"If a girl should move to Copenhagen, she shouldn't go anywhere near Holmbladsgade and its countless forbidding pubs," says an estate agent, but there are also locals who think the street used to do better and used to be safer:

"When I was a child, Holmbladsgade was a metropolis. I don't feel comfortable when I see the district today. You can't expect things to be unchanged after so many years, but it looks so bloody poor, and it was never so poor in the fifties when I was a child. There were lots of shops and small businesses. I see no future in the district today; on the contrary it is going further and further down. I feel I'm on alien territory in Holmbladsgade today. It's dreary and depressing," says Henrik Lange, born 1944, in *Sundbyfolk* (1999).

He remembers the factories that stood alongside private houses and market gardens. For instance the smelly meat meal factory Grand Danois near the Amager railway, which was never called anything but Great Dane Shit and had animals that had died of natural causes lying around in the factory premises. There was the Jensen & Møller biscuit works and factories that made metal manhole covers or washing soap or radios or rubber or beetroot salad. Schulstad's Bakery was special. "All the smells of the district came brutally together just here: bread, tobacco, paint, packaging, corrugated paper, galvanised zinc, tartar sauce, dead animals and so on. We used to pinch our noses, what we called *half a screw*, or we went with wide-open nostrils, what we

Eberts Villaby (the Ebert Estate). This small town-in-town, built by Amager-born magnate Hermann Ebert, still commands the highest prices on the island.

called a *whole screw*. Local people grew vegetables in small gardens, and they were anything but organic."

Amager was industry and countryside all at once. During the lunch break the workers from Maskinfabrikken Vølund bathed at Helgoland, where shivering schoolchildren opened the bathing season on 15 May irrespective of whether they wanted to or not, a place where a floating turd occasionally bumped against the pillars under the swimming baths. Øresund in the 1930s, 40s and 50s was not nearly as clean as it is now. There were countless firms, market gardens and hothouses, but towards the heart of the place near town the smoke, noise and stench rose into the air from a host of factories. The women of the island worked as helpers in the market gardens during the summer. In the winter they ironed shirts and pyjamas in the Swallow shirt factory in Holmbladsgade, made cigarettes on the night shift at Augustinus, packed biscuits in the biscuit factory or worked in the Valo experimental laundry. Or they made open sandwiches, worked as home helps, cleaners, canteen assistants or assistants in the maze of shops in Amagerbrogde.

A man who grew up on the island describes the hierarchy of 30 years ago, when Christianshavn was not much different from Amager. Both districts were for ordinary people. Islands Brygge, which is now so hot, was a place you didn't move to. It was the worst of them all. Then came Holmbladsgade and the low-built slums of Sverrigsgade and Norgesgade. "Now they're selling those tiny terraced houses for fortunes," he says in amazement.

But some things never change: there are allotment gardens on Amager, to which you move out in the summer. In a random block of flats in Amagerbrogade, three families have allotment gardens, but most don't have a car.

The Christianshavn people over on the other side of the moat are affluent, well educated, left wing in their politics, creative and as proud as peacocks of their historical district. On Amager, things look different. People earn less, are less well educated, do other

things, vote Social Democrat and are only here and there proud of their district. All the old things have gone, and only very few buildings are listed. Amager is new, shabby and burdened with a poor reputation. Even in 1902, the name of Amager had such a negative sound that a group of energetic businessmen suggested changing the name of Amagerbrogade to something quite different.

"I'm like a black fighting for Harlem," said the actor Jesper Klein. And Amager always needs prominent spokesmen who can surprise people by having chosen that place at all. "Oh? Does *he* live on Amager?" The place is constantly on the defensive and in conflict with its eternal and invisible enemy – a centuries-old tarnished reputation. It's something about Amager being outside town. Far outside. That the young men of the island wear gold chains and Adidas trousers, drive an Opel and live in red-brick apartment blocks. That the rockers are born out there in that flat, low-brow, filthy, ugly district.

A typical Amager story? It tells how *they* tread on you. That *they* come and pull the wool over the eyes of the fatalistic island population, who must simply put up with it – for instance the planning of the new town Ørestad, where politicians and planners sit drinking soda water and airing their big ideas and having to listen to the drunk on the back row shouting, "Go back to Copenhagen" and "You don't live here, man!" to everything they say. And nor do they. None of *them* live on Amager. Amager signals noise, cars and through traffic. Copenhageners never go there without a reason. The locals know that, and they are both relieved and insulted by it. House prices are kept down in that way, but why can't the sceptics realise that Amager is obviously a lovely place? A place where you escape career ambitions, elbows, boasting, swank and abstractions. At least that's what they say, and they make the island sound like the last refuge from modernity. An isolated old-fashioned Social Democrat island (with a touch of the Danish People's Party and the Danish Communist Party) with different values from those in town and especially

Amager always needs prominent spokesmen who can surprise people by the very fact of having chosen to live in that place.

those to the north, where people want something different, completely different, from their lives.

People with ordinary incomes can afford a little detached house on a little plot, and in the forty allotment associations it has always been still cheaper. But developments are taking place that look like those in Copenhagen, only on a smaller scale. The original allotment association residents are dying off and new people are moving into the increasingly expensive allotment houses. These include some academics. Some houses cost the unlikely sum of a million kroner or slightly more. Perhaps not those built of clay and scrap orange boxes from the harbour. "They look like shit," says one man, "but they keep the prices down."

"The allotment society Musikbyen out in Sydhavnen has for many years been modern in the eyes of the middle classes. We've never been that before. People thought it was too primitive out here. But now everything is quietly becoming better organised, although it's not exactly over-smart. At our general meetings we divide up into the old ones who don't think we should alter anything and simply believe we should live in peace, and the young ones who do want to," says Jørgen Øllgaard from the Sundbyvester Allotment Society.

In all Amager's allotment societies, a generation change is taking place. New, young people are coming in with other jobs than the classic Copenhagen industrial worker. One man comments that the allotment gardens at Kløvermarken and on Fælleden are being taken over by gays with their condi-bikes and hemp plants. And they are often the start of new trends.

"Amager has always been a market garden island, not to say a shit island. It's been considered a facility, shit with which you could simply do what you liked. There is no one who thinks that Amager is in fact the most densely inhabited part of Copenhagen. More people live there than in Østerbro, Vesterbro or Nørrebro, and it is taken less into consideration than any of them," says Jesper Klein – furious at the fact that the Metro on the island has been routed far away from the densely populated districts.

The other districts have always been given preference, ever since the first Danish coastal railway, which benefited the rich people living on the coast between Copenhagen and Elsinore. So did the original Number 1 tramline that ran to Hellerup and Charlottenlund. The first suburban railway line was Line A to Holte. Now, at long last, a Metro line is coming to Amager – and they are not even putting it where people live.

Amagerbro (Amager Bridge) lives with its martyrdom as a neglected place. This has established itself as part of the self-assurance of Copenhagen's fourth bridge district. Ignored by politicians, by fine folk, by trend-setters and all the others who just have to get through the island on the way to and from the airport, a notoriously unloved route: "We all know what it's like to have been to Rome or somewhere else and then drive back into Copenhagen from Amager, and Copenhagen looks like shit," says the poet Naja Marie Aidt.

In the "olden days" you couldn't get a taxi home because the taxi couldn't get a fare back from Amager. And there were no trains either. Everything was centred on Copenhagen apart from a single discotheque; that was where Bull Shit rockers were to be found. "*No one* from town goes to Amager," says one man. In reply, the island has built up a strong sense of local patriotism resting on stacks of local history periodicals and books. Amager traces its martyrdom back in time to the days when the island was also an appendix to the royal seat of Copenhagen. The island has been called Amacum, Amakæ and Amahaki. "Ama" meaning "to rub" (shoulders with Sjælland). Here lay the pantry that the king partly gave to a crowd of Dutch peasants with orders to keep it filled, and it continued to be rural right up to the 1960s.

Until 1658, this pantry lay in the midst of the kingdom, with flat fields and long, damp tidal meadows along the coasts, where cows and horses could graze. In the villages, the farms were built close together in rows just on the boundary between arable land

and tidal meadows, so that you could let out the cattle to graze through one door and bring in the harvest through the other. There Sundbyøster and Sundbyvester still lie, now completely disguised as urban districts on either side of Amagerbrogade, combined under the name of Sundby or Sundbyerne. Sundby-øster is on the left (on the water side), and the other on the right as you come from Copenhagen.

Until industrialisation and the spread of the city, the island's population lived on the land. Farmers grew rich by living right up against a large, wealthy customer that continued to grow all the time from the 15th century, when it became the country's capital city. They went across to Copenhagen a couple of times a week and sold their vegetables, fruit and meat on the market. It sounds delightful, but Amager was unprotected outside Copenhagen and was prone to being plundered and burnt by the enemy – and so it was. The proximity of Copenhagen also brought poverty.

Things went wrong in 1523, 1535-36 and 1658-60. In 1523, Amager, the source of provisions for Copenhagen, was, in the words of the enemy, "geplunderth und auszgebranth", (plundered and burnt out) and that was at a time when the Dutch peasants had just built some splendid new farms. It had all been rebuilt when the next war, the Count's War, broke out. Copenhagen was again besieged, its pantry plundered and Dragør burned. In1658, the Swedish king, Karl Gustav, landed at Dragør with 2000 men, and the people of Amager fled behind the city ramparts at Christianshavn taking with them everything they could carry. Their island was "the sole pantry for Copenhagen", and the Copenhagen military itself burnt Sundbyvester and Sundbyøster to prevent the Swedes from finding quarters so close to the ramparts. This inspired the enemy to burn down the rest of the houses and farms on the island so that "everything that

Villa idyll in the foreground. The Urbanplan high-rise housing scheme in the background.

In Amager you are not bothered by career ambitions, elbows, boasting, pumped-up false elegance and abstractions.

If there is a spare plot of land, there is a garden.

was found in there and which could not be carried away, such as corn, fodder and cattle, was devoured by the fire". Then came the typhoid epidemic in 1710 and 1711, which killed between a quarter and a third of the island's inhabitants.

At that time, too, Copenhagen moved some disagreeable things out to Amager. After a violent explosion, gunpowder was moved out of town, and from 1777 and for almost the next century, the city's night soil was carried out to the area at the start of Amagerbrogade and dumped there. The farmers spread the night soil on their hard-pressed, over-exploited fields, and an indescribable stench hung over it all. And to add insult to injury, a factory was subsequently built there for burning and grinding bones, and then came a glue factory, a burial ground for crimi-

nals and, in 1806, the Copenhagen scaffold. The last of about 35 executions took place in 1857, but people still say Ama'r and draw their hand across their throats. Cross my heart and hope to die.

When the ramparts were levelled, the great boom came to all other areas around Copenhagen. About 1870 the first urban housing was built at the entrance to Amager, and things got out of hand when the villages merged and became a town within a few years. By 1890 there were 13,000 inhabitants in the two Sundbys, which in size were only exceeded by towns like Århus, Odense, Aalborg, Horsens and Randers. But the streets ended blind in fields, and there were none of those things that belong to a town of that size. It couldn't afford it, for the people living there generally speaking only constituted a poor working class

The island has 40 allotment garden associations, where a change of generations is now taking place.

population. Vølund, the rolling mill, a biscuit factory, an aeroplane factory, dye works and so on and so forth all piled up, and the workers forced themselves into tiny two and three-room flats in Holmbladsgade and the streets off it. Finally, as a benevolent uncle, Copenhagen could not do anything but incorporate the impoverished bridge district into the city. This was done in 1902 and it was an expensive affair for the city, whereas Valby and Brønshøj-Utterslev provided better income from taxation. On the other hand, Amager brought a working class majority within reach.

In spite of all attempts, Amagerbro never really became elegant. In 1918, a merchant spent 400,000 kroner – an enormous sum at that time – on setting up the Café de Paris in Amagerbrogade. "In return, Copenhagen has been given an institution worthy of the city whose name it bears", wrote the press, but that kind of thing doesn't (didn't) work on Amager, and a few years later the new owner put up a notice on the marble façade: "Did you eat your fill? If not, ask for more. Two courses – 70 øre.

No tips." Experimental interiors on Amager are still few and far between. Much scarcer than in the two transformed and rehabilitated bridge districts of Vesterbro and Nørrebro. It's still a long way out there, even if it isn't.

Amager is at once tightly packed and very open. Seen from above, it looks green and bare because of the huge commons – Amager Fælled and Kalvebod Fælled – which are remains of the open and uncultivated tidal meadows along the coast. The military was quick to take them over in 1869 for target practice with cannon and handguns, but they quickly became too small and were reluctantly returned to civil use just over a hundred years later. Kalvebod Fælled accounts for a third of the present area of the entire island, but only dates from the Second World War, when it was used as an employment project for the unemployed. The area was under shallow water when the military wanted it as a new and bigger shooting range. In return, it was prepared to abandon the older Amager Fælled, which lay closer to town. A crucial poli-

tical condition for the enormous project was that as much of the work as possible should be done manually, partly to create work for people and partly to save on imported materials. The actual embankment with drainage channels and 77 kilometres of ditch was finished in 1945, but it had to be systematically pumped for 12 years before the common was dry enough to use, and by then it was already too small for modern weapons. The new town Ørestad occupies a belt 600 metres wide and five kilometres long across the two commons, and there is still room. Room for the abandoned fishing cutter on a fallow field and room for nine pin bowling. Room for wooden huts and small sheds, for large halls filled with second-hand furniture and for haulage contractors, bus depots, beer depots and enormous halls of residence. Room for market gardens in the shadow of the aeroplanes right out in West Amager and room for way-out names of distant warm countries – Ugandavej, Kongovej, Iranvej, Koreavej, Sudanvej, Liberia-vej, not forgetting Rhodesiavej, Pretoriavej and the others from the age of apartheid. And way out there is Kongelunden on land

set aside for "the cultivation of a forest" with firewood for tree-less Amager. Not a splendid natural forest with paths criss-crossing each other, but a well-arranged place with a road through. And out there is the little well tended fishing village of Dragør with room for 522 yachts and a conservative mayor. The rest of the island is run by Social Democrats. Now, not only Dragør but also large parts of Amager smell of money for the first time for a hundred years. The Metro is in the wrong place, they say, but it has opened Amager up. "Amager is not standing still. No longer. The insurmountable ocean of a strip of water that for hundreds of years has divided the so-called shit island from the rest of Copenhagen is today being erased by the Metro. It simply goes under the water and links the stepchild to the parent animal," writes Politiken in October 2002.

In his first book, *Fodreise fra Holmens Canal til Østpynten af Amager i Aarene 1828 og 1829*, Hans Christian Andersen writes that for him, Amager stands as "the best playground for my rushing young blood, this road seemed to me still not to have been travelled by any poetic horseman". And when he at last reaches the island, he notes that "finally, there lay the great, magnificent playground of the imagination, flat Amager, before me." A fact that still applies to the island today: there is space here. And that is valuable for a city that has used up all its space and needs more.

Ørestad

Copenhagen is a city built in a great circle because from the Middle Ages and right up until the 1850s it defended itself behind high ramparts. A city shaped as a narrow strip would be expensive to defend in this way; a circular one was cheaper. There can be more inside it. The intention with Copenhagen was defence. It is based on faith in God, the king and the plentiful herring in the Sound, but none of these three pillars is of any significance when a new town is to be founded today. So Ørestad is based on transport, the fact that you can move on quickly. The shape is linear because of the Metro – five kilometres long and 600 metres wide, so there is never far to walk to one of its five stations. Without this town there would be no Metro, and vice versa. The Metro is the life nerve of the new town, its icon and its raison d'être according to the town hall's own description. Ørestad's identity is that it is close to something else – Copenhagen, Sweden, the motorway, the airport. It is simply practical. But its planners are hoping with bated breath that it can also become something in itself and that it can gain its own soul instead of simply lying close to others'.

Ørestad has something all of its own, provided you can take it: it is modern, a complete contrast to the old town with its winding streets. And modern it is, right from the bright apartments with roof gardens and floating walkways to the way in which streets and roads are named after some of the outstanding names of modernism. The buildings seem to be transparent, the materials are granite, glass, concrete and steel, the art by Bjørn Nør-gard, Per Kirkeby and Hein Heinsen, the architecture by the best drawing offices in the country. This is to be a town to show others what we are capable of, a modern counterpart to Christianshavn and the Frederiksstad of the Enlightenment. "It will epitomise the ideals of its age," promises the town hall. No going back in time. Where critics say that they can't stand a place without a past and a history, adherents argue that Ørestad is the place of the future in Denmark. High-rise! New! Advanced! Everyone is new, everyone is helping to write their own history.

Not since the new towns of Christianshavn (1671) and Frederiksstad (1749) arose out of the mud has anything so alien and extreme been done in Copenhagen. Ørestad is three times the size of Christianshavn and Frederiksstad combined. All in all we are talking of building a town from scratch of a size of which Denmark has no experience. "We are talking of a million square metres of space indoors, so of course we're a bit nervous," says a high-ranking member of Copenhagen Town Hall.

The worry is that the city should simply be a flop and fail to appeal to real people's varying tastes. If they don't want to live there, the *wrong people* must ultimately move in, and then there will be a new ghetto with its resultant financial and social problems. The more attractive version of this is that the residents should be a mixture of owners, tenants and members of co-operative housing associations, of young people, old people and families with children. On the other side of the metro's overhead railway lies the Urban Plan as the antithesis of the hopes placed in Ørestad. It mustn't end like that. It must become neither a poor town nor a deserted town. The intention is to build such a beautiful, live and attractive town that the public will continue to stream out there and put the critics' pessimism to shame. Some will never be won over, for the brief history of the new town is that it was plonked down on a listed area of Amager Fælled

The metro is the nerve of the new city. Without that nerve, no city.

and Kalvebod Fælled. The neighbours found they had 600 metres further to go to get into open ground, and they had their views spoiled, and the rest of Amager was furious that the Metro was to be just where new people are moving in and not where the old inhabitants were living beforehand. The dream of one long, cohesive town of five kilometres is more like a piece of theoretical fiction. It is more likely hang together in some kind of transverse relationship with its traditional old Amager neighbours – if it is lucky.

And then there is its actual height in a town that is afraid of heights. Ørestad is being built to pay for the Metro. The Metro is expensive and so the town is built high and dense. A *great deal* has to be built to recoup the money, and the question is how people that have been accustomed to going around in their own houses and gardens will take to it. The Town Hall is anxious to know. The people there are hoping for a mini Manhattan in the southern end of the strip, where residences and offices are intermingled so that you can scarcely distinguish one from the other. The whole of this futuristic town is a protest against the divided town where work and home are sharply separated so that there is life in one place only during the day and in the other only in the evening. A large amount of housing doesn't automatically produce life, as can be seen in any huge building complex or suburb, but large numbers of people might achieve this, and there must be a constant stream of them in Ørestad. The planners hope for life throughout the whole twenty-four hours by combining the seat of business with the dormitory town – but it isn't certain that the two will accept each other. Commercial life has also grown accustomed to going around in its own environment – just think of the free-standing red blocks at Kalvebod Brygge. Perhaps companies will refuse to fit into a mixed block, surrounded by families, overturned bicycles and a general mess.

The builders in Ørestad are being very carefully told what to do. In relation to the failed and much criticised Kalvebod Brygge, which was planned and sold while Copenhagen was on its knees,

the city is now so successful that it can make demands. It doesn't *just* want to sell. It wants to have intelligent, inventive and experimental builders intent on trying this crazy new thing called life. But this is precisely where there is a danger of conflict. Members of the board of directors of the Ørestad Development Corporation are already horrified when they see a sausage stall in Kay Fiskers Plads. How will the leading figures in commercial life react to a circus next door? Or a concert? Or a playground?

Now the hunt is on for an essential thing for a town that wants to make an impression on choosy customers and attract 20,000 residents and 60,000 people working in Ørestad every day – an identity. "One of the most difficult aspects of planning a town from the start is that it has no prior history. All we can say is that this has been a military area where people have practised shooting across the common. But that story is important, because then you have something to get hold of," says one of the directors of the Ørestad Development Corporation, the architect Anne-Grethe Foss.

It is still difficult to catch sight of the story. Some envisage a cold, windy desert of stone and steel. Others notice those things that are not yet there. For instance, Claus Moesholm, former director of the advertising agency Home Sweet Home, says that he can't imagine himself walking around with a T-shirt inscribed *I love Ørestad*, for what is Ørestad about? "What is the emotional, real value? If you can sell a handbag for 10,000 kroner, then why not a whole district? Who on earth would have gone to Bilbao if it weren't for the Guggenheim Museum? One single building, and people come pouring in from all over the world. It's a fantastic example of a story that has clout."

Another person familiar with cities' eagerness for branding is the geographer Lene Strandsbjerg Wolff. She also has difficulty in placing Ørestad. "There is no story attached to it. The media are indifferent or mostly negative. Personally, I imagine endless rows of new buildings. There is no past, no ideology. Ørestad needs to

"We are talking about one million square metres, so of course our hand is shaking. It can go terribly wrong", says one city planner in Copenhagen Town Hall.

be taken over by some progressive, interesting people who can interpret the place, give it an identity and make it look smart in lifestyle magazines, like the lofts in New York. Gays are good at that. They have turned San Francisco into the city of gays. So if Klaus Bondam and Peter Frødin move in and create an Ørestad life style ..."

Not only must the town look extremely good, but it must also have a soul and life. So it is being provided with boulevards and paths, squares, schools and nurseries, parks and a library, sport, entertainment and, in time, a church. It will be given bridges, stations and multi-storey car parks. Lakes, canals and ponds are being dug. Trees are being planted. Benches and street lighting are being put in place. And this long strip of land is being divided into four segments that are not really intended to resemble each other, but perhaps to be reminiscent of the very different districts in Copenhagen itself. At the top is the Head, where students and academics buzz around in their halls of residence and universities in parallel with the media people from Danmarks Radio. This is a place to think, where the dominant builders – the university and DR (Danmarks Radio) – are making an effort to come together and to open their premises to people from outside. Ørestad Nord is the first completed area in town. Then there is the Neck – an untouched piece of green common with a lake and rare kinds of reptiles, plants, insects and birds. Then the Stomach (Ørestad City), where the practical, commercial life is centred on supermarkets, homes and offices. "There, they think a little more about themselves," says one well-informed source. They are not so wildly experimental as up in the Head, which has bought itself an extensive catalogue of ideas on life and actually appointed someone to create a link between them. In the Stomach, on the other hand, a Norwegian investor might have more difficulty in seeing why he has to pay to acquire life around his office. And at the bottom are the Feet waiting for high-density housing of nine to twelve storeys. So as not to build a block here and there and leave people to live on a building site for the next 20 years, one district is being finished at a time, and then on to the next.

That is what is being done with the outsides. The insides are different and more difficult. Ørestad has people appointed exclusively to create life, traditions and character. That is something new. You used to let people move into their new houses and leave the rest to them. They daren't do that in Ørestad. They are frightened to end at what Carsten Thau, Professor of Architectural History, fears: "Ørestad is not hopeless. It is really OK. Precisely that, OK. That is to say neat and elegant. It promises to be a study in good taste, all those things we are proud of in the tradition of Danish architecture and design. The risk is that it will all be so nice that people will start longing for some blotch, something out of place. When you see the plans and the projects so far, it is as though they have been laundered and ironed. Nothing gives you a kick up the backside."

Everyone has the same concerns: that the town will never really get off the ground and will suffer a polished death. That it will all be too architect-designed. That the buildings will be perfect, but the town a failure. That people will disappear in it. New towns and new districts in Europe have more often been a failure than a great success, and all undertake studies of each other to seek the recipe for that undefinable thing that makes a town interesting to move about in. It is madly difficult to build a soul.

In the Ørestad Development Corporation, the Department for Life is inventing a series of traditions – a Christmas tree, rolling the egg competitions, races, jumble sales – and is constantly hunting for new inspiration. "I'm appointed to look after the human things," says one of them. When, a few summers ago, a flock of children defied all regulations and set about bathing in one of the newly built canals, the planners were delighted. They talked about it for a long time. The Corporation allows the use of land free of charge, experiments with flexible gardens and movable playing fields and also helps new associations to get started. They are in contact with neighbours, present and future new residents and builders, dancers, entertainers, walkers, musicians and

"As a matter of fact it is a miracle that the place and those people have survived as themselves for that long", one woman says.

wickerworkers. Anyone who can breathe something that looks like real culture, intensity, variety or *action* into the growing town on the common is listened to and assessed. And one day, the Corporation hopes to be able to let go of its brainchild and watch it stand on its own feet.

Islands Brygge

A man moved straight from his mother's house in Klampenborg to Islands Brygge and had a shock. He says that at first he thought

people were nearly fighting all the time. Even when they only wanted to buy a packet of cigarettes. And there was often quarrelling and shouting and screeching somewhere or other in the block. But that was simply the general tone. It was nothing dangerous, quite the reverse.

Islands Brygge has always been a place for families of several generations living together, a place where parents, children, grandchildren and great-grandchildren got each other into the apartment blocks. It was an advantage if you had relatives there beforehand, for then they could vouch for each other. And the big

Part of the Harbour Park, where one doesn't exactly forget the busy past of this quayside as the place of call for boats to and from Iceland and the storing of coal, cobblestones, broken stones, cement and much, much more. The home of the great threat – and workplace – called Dansk Sojakagefabrik.

private landlords liked that. If you didn't know anyone at all, you could go down to the pub Ritta's cellar and give Kusse-Karl, Pussy-Karl, 1000 kroner. He knew some woman in the housing office. At other times, a bottle of bitters in the right place was sufficient. "People are linked to each in every way. Islands Brygge is sheer inbreeding," says one woman who got her flat in this latter way.

"Visitors coming in from outside think it's rough," says Bo Rasmussen, who has lived on Islands Brygge since he was a child in the 1960s. "In those days, the harbour was still used; there were lots of sailors, workmen and pubs. The houses overlooking the

water were known as snob row because they were for the slightly better-off. My father was only a window cleaner, so the big house looked down on us a little. That was where a postmaster lived, and a professor, but at school and at scouts we were all working class lads. We played on the rubbish dump, where the scavengers lived, and we delivered provisions to a meths drinker on the common when he had broken a leg. We also bathed in the harbour even if it was very polluted with discharge from the meat market on one side and the soya bean factory on the other."

There are not so many "ordinary" people in the streets now,

he believes. Not quite so many pubs and very little of permanence on Islands Brygge. This will change over the coming years, for the Metro has brought new energy, as have two major building projects and Ørestad further out in the back garden and Havne-badet, the harbour swimming facility. The big landlords have sold out, so the flats are either owner-occupied or co-operative ventures, which also changes the clientele. No one is any longer expected to take difficult but needy people in.

Islands Brygge is used for film sets because time stands still out there. It is used especially for the Second World War and the 50s and 60s. Virtually all the buildings were erected between 1900 and 1940, and nothing has changed since.

The area is a little bit outside everything. People out there used to call it "the forgotten district" and felt it was something of a martyrdom that the dangerous Dansk Sojakagefabrik was allowed to remain there so long and because nothing came of so many other things – planned sports halls, cultural centres, a completely new school, the suburban train. The very active residents had themselves to construct a primitive park on the deserted quay area in 1984, and the minute it was complete and professionally finished, some vast 12-storey buildings shot up on Kalvebod Brygge opposite and took the evening sunshine so that everyone had to move further over to the left. The same thing happened with Amager Fælled, Amager Common. When it was finally listed, the Ørestad Act was passed, and that took away a good section of the common.

At first sight, the broad, red streets of apartment blocks seem to be dominated by ladies' hairdressers, laundrettes and kiosks. The hairdressers have old-fashioned hair dryers, potted plants in the windows and curtains arranged in some a style out of the Ark. Even the laundry Smuts Ny-vask on the main road, Njals-gade, is enclosed in net curtains that completely shut it off. The number of pizza, burger and grill bars with laminated tables is legion. So is the number of closed-down shops, though some are

amazingly stable – the ironmonger from 1927 with its slightly dusty window display of coffee filters and electric light bulbs, the bookseller on the quayside, the camera shop and the fruit cellar with first-class goods where bananas still hang on hooks and where you can buy half a head of cabbage if that's what you need. The fruit is on shelves with mirrors behind and there are five kinds of potatoes in old-fashioned potato bins.

The first café opened on the harbour front as early as 1986 under the name of Café Liberation, but it was closed down three years later – by the police – during investigations into the crimes committed by a gang known as the Blekingegade Gang. Today, one of the district's new cafés is in these premises and serves something as atypical of the place as French culinary specialities. And wine. On the other hand, there are pubs with leaded lights and plenty of kiosks selling beer. Islands Brygge retains an old Danish beer culture in the midst of the café latte- and Chardon-nay-drinking metropolis, but it is changing now.

"In reality, it's a miracle that the place and the people have survived with their own identity for so long," says one woman. "We're not far from Rådhuspladsen. It must be the bridge and the wind that keeps the others away. Islands Brygge is one of the most windswept places in Denmark. It is *so* raw here. And then you have to cross that bridge every single time. It feels like you're walking for miles when you're on your way home. But it's also a nice, cheerful place where people appreciate some rather old-fashioned Danish things, different from in town."

From the big, bare windows in the café you can see a constant stream of men in blue overalls going in and out of a shop that sells beer on the opposite corner. A lot of them are carrying open sandwiches in greaseproof paper from the shop round the corner.

A kilometre further out along the endless quayside there are signs of old-fashioned working life. A firm with stores and silos is still working. An odd boat is tied up, and lorries drive to and fro. Islands Brygge has something that is rare in a city – space. Space for the deserted fishing cutter on a set-aside field and a space for bowling. Space for large halls containing second-hand furniture and for haulage contractors and bus garages. On the right lies the harbour, providing a breath of fresh air for this run-down, higgledy-piggledy area.

The asphalt turns into a gravel track with big potholes. We are approaching Nokken. Nokken is officially an allotment association and in reality a DIY community beyond the pale. It consists of Hovedgaden, Forgaden and Strandvejen, which run along Syd-havnen, the South Harbour, where short jetties jut out.

Funny wooden houses with miserable sheds and petit bourgeois copies of small houses surrounded by privet hedges and pressure-creosoted fences. There are fruit trees and kitchen gardens full of produce, and a rottweiler hurls itself at the fence. After the little village comes the common with some sparse shrubbery and tall, pointed poplars. You can return to civilisation along Artillerivej, past the carpet dealer, the car painter, car dealers, the Tuborg depot and a grill bar with bars in front of the windows.

It would be too much to say that the place has become chic, but there are signs. Small enclaves of more advanced city phenomena are moving into the major enclave that Islands Brygge has always felt itself to be. Like a local patriotic neighbourhood in Copenhagen.

By now, large numbers of photographers, designers, graphic artists, entertainers and painters have workshops and studios side by side with a bodybuilding centre, Amager Tyre Service and Jalo Guard Dog Service. "When I moved here six years ago, the building was full of light industry. There is still a printer, a sailmaker and some metal folk in the cellar, but every time one of the old ones goes, a new decorative artist comes in," says a graphic artist who has his office in an old cigar factory.

The place is on the move. A few years ago, people like him would have had premises in Vesterbro, but now the back yards have been cleared of garages, workshops and back buildings. In a few years, they will have to go out to the north-western districts or further out on Amager because the harbour will become an attraction that brings residences and undertakings of the more expensive kind. "Just as Nørrebro could change, so it can here. But just at the moment it's a sleepy area where you go to the baker's wearing jogging clothes and slippers. There's only a local pizza shop and four bakers here, but the rent is still affordable and there is space." The rents have already been put up once in view of the new, attractive status of the area.

In Njalsgade, which leads from central Copenhagen to the University, there is an enormous complex of old warehouses, stores, garages and offices that formerly belonged to the Co-operative Wholesale Society, and which are rented out to several hundred record producers, designers, IT people, galleries, advertising agencies and musicians. The Nicolai Wallner Gallery left Bredgade, that illustrious street of galleries, for premises in a low-built, unprepossessing back building here with a small, peeling nameplate. There are four other young galleries there as well, and none of them is listed in the telephone book. The complex is a field of energy of music, art and the Internet. "When the district becomes famous, we shall be thrown out. It's Soho all over again. The place will become too interesting and too expensive, and the Metro will put an end to us," says one man who designs web sites in typical minimalist factory premises done up entirely in white and black.

Smart people here slope across the street and keep things going in a sandwich bar that is unlike anything else in the district because it's modern, simple and serves lean food. Things proliferate like that. Round the corner, in Isafjordsgade, there is a new café with a rather Italian seasonal cuisine, white table-

The harbour swimming establishment and Islands Brygge. In the background, the much-criticised, clumsy Kalvebod Brygge.

Gardening in the allotments at Nokken at the end of the deserted kilometre-long quay.

cloths, candles and relaxed jazz. The two owners from central Copenhagen had never set foot in Islands Brygge before. You don't go there unless you live there. It is a well kept secret and it's so far away.

Before he moved into the actual harbour front with shop and office, the clothes designer Klaus Samsøe had a clear picture of Islands Brygge as the home of German shepherd dogs and beers. That turned out to be wrong, for lots of creative young people pass by. "I wouldn't have moved out here if I hadn't been 100 per cent convinced that this area will be one of the most attractive and exciting in Copenhagen. It's an old, slightly rough working-class district that will attract all kinds of creative people. People with money will be coming from the new apartments out near the Soya Factory," he says. And so he agrees with the trend-seeking Copenhagen magazine *Nat & Dag*, which asserts that "we guarantee it will not be many years before Islands Brygge's row of quays will be a super-exclusive promenade with expensive restaurants feeding the millionaires from the district's newly built and wildly expensive luxury flats".

Take it easy. For the time being, Islands Brygge's funeral director is next door to a shop that sells nothing but beer. In purely statistical terms the residents are frighteningly average. They earn the local average and exactly reflect the average state of health in the municipality. That is to say they smoke too much and weigh too much.

A harbour swimming facility at Islands Brygge? The local environmental authorities and the medical officer of health swear that the water is pure enough to bathe in. They say you have to think of the harbour as a river flowing quite rapidly past Amager and out to sea. There are immediate protests from Copenhageners with memories going back to the filthy 1970s and 80s: "But Amager's a mucky place. And the Sound's a pool of mud." That's a thing of the past. There are fewer industries in Copenhagen now, and the sewage works are better.

Only 15 years ago, the nursery at Islands Brygge had a special hot line to Dansk Sojakagefabrik next door. If there were a chlorine escape the factory was to ring immediately and give the alarm. The children were to be rounded up and taken inside and all doors and windows were to be closed. Escapes often happened. Today it seems crazy. The nursery school teachers were trained so that they all knew what to do. "Will the factory be fined when we're all dead?" asked the residents in demonstration after demonstration. And: "There's no chlorine in the air where the director lives. We don't want his filthy factory here."

One summer's day in 1980 it blew up with an enormous explosion that could be heard all over town. 27 people were injured, but the factory was rebuilt and only closed down 11 years later. That is the point in the transformation of Copenhagen. Industry closes down and leaves behind vast areas where something new has to happen. The City of Copenhagen directly considers Islands Brygge as a *reserve area*, both for leisure and urban development. Time is no longer standing still there. The last place in town where people with ordinary incomes can afford to live near the harbour expects the number of inhabitants to double from 7,000 to 14,000 within a few years. And they will not be the classical residents of Islands Brygge. The new ones will be well off for instance, which means that they will have things and services that you can hardly find in this part of town at the moment.

The two-kilometre long quay and the entire area behind it were so to speak built on the water, just as Christianshavn had been 300 years earlier. The harbour authorities and Privatbanken joined forces in 1901 to fill in the stretch of water from the old coastline out near Artillerivej. Copenhagen was short of quays for ships sailing to and from Iceland, and the intention was that a freight station should also be built there. Housing was built instead, arranged in a severe modern block structure alongside unusually wide streets. The first high-rise blocks overlooking the water were built in 1905. The fine big apartments were difficult to

The entrance to Copenhagen harbour looking south: Islands Brygge on the left, built about 1900 on an area of the entrance that had been filled in with rubbish. Kalvebod Brygge on the right, developed about 2000 as part of the new, much criticised Copenhagen – enormous, free-standing hotels, head offices, supermarkets. The picture shows Nykredit's magnificent glass cube.

let because people thought they were a very long way out. Copenhageners still have that feeling. The catastrophic factory was built there in 1910. At first it extracted oil from Manchurian soya beans, and later it started the production of chlorine.

The harbour promenade and the splendid flats failed to attract sophisticated residents as long as people were working and swearing and cursing on the quayside. But the same factory that provided the area with the unpleasant smell of an industrial district and kept it out of good company is now seeking to transform the place. The 200,000 square metres of harbour area from the soya factory are now one vast building site, where towering grey silos are being turned into luxury flats with a view, and where a long stretch of mud is gradually being transformed into a broad, elegant avenue with green flower beds in the middle. People have already moved into the old silo – a magnificent red block with coke-grey steel balconies just by the harbour's edge. *Honest* and rough industrial architecture is modern. And with a little determination it will be possible to change outsiders' views of this district: "Straight across Langebro and turn right. That's where Islands Brygge lies as a kind of mini Manhattan with straight streets and an impressive view of the harbour," it says in the first general history of the district, *Bryggen – den glemte bydel, The wharf – a forgotten part of town* from 1995.

This working class enclave with its wealth of traditions is about to undergo a total transformation, and the cranes are already working to make room for all the new things. Typically of the present building boom, the builders no longer talk about new single buildings, but of entire districts. Two of them are at Islands Brygge: one of them on the site of the soya factory, which is being transformed from a desolate, pestilential place to something to be called Havnestaden with its own design manual. The other is at Ny Tøjhusgrund near Amager Boulevard and the Hotel Scandinavia, which since 1990 has been left gaunt and ugly on its grass-grown foundations. The old military buildings were pulled down in the middle of the night 11 years ago because the

authorities were afraid of a new Christiania. The view from snob row on the edge of the harbour is quite new. Just before the new millennium you could look straight across the harbour from Islands Brygge at nothing at all. There were prostitutes, car parks and mobile homes. And a tall crane from which people practised bungee jumping.

Copenhagen underwent a profound financial crisis in the 1980s and early 1990s with deficits and debts of billions of kroner. Investors kept well away from the bureaucratic, left wing city. We had a recession, no money and a great many unemployed. Dansk Sojakagefabrik closed down in 1991 and was left empty for years. The only movement in the ruins of the factory were when weekend players played hardball out there or used the silos for rappelling. Everything changed in the mid-90s. Copenhagen started on a building boom that is still going strong. The city sold its land and finally found it had money in the bank and cranes working all out. In return, the builders in the harbour could have things as they wanted them. And the result is there for everyone to see.

This invigorating process started with the central mole at Langelinie in 1994 and continued with the renovation of Rådhuspladsen in 1996. The following year, Statens Museum for Kunst was extended and the sports town in Vesterbro was opened. Then still more residences were built at Langelinie and the process continued with company housing on Teglværksholmen at Sydhavnen and at Kalvebod Brygge – the harbour front opposite Islands Brygge. There, the 12-storey Marriott Hotel stands beside the headquarters of Nykredit. And so it continues all the way down to the shopping centre Fisketorvet, which is from 2000. Behind the supermarket the intention is to build a new district of offices and apartments.

Then there are also the enormous company residences at Kalkbrænderihavnen near Nordhavn, the Black Diamond, Henning Larsen's beautiful black office blocks along Christianshavn plus the residential district, Parken in Østerbro and a new ferry terminal, offices and luxury flats in Søndre Frihavn.

Having now been relinquished by the navy and the naval dock-yard, Holmen has been redesigned and taken over by a new public and schools of art. The airport is new, and Ørestad is coming with its university, Danmarks Radio, hospital, shopping centre, housing and offices. The Metro will link some of these. The bridge across the Sound is filling Copenhagen with Swedes, the new opera house has opened, and a new theatre is on the way.

In Islands Brygge and elsewhere near the harbour, ruined factories have been turned into "unique industrial architecture" in which it costs a fortune to live. From the 10th storey in the old seed silo you have a wonderful, distant view. The Soya factory is producing a thousand new apartments and yet again changing life in Islands Brygge. Where mounds of dusty coal and coke, sheds, containers and railway carriages once filled the actual wharf there is now the Harbour Park, where young musicians play wildly advanced German data music in the "outdoor industrial lounge".

Everything has been turned on its head within a very short time.

Index

The marked page numbers refer to photographs

Bibliography

Algreen, Lisbeth: Vesterbro. Gennem den flerkulturelle by. Mellemfolkeligt Samvirke. 1999.

Algreen, Lisbeth: Nørrebro. Gennem den flerkulturelle by. Mellemfolkeligt Samvirke. 1999.

Algreen, Lisbeth: Østerbro. Gennem den flerkulturelle by. Mellemfolkeligt Samvirke. 1999.

Andersen, Ulrich Storgaard: Dansk prostitutionsrådgivning 1874-1906. Speciale, Historisk Institut, Aarhus Universitet. 1997.

Arkitektens Forlag: Frederiksstaden 250 år. 1999.

Bang, Herman: Stuk. Schubothe. 1887.

Barlyng, Marianne og Schou, Søren: Københavnerromaner. Borgen. 1996.

Bering Liisberg: Christianshavn. Voldkomiteen og Foreningen til Hovedstadens Forskønnelse. 1918.

Bing, Erik Henriques: Evighedes Hus. En guide til den jødiske begravelsesplads i Møllegade. Forlaget Tågaliden. 1997.

Bramsen, Bo: København før og nu – og aldrig. Bind 1-12, Palle Fogtdal. 1987-91.

Broby-Johansen, R.: Men Broby gennem Ny-København, Frederiksberg, Broerne, Valby, Sydhavnen. Hamlet. 1986.

Broby-Johansen, R.: Med Broby i det gamle København inden for voldene. Hamlet. 1986.

Broby-Johansen, R.: Det gamle København. Thanning og Appel. 1978.

Christensen, Christian: En rabarberdreng vokser op. Hans Reitzels Forlag. 1961/1982.

Clemmensen, Carl Henrik: Mit København. H. Hirschsprungs Forlag. 1939.

Dahl, Henrik m. fl.: Københavnerlivsformer. Advice Analyse og Strategi A/S. 2003.

Ditlevsen, Tove: Barndommens gade. Athenæum. 1943.

Elmann Paddison, Sussie: Bryggen – den glemte bydel. Island Bryggges Lokalhistoriske Forening og Arkiv. 1995.

Federspiel, Søren m.fl.: Nørrebro – træk af en bydels historie. Knuths Forlag. 1997.

Fisker, Jørgen: Brikker til en mosaik om Zoologisk Have. Fisker & Schou. 1998.

Frandsen, Karl-Erik m.fl.: Amager. Nyt Nordisk Forlag Arnold Busck. 2003.

Gehl, Jan og Gemzøe, Lars: Byens rum, byens liv. Arkitektens Forlag og Kunstakademiets Forlag. 1996.

Hansen, Michael Bjørn: Krasnapolsky. Forlaget Per Kofod. 1994

Hvidt, Kristian: Pynt på gesimsen. Facader på københavnsk etagebyggeri 1860-1920. G.E.C. Gad. 1983.

Hvilsom, Frank og Engström, Anne-Li: Vesterbro. Byfornyelsescenteret. 2001.

Janssen, Jan E. og Thomsen, Allan Mylius: Nørre Kvarters Krønike. Nørre Compagnie og High Tech Prepress. 1997.

Jørgensen, Bent: Storbyens Stednavne. Gyldendal. 1999.

Kvale, Katja og Raahauge, Kirsten Marie: Et døgn på Rådhuspladsen. Kunstakademiets Arkitektskole. 2000.

Københavns Kommune: Bydelsatlas Indre by/Christianshavn. 1996.

Københavns Statistiske Kontor: Københavns bydele. 1999.
Københavns Universitet, Institut for Historie: Kongens og folkets København gennem 800 år. Forlaget Skipperhoved. 1996.

Lange, Bente: The colours of Copenhagen. The Royal Danish Academy of Fine Arts. School of Architecture Publishers. 1997.
Larsen, Ole: København skildret af danske forfattere. Carit Andersens Forlag. 1966.
Lind, Olav og Møller, Jonas: Bag hækken. Det danske parcelhus i lyst og nød. Arkitektens Forlag. 1996.
Lund, Hakon: Danmarks havekunst. Bind 1, Arkitektens Forlag. 2000.
Lützen, Karin: Byen tæmmes. Kernefamilie, sociale reformer og velgørenhed i 1800-tallets København. Hans Reitzels Forlag. 1998.

Madsen, Hans Helge: Østerbro før og nu – og aldrig. Fogtdal. 1993, 1999.
Mørch, Søren: Den ny Danmarkshistorie 1880-1960. Gyldendal. 1982.

Nexø, Martin Andersen: Pelle Erobreren. Gyldendal. 1904/1973.
Nørby, Ghita, Dahl Møller, Jette og Reich, Ebbe Kløvedal: Botanisk Have – en oase i storbyen. Lamberth. 1996.
Nørup, Majken Rude: Det københavnske værtshusliv 1857-1998. Strandbergs Forlag. 1999.

Olsen, Allan m.fl.: Skydebanegade – den pæne gade på Vesterbro. Udgivet af Andelsboligforeningen Skydebanen. 1996.
Olsen, Jens Peter: Frederiksberg Slot og Hærens Officerskole. Hærens Officerskoles Fond. 1997.

Raabyemagle, Hanne: Christian VII's palæ. Amalienborg I og II. Christian Ejlers' Forlag. 1999.
Raabyemagle, Hanne og Smith, Claus M.: Klassicisme i København. Gyldendal. 1998.

Rasmussen, Steen Eiler: København. G.E.C. Gad. 1969/1994.
Rifbjerg, Klaus: Amagerdigte, Fædrelandssange, Mytologi. Gyldendal. 1996.
Rosen, Wilhelm von: Månens Kulør. Studier i dansk bøssehistorie. 1628-1912. Rhodos. 1993.

Skak-Nielsen, Luise: Alle kender Blågårdsgade. Hans Reitzels Forlag. Københavns Bymuseum. 1989.
Skak-Nielsen, Luise: Tivoli og verden udenfor. Høst & Søn. 2000.
Strømstad, Poul: Københavnere fortæller. Erindringer fra det gamle København. Københavns Magistrats 3. Afdeling. 1972.
Svendsen, Susanne: Amager bybilleder. På kanten af byen. AK83 konsulenter A/S. 1995.
Sødring, Julie: Erindringer. Rosenkilde og Bagger. 1965.

Thimm, Jack: Sundbyfolk. Sundby Lokalhistoriske Arkiv. 1999.
Thomsen, Allan Mylius: Husmann's Vinstue og Pisserenden. Sommer og Sørensens Forlag. 1994.
Thorvaldsens Museum: 1796 København som kulturby. 1996.
Turèll, Dan: Storby-trilogien. Borgen. 1994.

Vasström, Annette: Holmens by. Nyboder og dets beboere – især i nyere tid. Orlogsmuseet. 1985.
Vesterbro Lokalråd: Hvidbogen om Vesterbro. En profil af et brokvarter 1989. Udgivet af Vesterbro Lokalråd. 1989
Vesterbro Handelsforening: Vesterbros Handelsforening gennem 90 år. 1990.

Weber, Ulla: Rådhuspladsen – et forsvindingsnummer. Kunstakademiets Arkitektskole. 1999.
Wivel, Ole: Guder i forårslys. Nordiske Landes Bogforlag. 1983.

Zerlang, Martin: Barndomsbyer. Samleren. 1998.

Åkerlund, Lene: Drømmene i Frederiksberg Have. Rhodos. 1991.

Biographical Data

Pernille Stensgaard (on the right) was born in 1960. She is a journalist and has worked for the Danish business magazine, Børsens Nyhedsmagasin. She now works for the weekly Danish newspaper, Weekendavisen. She is the author of *Skagen* (2003), a book about the Skaw, a northern fishing village in Denmark.

Anne Prytz Schaldemose (on the left) was born in 1971. She was trained as a photographer by renowned Danish photographer Rigmor Mydtskov. Photographer of *Skagen* (2003) and *Huse med sjæl* (2004), a book about the restoration of older houses. She is also the author of four children's nursery rhyme books. She works as a freelance photographer.

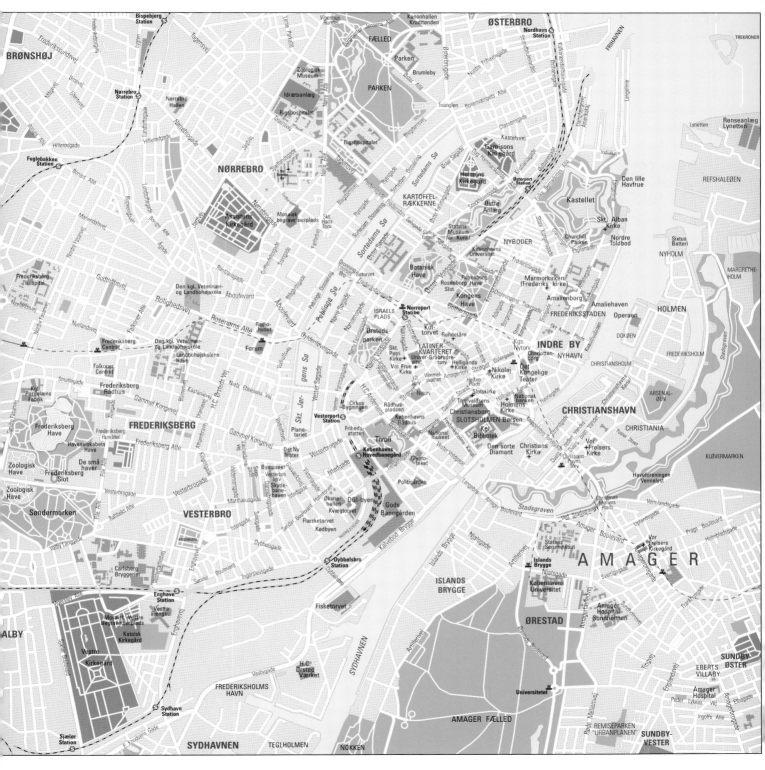